'Brilliant, discursive and wise'   Ben Goldacre

'ABSOLUTELY WONDERFUL. My face is stuck in a ridiculous grin of amazement. *The KLF* is dense, intelligent, well-researched, silly and, yes, magically profound'
Terry Gilliam

'A pop biography for people who don't read pop biographies'
Guardian

'Eccentric, bizarre, confusing, hilarious and more than a little pretentious but utterly irresistible and totally brilliant'
Cay McDermott, *The Quietus*

'The book brilliantly captures the anti-establishment attitude of Drummond and Cauty, and makes you wish the pop charts were full of such madness these days'
The Big Issue

'Wildly entertaining'   *Mojo*

'John Higgs's book about the KLF is – like its subject – a thing of endlessly fascinating, utterly demented genius'
Alexis Petridis

'I am going to bang on about *The KLF* rather a lot. Fascinating . . . Enthralling'
Robin Ince

T0301109

The KLF

Chaos, Magic and the Band
who Burned a Million Pounds

John Higgs

WEIDENFELD & NICOLSON

A W&N PAPERBACK

First published in ebook in Great Britain in 2012
First published in 2013 by Phoenix,
an imprint of the Orion Publishing Group Ltd
This edition first published in 2023 by Weidenfeld & Nicolson,
an imprint of Orion Publishing Group Ltd,
Orion House, 5 Upper St Martin's Lane, London WC2H 9EA
An Hachette UK Company

The authorised representative in the EEA is Hachette Ireland,
8 Castlecourt Centre, Dublin 15, D15 XTP3, Ireland (email: info@hbgi.ie)

3 5 7 9 10 8 6 4

A CIP catalogue record for this book is
available from the British Library.

ISBN (Hardback) 978 1 399 61035 3
ISBN (eBook) 978 1 780 22656 9
ISBN (Audio) 978 1 409 18040 1

Typeset by Input Data Services Ltd, Bridgwater, Somerset

Printed in Great Britain by Clays Ltd, Elcograf S.p.A.

www.weidenfeldandnicolson.co.uk

To the Prettiest One

CONTENTS

'Reality is not enough; we need nonsense too. Drifting into a world of fantasy is not an escape from reality but a significant education about the nature of life.'

Edmund Miller, *Lewis Carroll Observed*

PROLOGUE:

The Fuckers Burned the Lot

▲

Jim Reid retired to his hotel room at around midnight on 22 August 1994. Half an hour later there was a knock at the door. It was Bill Drummond and Jimmy Cauty and they had the suitcase with them.*

---

* Welcome to the footnotes. I am writing these ten years after the book, as I look again at the text to see what I make of it now. The idea is that these footnotes will act like a director's commentary and give some insight into the book – why it is like it is, and how it was written. You may want to skip them entirely if you are new to the book – it's odd enough in normal circumstances and reading it for the first time with an extra meta layer may be a bit much. Or, conversely, this may be the greatest, most hardcore way of reading the story. Who knows? Let's hope for the best and see how it goes.

'Come on, we're going to do it now,' said Drummond.*

Reid asked why. 'There's just a time when you instinctively know it is right,' Cauty replied. The plan had been to get up early on the morning of the 23rd and climb, with the suitcase and its contents, to the top of one of the mountains that dominate the island of Jura. Well, it was now technically the morning of the 23rd. The mountain was unimportant.

'Do you remember Christmas when you were a kid, and you just couldn't wait for morning?' Drummond asked.

Reid was a journalist who had been taken to Jura by Drummond and Cauty in order to act as a witness. He grabbed his Dictaphone and followed. They left the warmth of the hotel and went outside into the night. Here they met the fourth member of their party, Alan Goodrick, a Falklands War veteran and rock tour manager more commonly known as Gimpo. It was raining.

Drummond did not look like one of the most successful and credible pop stars on the planet. He was forty-one years old with an Everyman haircut and the sort of thoughtful, respectable demeanour you might associate with a secondary school teacher. Nevertheless, he had produced a string of global number one singles and had just come first in *Select* magazine's '100 Coolest People' list. Jimmy Cauty, the other half of the duo known as The KLF (among other things), was a few years younger with wild dark curly hair and a more anarchic sparkle in his eyes.

---

* That said, we're building to a dramatic bit, so I'll keep quiet for a moment.

The suitcase went into the hire car's boot. Reid had still not seen the contents of the case at this point, but he was pretty sure he knew what was inside. Gimpo had also guessed. During the flight to the Hebridean island the thought of killing Drummond and Cauty in order to steal the suitcase had entered his head. He didn't do that, of course. He just thought about it.

Well, you would, wouldn't you?

Gimpo drove them away from the hotel, down a rough track and across the Scottish island. The night was pitch black. 'This just feels better,' Drummond said, 'going out in the night when it's pissing down with rain.'

A few minutes later they pulled up by a deserted stone boathouse. Cauty had discovered it earlier in the evening when he and Drummond had been searching for the remains of a giant wicker man they had burned three years earlier, in front of dozens of robed and hooded members of the music press. They stepped out into the cold. Gimpo left the car lights on and they illuminated the rain, the bracken and the boathouse. They took the suitcase out of the boot.

They went inside. The flame from a cigarette lighter revealed rough stone walls and an earth floor. Ropes hung from old wooden rafters. And at the far end: a fireplace.

The suitcase was opened and its contents were dumped onto the ground. The four men stared down at the heap of paper at their feet.

It was a million pounds.

Very few people get to see a million pounds sterling first hand. Even fewer get to dump it onto a dirt floor in a remote abandoned building in the middle of the night. Those fifty-pound bundles were power and potential in its purest form. They were countless acts of compassion and charity, or a lifetime without work. The amount was highly symbolic. It was the amount that is associated with success; the quantity of money needed not only to escape the rat race, but to win it. That money was freedom, both physically and symbolically.

Cauty opened the first bundle and took out two fifty pound notes. He handed one to Drummond and set fire to both with his lighter. Despite the cold and damp, the flame readily ate through the paper. More notes were placed in the fireplace and, over the course of the next two hours, the fuckers burned the lot.*

On their return from the Isle of Jura, Drummond and Cauty found themselves at the start of the long, hard process of coming to terms with what they had just done. As Cauty told the BBC six months later, 'Every day you wake up and

---

* This phrase 'The fuckers burned the lot' did the book a great deal of good, I think. It tells the reader that the book is on their side, and that it understands how they are reacting to these events. There is a danger with a story like this that it could be told from either the perspective of fan worship, or through impenetrable academic art speak. 'The fuckers burned the lot' reassures us that this story might avoid those traps. There was talk at one point about using it as the book's title, I recall. The idea was abandoned on the grounds that we'd have to asterisk out the swear word, at which point it loses its charm.

think, "Oh God – I've just burned a million quid." Nobody thinks it was good. Everyone thinks that it's a complete waste of time.' The heart of the problem was that they did not know why they had done it. 'I don't know what it is, what we did. Some days I do. Bits of it,' Drummond said. 'But I've never thought that it was wrong.'

Drummond and Cauty's inability to justify or explain their actions is one of the most intriguing aspects of what happened on Jura. It echoes the fates of the founders of Dadaism, the small group of artists and radicals who opened the Cabaret Voltaire in Zurich in the middle of the First World War.* The Cabaret only lasted for six months, and no recordings were made of what happened there, yet those present spent the rest of their lives trying to come to terms with what they had done. They never really did. As the American author and music journalist Greil Marcus points out, 'This is the best evidence – the only real evidence – that something actually happened in Zurich in the spring of 1916.'

The money burning was recorded. Gimpo had filmed the event with a small camcorder. In the months after the burning, as Drummond and Cauty searched for some context or insight to allow them to understand their actions,

---

* This sudden reference to early twentieth-century Dadaism is an unexpected swerve, isn't it? If your book is going to be stuffed full of unexpected swerves, you need to establish that from the very beginning. Readers are very accepting of odd things that are established at the start. It's when weirdness kicks in halfway through that they have a problem. When that happens, it feels like the world of the book has been mis-sold.

the idea that they should show people the film arose. Perhaps if they showed the film and asked for help, someone might be able to explain to them what they had done?

This was a terrible idea, but they were hardly in their right minds at the time. They set about organising a film tour of arts venues and unusual locations around the British Isles. The first screening, on 23 August 1995, would be in the village hall back on Jura.

People were, by and large, rather angry. This is not surprising. If you ask a crowd to tell you why you burned a million pounds, when members of that crowd would very much like to have a million pounds themselves and know that they never will, then there is not going to be a huge amount of sympathy in the room.

It was the pointlessness of the whole thing that got to people. When it was revealed in a court case in 2000 that Elton John had somehow spent £40 million in twenty months, including £293,000 on flowers, people reacted differently. There was much head shaking, tutting and many jokes, but generally speaking nobody took it personally. It was Elton John's money after all, and his extravagance seemed in keeping with the personality that earned him that money in the first place. His wasted money, at the very least, had made a number of florists happy.

When Cauty and Drummond wasted their money it felt different. Seeing video footage of the burning was a genuine shock. Their money looked like kidney dialysis machines, beds in homeless shelters or funding for young artists in a way that Elton John's wasted money didn't. This wasn't money being wasted; it was money being negated. The argument that it was their money, and they could do what they liked with it, didn't ring true. What they had done felt wrong.

The adverts for the film screenings read, 'Jimmy Cauty and Bill Drummond urgently need to know why did the K Foundation [Drummond and Cauty's post-KLF name] burn a million quid? Was it a crime? Was it a burnt offering? Was it madness? Was it an investment? Was it Rock 'n' Roll? Was it an obscenity? Was it art? Was it a political statement? Was it bollocks? There will be screenings of the film *Watch The K Foundation Burn A Million Quid* at relevant locations over the next twelve months. Each will be followed by a debate attended by Messrs Cauty and Drummond where the answers to the above questions and others will be sought.'

Debate did follow, but very little of it seemed helpful to Drummond and Cauty. There was some talk of art, pranks, scams and promotion, but nothing that really held up to scrutiny. Many wondered if the whole thing was a hoax, or if they even burned money at all (this idea was discredited by a later BBC documentary, which produced a trail of evidence showing that the money was genuine).*

---

* Here I am referring to the forensic analysis the BBC commissioned, in which the ashes collected from Jura were examined in a lab and declared to be the burnt remains of a large amount of fifty-pound notes. With hindsight, I should probably have included more about this. If the past

Very quickly, a consensus view formed. It was a view that explained to most people's satisfaction exactly what had happened. This consensus arose spontaneously from many different audiences and it allowed most people to put what had happened behind them and move on. The consensus was this: *Drummond and Cauty are a pair of attention-seeking arseholes.**

It did seem like a power trip. As the pair sat behind a desk at the screenings it was easy to imagine that they were thinking, 'We had a million pounds, something that you will never be able to obtain no matter how hard you work. And we didn't want it. But we wouldn't give it to you. We'd rather burn it than give it to you. So we did. Because we could.'

---

ten years is any guide, the percentage of people who still believe that the money burning was a hoax remains a significant constant. I can certainly understand the intrinsic belief that *people just wouldn't do something like that*. The details of the hoax, which are almost always declared with absolute certainty, vary a fair bit. One common story is that the Bank of England were complicit in the hoax, and that they gave Bill and Jimmy money that was already marked to be destroyed. In this version of the story, Bill and Jimmy approached the Bank of England and asked for a million pounds of used notes, which were going to be burned anyway, to use in an art project. The Bank thought this sounded reasonable and handed over a million pounds. If anyone else wishes to try this, I would love to hear how the Bank of England reacts. While writing the book, I took the view that they did indeed burn the money. That hasn't changed over the past decade.

* It's rare for a book to raise the question of whether its subjects are just attention-seeking arseholes. This is a shame. Quite a few books would be improved by this.

The fact that they didn't know why they burned the money did not really figure in this reaction. Very few believed that anyway. Were not the pair, according to almost every article written about them, some form of 'master media manipulators'? The KLF, it was understood, were people who definitely knew what they were doing, for how else could you explain their success? From this perspective, their claim to be unable to justify their actions appeared to be an excuse to hold screenings and rub people's noses in what they had done.

There were some supporters, of course, who praised the burning sincerely and genuinely. They often had some pet critical theory, a personal tower of cards, which allowed them to view the burning as artistically important. They were very much a minority, however, and nothing they could do or say could compete with the *pair of attention-seeking arseholes* interpretation.*

And really, who could say that that interpretation wasn't

---

* It's quite sweary, this book, isn't it? I tend not to swear in the books I've written since, except in direct quotations of the speech of others. This is because swearing tends to make your author's voice very prominent in the storytelling. A lot of the time, I am trying to make myself as invisible as I can, in order that there is as little as possible between the events of the story and the reader's attention. For a book to really work you need the reader's attention to be on the narrative, not the author. There are, of course, moments when you butt in, indulge your authorial voice and make yourself present, but a judgement call is needed as to whether these improve or damage the ultimate effect. I am aware, needless to say, that adding an author's commentary in footnotes is a great crime in this context. But hey.

true? Perhaps that was the crux of the matter. Perhaps there was nothing else to add.

The futility of it all came to a head while they were sitting in a Little Chef diner near Aviemore, in the Scottish Highlands, the morning after a screening of the film in Glasgow. Drummond and Cauty had had enough. The screenings, they finally understood, were not going to achieve anything. They began to draw up a contract that would force them to walk away from the whole thing. The contract read:

> For the sake of our souls we the trustees of the K Foundation agree unconditionally, totally, and without hesitation to a binding contract with the rest of the world, the contract is as follows.
>
> Bill Drummond + Jimmy Cauty agree to never speak, write or use any other form of media to mention the burning of one million pounds of their own money which occurred on the Island of Jura on 23 August 1994 for a period of 23 years after the date of signature.*
>
> Bill Drummond + Jimmy Cauty are free to end the K

---

* This was signed on 5 November 1995, meaning that the twenty-three-year-old moratorium would end in 2018. Bill and Jimmy returned in 2017, however – twenty-three years after the burning, instead of twenty-three years after signing the contract. As always, poetic licence beats legal formality in their world.

Foundation in all respects for a period of 23 years after the date of signature.

Bill Drummond + Jimmy Cauty agree to store all assets of the K Foundation, including the ash of the one million pounds burnt on Jura, for a period of 23 years from the date of signature. This is to be completed within 14 days of signature.

Bill Drummond + J Cauty agree to allow Alan Goodrick use, for whatever purpose, the film 'Watch The K Foundation Burn A Million Quid' and all film rushes.

Bill Drummond + Jimmy Cauty agree to publish this contract as a one page advert in a broadsheet of their choice within 14 days of signature and to cover costs.

It is agreed that in signing this contract, the postponing of the K Foundation for the said period of 23 years, provides opportunity of sufficient length for an accurate and appropriately executed response to their burning of a million quid.

All that remained was to sign the contract and confirm the agreement. Cauty and Drummond had an idea about how to do this. They would write the contract on the hire van and then push that van over the cliffs at Cape Wrath on the northern tip of Scotland. That, it was felt, would be a suitable end to the matter.

Gimpo reacted to this idea by immediately returning to the van, which contained his film, and driving back to London, leaving Drummond and Cauty stranded. This is one of the few sensible acts in this story.

Nevertheless, a G-reg Nissan Bluebird was soon hired

and the contract was written across its entire body and windscreen with a gold pen. Cauty and Drummond signed the contract and the poor car was duly pushed over the cliff to fall hundreds of feet into the crashing North Atlantic surf. Cauty had first removed the radiator cap because it would 'smoke better' as it fell.*

And that should have been that.

Except . . .

Except that *the pair of attention-seeking arseholes* consensus doesn't really explain a great deal. It's an incomplete picture. There are many attention-seeking arseholes about but, by and large, they don't go around burning their last million pounds.

Then there's the matter of their inability to come to terms with what they did. The music journalist Andrew Smith described in the *Observer* how a long-time friend and associate of The KLF told him that they knew the burning

---

* When you're writing a book like this, you need to have as strong a sense of what not to include as what material you do. It's easy to lose control of the narrative if you don't set definite boundaries, in which case the story could spiral out endlessly. One of the boundaries I set myself here was not to include anything that Bill and Jimmy did after this Nissan Bluebird incident. That's why there's nothing about the 1997 2K comeback single 'Fuck the Millennium', the 'K Cera Cera' record, Jimmy's acoustic weaponry, or any of their other many adventures. This might seem harsh on a bunch of good stories, but it doesn't stop other people from writing about those things elsewhere. Whatever book I write, I always get asked the question, 'Why did you not include such-and-such?' Usually I attempt to give a reasonable and respectful answer, but often what I want to say is, 'Because the book would have been worse if I had.'

was real 'because afterwards, Jimmy and Bill looked so harrowed and haunted. And to be honest, they've never really been the same since.' Like the founders of the Cabaret Voltaire, the fact of their bewilderment is evidence that they were swept along by something larger, and something not of their design.

The fact that their actions are so incomprehensible suggests that we must be missing something. Somehow our view of our world or our culture is incomplete. Even if we accept that Cauty and Drummond were attention-seeking arseholes, there still must have been some strange influences pushing them in that particular direction. We can be fairly certain, given the end result, that these influences will be disturbing and irrational. But if we pursue those influences, what will we find? Will they be interesting? More importantly, will they be useful?

How do you tell a story such as this?

In December 1995 I was fortunate enough to spend an evening with the American counter-culture author Robert Anton Wilson.* At the time, I was researching a book about the Harvard psychologist turned psychedelics

---

* Here's Bob! When this book was written, his books were not always easy to get hold of in the UK. Often it was easier to download a pirate PDF than wait months for an online order that might never arrive. Since then, Hilaritas Press have begun methodically republishing the bulk of his work in really nice editions, which I heartily recommend to all. *Cosmic Trigger 1* – for which I wrote a foreword – is a great place to start with RAW's work.

advocate Timothy Leary, and Leary was a good friend and a major influence on Wilson.

It occurred to me to ask him his thoughts on The KLF. Robert Anton Wilson, it was generally understood, was a major figure in the KLF story. He co-wrote *The Illuminatus! Trilogy*, an underground but influential series of novels which had acted as inspiration and as a guiding philosophy for Drummond and Cauty's musical adventures. The first name they used together, The Justified Ancients of Mu Mu, was taken directly from this work.

The reason I asked Wilson about The KLF had nothing to do with Timothy Leary. It was because I was intrigued by a rumour that I had heard via a friend of Cauty. The rumour was this: although it was frequently claimed that the initials 'KLF' didn't mean anything, or that they meant different things at different times (Kings of Low Frequencies, Kopyright Liberation Front, and so on), the initials did actually have a specific meaning. According to this rumour, KLF stood for 'King Lucifer Forever'.*

I was unsure what to make of this, but it didn't feel right. The idea that there was a hidden secret at the heart of the band contradicted everything else I knew about them.

---

* That detail is a nice sinister twist, isn't it? Another version of this that I've heard is that KLF stood for 'King Lucifer's Forces'. Whether there's any truth in these rumours I don't know, but hearing them was a major factor in deciding to write this book. They also influenced the two-part structure, with The JAMs being 'Rabbit Ears' and The KLF being 'Horns' – which I'll talk about later.

It implied that they had a purpose, and that they knew what they were doing. This seemed deeply out of character. Still, it was an odd thing for a friend of Cauty's to claim, and an odd thing for someone to invent. I wondered if there was an air of 'Chinese whispers' about the phrase. Perhaps someone had made this suggestion as a joke after the band had ended, and the nature of word of mouth morphed it into the more interesting and definitive version which I heard? I asked Wilson what his thoughts about The KLF were.

'I've never heard of them,' he told me.*

'They were a British band who first called themselves The Justified Ancients of Mu Mu? They went on to burn a million pounds?' I prompted.

He shrugged. He explained that there were an awful lot of bands who played around with that imagery, and that he couldn't keep track of them all. He also said that punk bands seemed particularly keen on it, which surprised him a little as he wasn't really into the punk thing.

I hadn't expected that. Almost every account of the origins of The KLF mentioned Robert Anton Wilson. He was, I was sure, an integral part of their story and it seemed reasonable for him to be aware of this. The fact that he wasn't provided the first hint into how this story could be told.

It is not necessary for a character in a story to be aware of that story. This is not something that we understand

---

* A reminder that these events take place in the pre-internet world, back when the pleasures of blissful ignorance were normal and unremarkable.

instinctively or intuitively. The films we watch are focused on a hero's journey, and we automatically interpret the other characters as being part of that hero's story. If we see merchandise from the *Harry Potter* movies (for example) which shows minor characters from the films, then this does not strike us as odd. That character is part of those films, after all, and therefore part of Harry Potter's story.

Often, however, those characters should have no knowledge of the story that they are in. They may feature in an early scene and never be seen again, remaining ignorant of the events that follow. They would have no more reason for thinking that they were part of 'Harry Potter's story' than the story of anyone else that they met. Indeed, the idea that this was 'Harry's story' would seem ludicrous because, as far as they are concerned, they are in the middle of their own story. Their story could conceivably be more dramatic and exciting than Harry's. To them, Harry would be a bit player in their own story, not vice versa. This is certainly the situation in narratives which deal with real, as opposed to fictitious, people. We are all forming our own narratives and we can't be expected to keep track of everybody else's narratives, no matter how much they would like us to.

In the light of Wilson's comments, I started to wonder if there was such a thing as a story that no one knows they are in – least of all the main characters. Could a complete narrative develop by itself with no one guiding it or steering it? You would instinctively think not, yet whenever I thought about the KLF story and Cauty and Drummond's confusion about their actions, I couldn't shake the idea that there was nobody involved who could hear the story that was being told.*

On one level the story of The KLF is easy to tell, because almost everything they did between 1987 and 1994 was well recorded. Almost every song they produced, interview they gave, video they made or press release they issued is archived on the internet somewhere (or at least was and will be again – KLF websites and .ftp archives† have a habit of appearing and disappearing). For this we must thank Drummond and Cauty's championing of Situationist ideas, particularly with regard to their views on copyright.

---

* This is basically a warning that what follows isn't really a book about The KLF. Or, at least, it is going to wander far from the usual path that music biographies are supposed to follow. I remain pleasantly surprised at how accepting people have been about this – whatever this book is, it seems to work on its own terms sufficiently well for it to become as accepted as it has. It helps that there are now 'proper' books about The KLF available, for those who want them, such as Ian Shirley's *Turn Up the Strobe* (2017). I'll talk about what the book actually is as we go along, because its boundaries and limits are more solid than usually suspected. For now, though, I'll say that although this may not really be a book about The KLF, I still think it is exactly what a book about The KLF should be.

† .ftp archives! That's dated the book a bit. The modern internet is good at hiding all this stuff from us now. I seem to remember that back then I had to use software like CoffeeCup Free FTP to get hold of a lot of KLF stuff. This is triggering waves of nostalgia for the Web 1.0 days . . .

The Situationists were a small but influential group of avant-garde thinkers from the 1950s who thought that culture was forced upon us, and that we needed to take control of it. These ideas sufficiently influenced KLF fans so that, when the internet grew in the years after the band split, they digitised their collections and shared them with the world.

Thanks to these copyright-ignoring KLF fans, it is possible to download the entire story of The KLF, as it played out in the media, in an afternoon. Then, with every press article, photograph and interview laid out before you, you can begin to pull a narrative out of all that data. The Situationists would have made a distinction between this mass of cultural data, what they would have called the *spectacle* of The KLF, and the actual events that caused this spectacle. What we have is not what happened, but it is all we can know about what happened. As the Situationists saw it, it is all that you can ever have to go on.

This made sense to me because of my experience researching the Timothy Leary biography. For that book, I behaved as you would expect a conscientious biographer to behave, and for a very good reason. I had never written a book before, or indeed any text of length. I didn't know what I was doing, and wanted to hide that fact from people. I worked diligently and tracked down people who had first-hand knowledge of events, formed a good relationship with Leary's estate and gained access to a number of archives, including his own. I travelled thousands of miles and I got to know as many people as my budget and time frame would allow, because basically that is what you are supposed to do.

As I progressed with this research, I noticed a surprising pattern in the data. Time and time again, older books, letters and interviews proved to be far more illuminating than first-hand interviews. It soon became apparent that accounts of events changed over time, and that the 'truth' of what happened depended very much on the date of your source. This was clear to me because I had access to Leary's own archive of papers. I could read letters and diary entries written at the time, find later magazine interviews about the same period, and also speak to surviving witnesses thirty or forty years after the event. These differing sources revealed a drift away from the raw chaos of what actually happened into a neater, simpler narrative which didn't always match the original sources. Even though later sources could offer greater perspective and illuminate things that were not apparent at the time, I adopted a rule of favouring the older sources whenever possible. They captured the flavour of the times, somehow, in a way that the more considered later versions didn't.

Psychologists have studied this drift of memory into error in great detail and found it to be an undeniable fact of our lives – even if most people refuse to accept it about their own memories. This drift has been found to be so precise and predictable that it can be plotted on a graph, known as the Ebbinghaus curve of forgetting.*

---

* I believe that technically this is usually known as the 'forgetting curve', or sometimes the 'Ebbinghaus forgetting curve'. However, I personally

What happens is that witnesses slowly absorb events into their own narrative, losing the loose ends and unexplained incidents and making sense of what they can with respect to their own lives and prejudices. We all do this. Indeed, if modern neuroscience is correct, it is something that we do far more than we think. The role of the ego, it appears, is less like a president or a prime minister deciding on a course of action, but more like their spin doctor explaining the action afterwards in the best possible light. We rationalise the actions of our unconscious minds and present them as an entirely correct, politically consistent course of action regardless of what it was or how uninvolved we are in the decision.

All this needs to be considered in any attempt to discover why The KLF burned a million pounds. If the central protagonists were as baffled as everyone else about their behaviour, and if other characters are not even aware that they are in this story, that leaves us with something of a problem. In this instance, asking the protagonists what happened all these years later would not only fail to illuminate those events, it would almost certainly take us decidedly off course. Many journalists have already tried this approach, interviewing Cauty and Drummond at length about the burning, and it hasn't really got them anywhere.

---

feel that the 'Ebbinghaus curve of forgetting' is a much better name and, as such, I always wilfully use it despite knowing it might be technically wrong. 'Ebbinghaus curve of forgetting!' It's just a magnificent phrase.

What is the alternative? We are left with the spectacle, and it is from within this spectacle that any answer to why they burned a million pounds must be sought. This approach seems particularly well suited to this story, because taking an encyclopaedic, academic approach to The KLF is not going to reveal the things that we're searching for. Drummond and Cauty stumbled mapless through their own stories, taking and using whatever they felt useful, so that is the approach we shall take as well. We are attempting to find the spirit of those events, and we can only do that by invoking them ourselves.*

Here, then, is a story that the cast were not told they were in.

---

* This point is probably worth stressing. The encyclopaedic, academic approach to biography can, of course, be powerful and important. Sometimes, however, it can fail to capture something significant about its subject. Attitude is more important than details, in some stories, and this can evaporate under a methodical, dry authorial voice. In a book like this, while I was trying to tell the story of what happened, I was also trying to sketch a portrait that would capture this attitude and leave the reader with an impression of The KLF that was immediate and vivid. I was trying to capture what it felt like to me, because that was the reason I thought the book should exist. As a result, it was written and originally self-published digitally without any attempt to contact Bill and Jimmy – because that was what they would have done. They were not ones to ask for permission. Dutifully seeking approval, in this instance, would have been against the spirit of the thing. Here I was also helped by Bill and Jimmy touring the country in 1995 to show the film of the burning, because they specifically asked the public for a reaction to what they had done. Using living people's lives in your work without their permission is ethically horrible, but their request for a response excused it, to my mind at least. It may have taken me seventeen years, but this was my reaction.

PART I
Rabbit Ears

1

Eris and Echo

▲

Bill Drummond and Julian Cope drove across Liverpool in an old, battered Transit van. In the back was a stolen mattress which they were taking to Devonshire Road in Toxteth. This was a row of grand Georgian mansion houses that had been built from slave-trade wealth, but which had long since decayed into squats and cheap, rundown flats. The mattress was for Cope, who was moving into the top floor of the house with his new wife. It was 1978, and Drummond was twenty-five. In the eyes of teenage punks like Cope, he was already old.

Drummond may have been old, but he had plans. He had achieved a touch of local fame with a band called Big in Japan, which also included future pop stars Holly Johnson, Pete 'Budgie' Clarke, Ian Broudie and Pete Burns either in the band or as part of its entourage. It was a highly creative mix of individuals who would go on to have more than their fair share of hit records. They had played regularly at the influential Mathew Street club, Eric's, and they had released one song as part of a split 7-inch single, but ultimately they were a shambolic affair which had split up, leaving behind a semi-legendary reputation and a string of debts. It struck Drummond that he could raise money to pay these debts by setting up a record label and releasing a Big in Japan EP. This seemed an obvious next step for a man of his age. He still loved music but, being twenty-five, he was clearly too old to make music himself.

More than anything, Drummond loved 7-inch vinyl. Singles possessed a magic that indulgent, career-minded albums sorely lacked. They were immediate, cheap and democratic. They could be terrible, of course, but the best ones had power over their owners which no other art form could compete with. There's nothing vague about the love you feel for a perfect pop song. It does not need explanation or context. And what other art form, in the late twentieth century, could make similar claims?

If Drummond was going to start a record label then he would do so with the same attitude that musicians should make music, keeping one eye on personal honesty and the other on the far horizon.* His label would only release

---

* Oof, that's a horrible sentence. It makes it sound like Bill Drummond had a lazy eye. Quite how that made it past the first draft, I don't know. Oh, the shame!

singles, for a start. And it would only sign bands that possessed an otherworldly something, bands that sent shivers down his spine. It was not necessarily the music that these bands created that he was interested in, for that was out of his hands. It was the idea of the bands that was important. This was why he needed Julian Cope.

Punk had arrived in Liverpool. It was the sudden return of all the feelings and emotions that the hippy culture had tried to repress, a reawakening of all the disrespect and raw frustration that the peace and love generation believed they were above. The punks may have kept the hippies' DIY attitude and their contempt for the older generation, but they were quick to rip down their indulgent fantasies with an ugly blast of blunt realism and angry mockery. They had no intention of putting up with the bullshit any longer. They wanted to do stuff.

History has adopted a very limited definition of 'punk', one which boils down to a spitting kid with a Mohawk haircut and a safety pin through his nose. Modern punk bands recreate the raw guitar music and confrontational fashion that were created before the original punk spirit faded, but this is to recreate the result of punk rather than punk itself – the symptoms rather than the disease. The attitude and look of the Sex Pistols came to be adopted as the definitive archetype, but away from the King's Road and outside London the punk ethic found many different ways to display its contempt for conformist society. In Belfast, for example, the Troubles were at their peak in the late 1970s and early 1980s, and slight nuances in speech or dress were enough to indicate sectarian allegiance and, potentially, bring violence or even death. Against this background a woman walked around the city dressed in a bin bag and flippers, carrying a kettle for a handbag. That was pretty damn punk.*

Liverpool, too, had its own local flavour of punk, and it was one with strict, self-policing ideas about what was acceptable. Fierce competition between local egos created an atmosphere where anything gimmicky or fragile was immediately leapt upon and torn to shreds for sport. There was a general contempt for anything from outside the city, with the notable exception of Manchester, with whom Liverpudlians shared an uneasy respect disguised as a bitter rivalry.† The Liverpool scene worked on the principle that great things were just around the corner. They were still out of reach, admittedly, but they were definitely getting closer. The big question was not what the future held, but who would be the first to claim it. The Liverpool punks were driven by a fear that their enemies would achieve great things first – or worse, their friends.

It was into this world that Julian Cope arrived in the summer of 1976, a well-spoken student teacher from middle-class Tamworth with an upper-class name and a

---

* At least one person has questioned the truth of this. I can report that my wife saw this person with her own eyes in the late 1970s, outside Leisure-World on Queen's Street.
† Incredibly well disguised, most of the time.

fondness for wearing a noose around his neck.

Despite these drawbacks, Drummond recognised two important things about Cope. The first was his obvious talent, raw and untamed as it was. The second, and most important, was that he had put a band together called The Teardrop Explodes and, in Drummond's estimation, this was by far the best band name in Liverpool. True, The Teardrops had not yet recorded, played live, or indeed learnt how to play their instruments, but this was pretty normal for the Liverpool scene. Most bands that Drummond's friends talked about didn't actually exist beyond the idea and a self-printed T-shirt. Cope was ahead of most, as he had already written the best part of three songs and was showing no signs of getting bored and giving up.

So as the pair drove towards Toxteth, Drummond explained to Cope his aspirations for his label, and why he wanted to put out records by a band called The Teardrop Explodes. Cope was initially wary, conscious of his band's inability to play and of his own current inability to sing. He had once been in a band with Ian McCulloch, a young Scouser who definitely could sing, so Cope suggested Drummond release a record by McCulloch's new band. Drummond was initially wary. McCulloch was known to be a fan of David Bowie, which at the time was unforgivable. Still, he asked what the band was called and Cope told him. They were Echo & the Bunnymen.

Echo & the Bunnymen. The name was not quite as good

as The Teardrop Explodes, but it was good. It was mysterious yet, at the same time, strangely confident. Something about the name struck a nerve in Drummond, and after he founded Zoo Records he released singles by both The Teardrop Explodes and Echo & the Bunnymen. The singles were 'shit', at least in Drummond's opinion, but he loved the bands that made them. Or, more accurately, he loved the idea of those bands.*

In the mid-1960s a photocopier was state-of-the-art technology, and having access to one was something of a privilege. Using an office photocopier after-hours for personal projects, without the boss knowing, was far riskier and more rebellious than it would be today. This was certainly the case for Lane Caplinger, a secretary of New Orleans District Attorney Jim Garrison.†

---

* That was a fairly straightforward bit of music biography writing, wasn't it? It helps to make the coming swerve seem even more abrupt. I don't think anyone at this point would be expecting the next paragraph. I still like how unapologetic the book is about this sudden shift.

† I recall feeling very cocky about this section. I remember thinking, 'If people make it through this bit, then they're mine. I'll have them for the rest of the book.' It was easy to be arrogant about readers at this stage in my career because I didn't have any – the subject was all theoretical. Now that I have some, I worry far more about how they are getting on and what they are thinking. There's a danger that this makes you a more timid writer, but I think in practice it makes you think harder and take more care over how you cause trouble. Yes, you could just shove your readers into a minefield. But I think the author's role instead is to take them by

In 1991 Garrison would be portrayed by Kevin Costner in Oliver Stone's movie *JFK*, which was based on Garrison's book *On the Trail of the Assassins*. But this was 1965, a year before he became involved in Kennedy conspiracies and two years before the Summer of Love thrust hippies, psychedelic drugs and alternative lifestyles in front of an unwary public. Things had not yet begun to get weird, in other words, and for a respected figure like Garrison there was little to indicate what surprises the future had in store. He would have been quite unprepared, then, for the book that Caplinger and her friend Greg Hill were producing in his office.

This book was the original version of what would become known as the *Principia Discordia, or How I Found The Goddess and What I Did To Her When I Found Her*, by a writer named Malaclypse the Younger. They made a first edition of five copies. At the time it was little more than a joke for some of their friends, but its influence is now scrawled in a haphazard and frequently illegible manner across the history of the late twentieth century.

There was some debate in the 1970s, when the book's fame began to spread, as to just who this Malaclypse the Younger was. Some believed that the book was the work of Timothy Leary. Others claimed it was written by the British-born Eastern philosopher Alan Watts, or by Richard Nixon during 'a few moments of lucidity'. It is now

---

the hand and be with them in a reassuring way while you walk them into a minefield.

generally accepted that the book was largely the work of Caplinger's friend Greg Hill, and that some parts were written by Hill's old school friend Kerry Thornley.*

The ideas behind the book can be traced back to the late 1950s, when Hill and Thornley attended California High School in East Whittier, a rural Southern California town that then nestled among vast orange groves. At school they were viewed as nerds. Hill was short, squat and introverted, while Thornley was tall, very thin and bursting with a nervous energy. They shared an enthusiasm for pranks and strange ideas. They were also both keen on bowling alleys, largely because they served alcohol and remained open until two in the morning.

It was in one such bowling alley in 1957 that Thornley showed Hill some poetry he was writing. It included a reference to order eventually arising out of chaos. Hill laughed at this. He told Thornley that the idea of 'order' was an illusion. Order is just something that the human mind projects onto reality. What really exists behind this fake veneer is an infinite, churning chaos. For Hill, an atheist, the failure to understand this was the major folly of the religions of the world, all of which claim that there is an organising principle at work in the Universe.

Hill also told Thornley that the ancient Greeks were an exception to this rule, for they had a Goddess of Chaos. Her

---

* There's been no attempt yet to explain why we have made this detour or how it connects to the story of The KLF. That's either pretty confident or pretty stupid. Let's see how long this lasts.

name was Eris, which meant 'strife' and which translates as 'Discordia' in Latin. Clearly, if anyone wanted to worship a deity who was genuinely active in this world, then Eris was the only credible option. All that was needed was for someone to create a religion around her which, naturally, they decided to do. They called it Discordianism.*

Discordianism is, at its heart, wilfully contradictory. It claims that chaos, confusion and uncertainty are the true nature of reality. This claim does tend to raise the question as to how Discordianism itself, and all the assumptions that it is based on, can be accepted with any authority. Or to put it another way, if someone tells you that there can be no certainty, then believing in what they've told you becomes a paradox. Hill and Thornley were not put off by such problems. If anything, they enjoyed them. As they developed their ideas over the following years, they found that there were ways around such things, if they only kept their sense of humour about them.

One such innovation was Hill and Thornley's invention of the concept of 'catmas'. Catmas are similar to dogmas, but they are considerably less rigid. Normal religions consider dogmas to be absolute, unquestionable truths. Discordians

---

* My source for all this was Adam Gorightly's hugely important book *The Prankster and the Conspiracy*. There are now many more sources of information about the history of Discordianism readily available, of which Gorightly's *Historia Discordia* deserves a special mention.

consider catmas to be absolute, unquestionable truths, for now at least. This is an approach that echoes the philosophy of the American writer and radical sceptic Charles Fort, who in 1932 wrote, 'I conceive of nothing, in religion, science or philosophy, that is more than the proper thing to wear, for a while.' Discordians understand that every catma may one day be discarded on the grounds that it is nonsense. Until that day comes, it should be accepted and respected. Some Discordians may even genuinely believe catmas on occasions, should the mood take them, but this is certainly not compulsory.

For one example, consider the Discordian catma regarding food. Most religions include strict dietary rules. Jews are forbidden to eat pork. Catholics should eat fish on Fridays. Certain sects of Buddhists, Sikhs and Hindus are vegetarian, and Hindus cannot eat any part of a cow. In the same spirit, Discordians are forbidden from eating hot dog buns.

There is a 'reason' for this catma. It originates in a story in which Zeus held a party for the gods but did not invite Eris on the grounds that she tended to cause trouble. Thus Eris experienced what Discordians refer to as the 'original snub' and was reduced to eating a frankfurter sausage by herself, sitting alone outside the party. Nobody believes a word of this, of course, yet Discordians have respected the catma of the forbidden hot dog buns for over forty years. They don't respect it particularly thoroughly, admittedly, and indeed you'd be hard pressed to find a Discordian who has never eaten a hot dog bun. Nevertheless, at Discordian events and special occasions, people still make a show of eating frankfurters with no buns. The reason for this is that the catma, despite being nonsense, is useful. It is a terrific satire against the forbidden food dogmas of established religions.

For those who've found it funny, it becomes that much harder to take seriously any claims about food being unclean, kosher or halal. It helps make any religious leader who expresses belief in similar dietary rules appear ludicrous, and this makes any other dogma that they may preach appear equally suspect. Should Discordians ever find a better catma to ridicule religious dietary dogma, then the hot dog rule will no doubt be unceremoniously dropped. But until that day, Discordians keep the 'no hot dog buns' catma – not because it is true, but because it is powerful.

Slowly Hill and Thornley recruited a few like-minded friends into their new religion. Their aim was to undermine existing belief systems by spreading confusion and disinformation with as much humour as possible. To this end they each adopted a host of new names under which their Discordian endeavours were credited. Hill became known varyingly as Malaclypse the Younger, Rev. Dr Occupant, Mad Malik, Ignotum P. Ignotious or Professor Iggy. Thornley became Omar Khayyam Ravenhurst, Rev. Jesse Sump, Ho Chi Zen or the Bull Goose of Limbo. Many different Discordian chapters were founded. The majority of these contained only one member, and some contained none at all. Discordians then wrote essays and letters under these aliases, only to then follow them with completely contradictory essays and letters under a different alias. Gradually this process spread and, by the time it reached its height in the late sixties and early seventies, it had become known as Operation Mindfuck. The aim of Operation Mindfuck was to lead people into such a heightened state of bewilderment and confusion that their rigid beliefs would shatter and be replaced by some form of enlightenment.

That was the aim, anyway. In practice it rarely worked out so well, with those heavily absorbed in Discordianism proving more likely to succumb to paranoid schizophrenia than to any form of enlightened bliss. Still, they meant well.*

Discordianism was a joke, at least to start with. Discordianism is often described as being either an elaborate satire

---

* It's interesting to look back on this from the other side of the Trump and Covid-19 lockdown era, after 'fake news' and algorithmically targeted misinformation gave us all a pretty miserable time. Clearly, this doesn't look quite as funny now as it did when I wrote this. It's worth saying, however, that a working knowledge of Discordianism and Robert Anton Wilson has proved to be valuable throughout this trying time. We probably all saw people we know fall into the tar pits of QAnon, 5G, anti-vax or other bleak, paranoid conspiracy theories. Political and New Age-type people seemed to be particularly susceptible to this, especially during the Covid lockdown period when people spent more time online and less time talking face-to-face with friends. From my experience, however, readers of Robert Anton Wilson have come through this era well – his work gives us vital antibodies that protect us from catching these belief systems. Wilson's readers may be interested in these conspiracies, and they may be knowledgeable about them, but they sure as hell don't believe in them.

disguised as a religion or an elaborate religion disguised as a satire, descriptions which wrongly assume that it cannot be both at the same time. The whole concept was a satire or, at most, a way to deal with nihilism by wrapping it up with a goddess and a sense of humour. As events unfurled, those at the heart of Discordianism stopped making this distinction. As Discordianism started to take on a life of its own, it became harder and harder to claim that what was going on was 'just' a joke.

Eris, or, rather, the concept of chaos, had a busy second half of the twentieth century. Clearly, she was making up for lost time. Chaos had not been recognised academically since the time of the ancient Greeks. The closest subject you could find in engineering or physics literature was *turbulence*, and this was only described as something to be avoided.

During the 1970s the concept was embraced in places as diverse as university maths departments and occult sub-cultures (or perhaps those places aren't so diverse after all, for in the 1970s, university maths departments and occult sub-cultures were both places where young men took lots of LSD). Regardless, whole new fields such as *chaos maths* and *chaos magic* sprang up. The relationship between chaos and order was being modelled mathematically, and the results were surprising. In what was thought to be order, people found chaos, yet when they then looked into chaos they found order. Phrases like 'the Butterfly effect' became universally known, if perhaps not universally understood. Hill and Thornley were only joking when they talked of helping chaos manifest itself in the modern world, but that is precisely what happened.

For the first time since the 1960s, music journalists from London were travelling to Liverpool to write about Liverpool bands.* They had to, for something was definitely happening – just as those in the Liverpool scene always knew it would. Every one of the early singles that Drummond released from Echo & the Bunnymen and The Teardrop Explodes was hailed as the 'single of the week' by the influential British music weekly the *NME*.

Those journalists wanted to know what the name 'Echo & the Bunnymen' meant. It didn't actually mean anything. Cope had gone against the tide of the usual, 'blunt' punk band names when he came up with The Teardrop Explodes and now other Liverpudlian bands were creating similarly elaborate and psychedelic sounding names in an effort to compete. Echo & the Bunnymen was one of the better attempts, while names such as Frankie Goes To Hollywood or Orchestral Manoeuvres in the Dark were perhaps less impressive.† Echo & the Bunnymen was just one of a handful of names suggested by a friend of the band known as Smelly Elly, and was adopted on the grounds that it was

---

* And back to Drummond, with no attempt to explain what all that was about. This was either very ballsy, or I just didn't know any better.

† This is subjective opinion, of course, but in the decade since this book came out no one has taken me up on it, so I think it stands up okay.

the best suggestion that they had. The band wanted a better story than this for journalists, so they claimed that Echo was their drum machine, and that they were Bunnymen in a similar way that *Playboy* models were Bunnygirls.

The spreading of this story did not please Bill Drummond. He had his own personal meaning for the name, and he far preferred his version. It was triggered by the sleeve of their first single, 'Pictures On My Wall', which featured a scratchy silhouetted drawing of a strange, powerful beast.* The two shapes emerging from the top of its head would perhaps normally be interpreted as horns, but in the context of the band could be considered to be rabbit ears. But what a rabbit! This strange beast was sinister and powerful, and Drummond intuitively knew that this creature, whatever it was, was Echo. The Bunnymen, therefore, were his followers.

At the time Drummond liked to spend hours in the Central Library in the centre of Liverpool, searching through the shelves marked Religion, Myth and Tribal. As he wrote in 1998, 'I was on the hunt for real or even imagined information on who this weird Echo character was.' He quickly discounted a Greek mountain nymph and lover of Pan who was called Echo. That story did not connect with him in any way. But there were stories that did make an

---

* I saw Echo & the Bunnymen over forty years later, at Manchester Albert Hall in February 2022, and they were still using this image as their backdrop. According to their guitarist Will Sergeant, it was inspired by the film *Quatermass and the Pit.*

impression, stories of a mythical trickster being who could take the shape of a rabbit. These stories came from native people from the far north, from Siberia, north Canada and Scandinavia. Drummond began merging these separate tales in his head, creating a clearer image of this elemental spirit from dark, cold landscapes.

He didn't tell anyone this, of course. That would be crazy.

So when the band gave the press their version of the story, Drummond held his tongue. 'I had to stop myself from butting in and saying, "No, no, you've got it wrong. It's nothing to do with Bunnygirls. Bunnymen are the scattered tribes that populate the northern rim of the world and are followers of a mythical being, divine spirit, prime mover who takes the earthly form of a rabbit." But I didn't.'

In 1980 Echo & the Bunnymen released their first album, *Crocodiles*.* Drummond had licensed the album to Warners, thus keeping Zoo pure and free from such self-indulgent projects as albums. But it still felt like a compromise. McCulloch and the band clearly had very different dreams from Drummond. They wanted to make albums, tour the world and become hugely rich and successful. As their manager, Drummond had to accept this, but he was still of the impression that a real band should just make a few perfect singles and then split up.

---

* The final section of this chapter is probably my favourite part of the book.

The album sleeve was lying on the floor of his office when Drummond glanced at it, its image foreshortened by the angle. The cover photo showed the band in a forest at night, lit by strong red and yellow light. In the centre of the frame bassist Les Pattinson sat leaning against an ash tree which, strangely, had two primary trunks which gracefully curved around each other.

Then suddenly – the picture changed.

Red and evil, a huge rabbit's head stared at Drummond, solid and unblinking. Instantly he knew who he was looking at. It was Echo.

And then, in a blink, the band photo returned. Picking up the sleeve, Drummond realised that it contained an optical illusion. The tree trunks looked like the head and ears of a rabbit, one that appeared evil thanks to the downward angle of its eye, the sharp elongated point to its face and the red light on the tree. Once he had seen it, it seemed incredible that no one had ever noticed it before.

This was weird. Echo was supposed to be an idle fantasy of Drummond's, a strange personal thought that he kept to himself. It was not supposed to appear out in the world, eyeing him coldly from an album sleeve. He spoke to the photographer to determine whether it had been done deliberately, and learnt that it had not. The final cover photograph had been one that no one had wanted, but which had eventually been accepted as a compromise. No one had seen the rabbit head in the image before Drummond pointed it out.

He was discreet when he spoke to the photographer,

of course. He knew that the idea of Echo was a personal fantasy from his inner life, an idea that could survive in his mind but not withstand the scrutiny of others. But the appearance of the rabbit in the world outside him had strengthened the idea, giving it the potential to grow and evolve and become more elaborate and intricate. Such constructions grow secretly in many minds, acknowledged and understood only by their creators. Their imaginary nature does not mean that they are unable to affect the world at large.

2

Illuminations and Illuminatus

▲

The psychologist Carl Jung credited a particular dream as being a turning point in his life, one which convinced him to embark on the study of synchronicity and the subconscious. He wrote about this dream in his book *Memories, Dreams, Reflections*. In due course the Liverpudlian poet Peter O'Halligan read about the dream in that book, and came to view it with equal significance.*

In his dream, Jung found himself 'in a dark, sooty city.

---

* By this point the book can take any detour that it likes, and the reader is okay with it – perhaps even eager for it. That this diversion into Jung swings back to Liverpool certainly helps, though. This chapter starts to connect the various strands together, reassuring the reader that this is all going somewhere and that the book knows what it is doing. Chaos is great, but it is best enjoyed in short bursts.

It was night, and winter, and dark, and raining. I was in Liverpool. With a number of Swiss – say half a dozen – I walked through the dark streets.'

Like many Scousers, O'Halligan's home city was a significant part of his personal identity, so Jung's mention of Liverpool immediately grabbed him. In later years, he researched Jung's life in an effort to discover if there was a link that explained the setting of Liverpool in this dream. But he did not find any. Jung had never been to Liverpool and didn't have any obvious connection to the place.

The dream continued. 'It reminded me of Basel, where the market is down below and you go up through the Tottengässchen (Alley of the Dead), which leads to a plateau above and so to the Petersplatz and the Peterskirche.' The 'Peter' in these street names gave Peter O'Halligan a personal connection to the dream. 'When we reached the plateau, we found a broad square, dimly illuminated by street lights, into which many streets converged. The various quarters of the city were arranged radially around the square.' O'Halligan later searched Liverpool for the best candidate for such a place, and came to believe that Jung referred to the square* at the end of Mathew Street. This was an area that then consisted of old warehouses between the centre of the city and the waterfront. This was the exact same place where O'Halligan had recently leased

---

* It's pushing it to call this a square. It's basically a pedestrianised crossroads. But myth is more powerful than pedantic niggles like this, so the story lives on.

a building, and the location of Eric's, the club where Bill Drummond would perform with Big in Japan. Some years after Jung's dream, one of these warehouses would become a club called The Cavern, from where the Beatles would emerge to change the world.

Jung continued. 'In the centre was a round pool, and in the middle of it, a small island. While everything around was obscured by rain, fog, smoke and dimly lit darkness, the little island blazed with sunlight. On it stood a single tree, a magnolia, in a sea of reddish blossoms. It was as though the tree stood in the sunlight and was, at the same time, the source of light. My companions commented on the abominable weather, and obviously did not see the tree. They spoke of another Swiss who was living in Liverpool, and expressed surprise that he should have settled here. I was carried away by the beauty of the tree and the sunlit island, and thought, "I know very well why he has settled here." Then I awoke.'

Jung felt that his subconscious had showed him something of profound importance. 'Everything was extremely unpleasant, black and opaque – just as I felt then,' he wrote. 'But I had had a vision of unearthly beauty, and that was why I was able to live at all.' Jung had found, bubbling up from his subconscious, an image of illumination that inspired him. It was no more than a dream image, but it was more powerful and had a greater impact on him than things which physically exist.

Jung's dream also had a profound effect on O'Halligan, because he, too, had had a dream. He had dreamt that he saw a spring bubbling forth from a cast-iron drain cover in the middle of the road where Mathew Street, Button Street and others converge. He came down to Mathew Street the next day and, sure enough, there was a manhole cover where he had dreamt one. He also saw that one remaining warehouse had a 'To Let' sign outside. He had then gone to the bank, got a loan and leased the building. He turned the downstairs into a market and opened a café above it. The market became known as Aunt Twackies, a pun on the Scouse mispronunciation of 'antiques' as 'an teek wees'. He would later discover that there was an ancient spring underneath the building, which fed into an old brick-built reservoir.*

When he later read of Jung's dream, he was struck by the way that Jung seemed to have dreamt of the exact same location, and that he, too, had linked it to some elemental source of life. This seemed deeply significant to O'Halligan. He arranged for a bust of Jung to be placed in an alcove in the outside wall.

*

---

* According to Spencer Leigh's book *The Cavern Club: The Rise of The Beatles and Merseybeat* (2015), 'when The Cavern was excavated in 1982, the builders stumbled upon an old shaft that led into a huge hole, a cavern underneath The Cavern as it were. It was filled with water and the architect and the site-agent bravely investigated it in a rubber dinghy. The lake was 120 feet long and 70 feet wide and, in parts, eight foot deep. There was no other exit and because of the scrapings in the sandstone wall, they could tell it was man-made. But why was it constructed?'

The market began to attract members of the local music scene due to its proximity to Probe Records and Eric's nightclub, and because they could spend a day talking and planning in the café for the price of a cup of tea. Bill Drummond, then twenty-three, was one of many who would spend hours in the place. Drummond was working as a set builder at the Everyman Theatre. He had returned to Liverpool, where he had attended college, after a short period working on trawlers in his native Scotland. One day he wandered in and found O'Halligan hammering a nail into a piece of wood. O'Halligan told him that he was planning to open what he called the 'Liverpool School of Language, Music, Dream and Pun'. He also told him about Jung's dream. 'I didn't really understand what O'Halligan was on about,' Drummond recalled later, 'but it resonated and I remembered it almost word for word. Also, he didn't look like a hippy, more a Scouse Beat, so he was okay with my prejudices at the time.'

The Liverpool School of Language, Music, Dream and Pun was planning on staging plays. O'Halligan had persuaded the actor and director Ken Campbell to base his next project there. This was quite a coup, as Campbell's previous touring show, *The Ken Campbell Roadshow*, had been something of a success. It had featured Campbell, together with a troop of actors including Bob Hoskins and Sylvester McCoy, dramatising weird and wonderful 'friend of a friend' stories. The reason why O'Halligan wanted to stage plays was, naturally enough, another one of his dreams. This dream had featured a building with a raging fire upstairs and a play being performed in a theatre in the basement. There had been a copy of *Playboy* magazine on a seat in the theatre. This didn't immediately make a great deal of sense, but in the world of the dream it was in some way significant.

The editors of the *Playboy* 'forum' letters pages during the mid-to-late sixties were Robert Anton Wilson and Bob Shea. In many ways their positions were not that different from most office jobs, except that the secretaries tended to be prettier and every week or so they'd be invited up to Hugh Hefner's mansion to 'watch movies and stuff'.

A lot of the readers' letters they received, though, were decidedly odd.

In part this was because some of these were from the small, initial group of Discordians. The two Bobs found themselves in frequent correspondence with Kerry Thornley. They soon became committed Discordians themselves, with Wilson adopting the Discordian name Mordecai the Foul and Shea calling himself Josh the Dill. It was not long before the *Playboy* forum took, under these two editors, a decidedly weird turn. Letters were printed that proclaimed deeply complicated and contradictory conspiracy theories, not because the writers believed what they were claiming, but because they wanted to mess with the heads of the people who read *Playboy*.

Context is important here. Those letters appeared considerably more surreal simply because they were part of the *Playboy* letters page. To use the April 1969 edition as an example, there are the usual letters which begin: 'After an hour or so of heavy petting, I often find myself in substantial pain in the area of my testicle and lower abdomen', and 'The girl who lives across the street from me has been my friend since childhood. Now that we've both reached maturity, I see our relationship in a new light.' These letters are then followed by one that starts, 'I recently heard an old man of right-wing views – a friend of my grandparents' – assert that the current wave of assassinations in America is the work of a secret society called the Illuminati. He said that the Illuminati have existed throughout history, own the international banking cartels, have all been 32-degree Masons and were known to Ian Fleming, who portrayed them as SPECTRE in his James Bond books – for which the Illuminati did away with Mr Fleming.' This was then followed by a lengthy reply, detailing the history of the eleventh-century Islamic Hashashin sect and pointing out that Ian Fleming died of natural causes.*

The strange thing was, though, that Thornley and friends weren't writing all these letters themselves. While many could be attributed to their small core of Discordian colleagues, there were many others which appeared to be from complete strangers. Or were they? This was a problem with Operation Mindfuck, for you couldn't trust your

---

* I'd completely forgotten about all this, even though I've just spent a year writing about Fleming and James Bond (see *Love and Let Die: Bond, the Beatles and the British Psyche*, 2022).

friends to be honest about their activities. But still, judging by factors such as the postmarks on letters and unknown handwriting, there appeared to be many conspiratorial letters arriving from people that they didn't know. The Discordian ideas, which Thornley had been spreading in printed handbills and, eventually, in the *Principia Discordia*, were starting to spread. They were spreading to people who liked to write letters to *Playboy*.

Wilson and Shea did their best to make sense of what was going on. The concept we now call 'conspiracy theory' was emerging, fully formed, just a few brief years after the flaws in the Warren Commission report into the JFK assassination had become evident. People were now openly accusing sections of the US Government of being involved in Kennedy's death, an idea that would have been unthinkable to the average American when the murder occurred in 1963. To Wilson and Shea, as they waded through all the different accusations, it started to look like *everyone* had killed Kennedy. Some blamed the CIA, others the Mafia. Some claimed that it was Castro, while others pointed to anti-Castro forces. As they joked to each other, what if every conspiracy was true? From all this came the idea for the trilogy of novels that they wrote together between 1969 and 1971, the award-winning *Illuminatus!* trilogy, which they dedicated to Hill and Thornley.

The wilfully complicated plot of the book boils down to a struggle between order and chaos. It features an organisation of enlightened beings called the Illuminati, who secretly rule the world for their own evil ends. The

Illuminati was a real organisation which had been founded in Bavaria in 1776 with the aim of exploring and spreading Enlightenment ideals. Shea and Wilson claimed that the organisation has existed in secrecy ever since, and indeed for centuries beforehand, although most historians insist that it only lasted for about ten years.

In the book, the Illuminati are opposed only by small groups of Discordians, who have to prevent the Illuminati from bringing about the end of the world. The Discordians, in true Discordian fashion, go under many names, such as the ELF (the Erisian Liberation Front), the LDD (The League of Dynamic Discord, also known as Little Deluded Dopes) and The Justified Ancients of Mummu, otherwise known as The JAMs. The JAMs had helped organise the assassination of JFK. They were 'at least as old as the Illuminati and represent the primeval power of Chaos'. They had once been part of the Illuminati, but they had rebelled in a similar way that Satan rebelled in Heaven and had either left, or been kicked out. As a sideline, they had set up a record company to create some decent music. The rest of the music industry was controlled by the Illuminati, the book explained, which was how they were able to incorporate the anti-JAMs slogan 'Kick out the Jams, motherfuckers!' into MC5 records.

Or, at least, that's a typical interpretation of the plot. In true Discordian style, these things are fluid and open to interpretation. The book likes to play tricks with its narrative, happy to contradict itself in order to generate confusion and paranoia in the reader. Nevertheless, the idea that The

Justified Ancients of Mummu represent chaos, and are at war with order or control, is a core idea that most take away from the book.

Unsurprisingly, publishers were baffled by the whole thing. Eventually, after four years of effort, the first volume was published in 1975. It has remained in print ever since, won awards and inspired conspiracy fiction from *Foucault's Pendulum* to *The Da Vinci Code*, as well as countless video games and comic books. It planted the idea of the Illuminati as an organisation who are currently active, and who secretly run the world, into modern culture.* This idea was intended as no more than a joke or a 'mindfuck'. Nevertheless, there are now countless conspiracy theorists around the world who believe that it is true. Imaginary ideas have a way of being just as influential, it seems, as more grounded ones.

Ken Campbell was paying for a stack of books in Compendium,† an independent, esoteric bookshop in Camden,

---

* It seems funny now that it was necessary to explain all this and describe who the Illuminati were supposed to be. Now, it's probably fair to say that most people have heard of them and that they associate them with the 'eye in the pyramid' symbol. I blame Beyoncé.

† Ah, the much-missed Compendium. It's hard now to overstate how important that shop was in terms of plugging people into alternative ideas and perspectives. You could spend hours browsing before deciding what to buy, knowing that the book you chose would change you and your understanding of the world, even if you didn't yet know how. Before our

north London, when he noticed a copy of *Illuminatus!* on display by the till. He was searching for some science fiction that might be suitable to adapt for his next project because, following a pleasant evening drinking with the sci-fi author Brian Aldiss, he had decided that he quite liked the company of science fiction people. So it was that in 1976 Campbell and the writer and actor Chris Langham formed the Science Fiction Theatre of Liverpool, with the intention of creating a play to stage at Aunt Twackies. All he had to do now was find some science fiction.

His eye was drawn to this one book because it had a yellow submarine on the cover, which has obvious connections to Liverpool. The book itself was not science fiction, but booksellers had not known what to make of it and had placed it on the science fiction shelves for want of anywhere better. This, it seemed, was good enough for the Science Fiction Theatre of Liverpool.*

Of all the books he bought that day, it was *Illuminatus!* that grabbed Campbell. It affected him in a way that none of the other ones did. Reading it made him see the world

---

modern era, where you can get pretty much any book with just a few clicks online, a place like this was incredibly valuable. You don't tend to think of shops as being significant influences in your life but, looking back, I think it's true that both Compendium and Probe Records in Mathew Street helped make me.

* As Ken would later explain, 'When you think about it, normal theatre is basically about people walking in and out of doors. Science Fiction is about everything else.'

differently. What had previously appeared to be hierarchical, ordered and neatly categorised now appeared as random connections of chance and ignorance. This effect was not just limited to the world in the book. The real world itself was changed, or at least how he perceived it. *Illuminatus!* made him simultaneously wiser and more baffled. It was good stuff.*

Campbell decided to turn the entire trilogy into a cycle of five plays, lasting a total of eight and a half hours. There would be twenty-three actors playing over three hundred distinct parts. This epic tale of global domination would be told on a small stage at the back of a warehouse café. Most people would not consider this to be a plausible goal, but Campbell went ahead and did it anyway. As he saw it, things were only really worth doing if they were impossible. To quote Chris Langham, who co-wrote the play with Campbell, 'if it's possible, it will end up as some mediocre, grant-subsidised bit of well-intentioned bourgeois bollocks. But if it's impossible, then it will assume an energy of its own, despite everything we do or don't do.'

The cast and crew were recruited, often in ways as strange and disorientating as Wilson and Shea's writing. The actor Bill Nighy, for example, was flat-sitting in London when he

---

* Seeing as I'm now writing in the 2020s, I should add that a lot of it really hasn't aged well, particularly the portrayals of women. It's still an important book, of course, but there is no hiding the fact that it was written in the 1960s by two staff writers at *Playboy*.

came across a copy of *Illuminatus!*. After spending a day reading it, he turned on the TV and was confronted by a different image of something from the book every time he changed the channel, such as the bank robber John Dillinger or an American dollar bill (the symbolism of which the book discusses at length). Disturbed, he decided to turn off the TV and go to the pub. He took the book along with him, only to be approached by a strangely dressed bloke with bushy eyebrows. It was Ken Campbell. When Nighy told Campbell that he was an actor, he was hired on the spot.

Other cast members included David Rappaport, Jim Broadbent and Prunella Gee, who played the Goddess Eris and later had a daughter with Campbell named Daisy Eris.* It was at this point that the twenty-three-year-old Bill Drummond also came into Campbell's orbit. The pair spent a day down by the Mersey and by the end of it Drummond had been recruited to produce the sets for the show.

It was never going to be easy. Campbell's key piece of direction to the cast and crew was, when thinking about the tone of what they were doing, to keep asking the question: 'Is it heroic?' Drummond went back to the table in the back room that doubled as his workshop and painted the

---

* Since 2017, Daisy has become Bill and Jimmy's go-to director for their various shenanigans. Daisy often tells the story of how she was conceived backstage during a performance of *Illuminatus!*. Her parents explained to her that 'it was a very long play and there were some boring bits.'

phrase 'Is it heroic?' on the wall in white paint. He then got to work.

'And fuck me, did he deliver!' to quote Bill Nighy. Drummond's solution was to build the sets in strange scales, utilising tricks such as foreshortening and strange angles, all of which perfectly suited the disorienting style of the play. Tables or beds were upturned and stuck to the rear wall, giving the audience the impression that they were looking down on the action from the ceiling. Given the seemingly contradictory scales of the story and the café stage, Drummond took Ken Campbell's advice, assumed that the impossible would be possible and just knuckled down and did it. And why not? Everyone was achieving things previously unimaginable. Jim Broadbent recalled the production of *Illuminatus!* working on a 'genius level . . . It wasn't that Ken was being a genius . . . it was the whole creation of doing the greatest show yet done on Planet World . . . his creative imagination was just stunning.'

The success of the play led to a move south, and a sold-out run at the National Theatre in London began in March 1977. It now featured a pre-recorded prologue performed by John Gielgud, who played a computer called the First Universal Cybernetic Kinetic Ultramicro Programmer, or FUCKUP ('The best anarchist joke ever perpetrated at the heart of the National', in the opinion of Campbell's biographer Michael Coveney). It also featured Robert Anton Wilson himself, who was given a role that involved lying naked on the stage shouting the maxim of the notorious

English occultist Aleister Crowley, 'Do what thou will shall be the whole of the law!'*

Wilson also brought a large amount of acid with him, which he offered to the cast. Bill Nighy recalls that 'everyone went very quiet and then . . . "Yeah, why not, thanks," and we all dived in. So we were all tripping. It's a terrible idea if you want to act, but there you are . . .' Nighy's position was made more difficult because he had a scene with Neil Cunningham where they had to 'act' tripping. 'How do we act tripping as we already are anyway?' Nighy asked. Cunningham suggested that they just stood there and held hands. So the pair of them stood on the stage, and held hands.

For many in the audience of the National Theatre run, this was their first exposure to Discordian ideas. Among them was a young artist called Jimmy Cauty.† Cauty,

---

* Because the patron of the National Theatre was then Queen Elizabeth, a common story in accounts of Robert Anton Wilson's life is that he got naked in front of the Queen. Alas, the Queen did not regularly attend National Theatre productions and did not turn up for Campbell's production of *Illuminatus!* A shame, but it was her loss.

† Over fifty-seven pages in and – the introduction aside – I'm only starting to mention Cauty now. The portrayal of Jimmy is one of the great failings of this book. Or at least, it is if we keep up the pretence that this is a book about The KLF. It doesn't help matters that a lot of what is in here about him comes from Bill's writings, so we're often getting Jimmy filtered through Bill's eyes. The sense that this can give – that Jimmy was the practical, more grounded member of the band – is one I know Jimmy would disagree with. Hopefully someone will step up and write a full biography of Jimmy one day, covering his entire artistic career. That, I think, would be fascinating.

originally from Liverpool and then aged twenty-two, had already had some success painting bestselling *The Lord of the Rings* and *The Hobbit* posters for Athena (they were bought, he said, 'mainly by student nurses'). He did not meet Bill Drummond at this performance. Drummond had disappeared from the project back in Liverpool. After the sets were completed and as the premiere of the play grew nearer, Drummond announced that he was just popping out to get some glue and never returned. It was the late 1970s and punk was starting to rumble. As radical as the book and play were, the spirit of the age was not emerging in the form of eight-and-a-half-hour plays. Together with Ian Broudie, then a young guitarist whom Campbell had recruited to perform music for the play, Drummond formed the band Big in Japan.

Campbell had shown Drummond that the impossible was only impossible if you did not stand up and do it. It did not matter how big the practical problems were, or how crazy the enterprise may seem. This was an important lesson in Drummond's education. He took that attitude, picked up the Gibson 330 guitar he had bought in Tin Pan Alley in 1969 and went off to make music.

3

Sirius and Synchronicity

▲

In October 1966, Jim Garrison sat down to read the Warren Commission Report and tried to make sense of the assassination of the president. The Commission had published twenty-six volumes of hearings and evidence. This was a lot of data, but Garrison was an experienced district attorney and he was used to working with large and complicated sets of information. Methodically, he read through every witness statement and examined every photograph. With all the evidence mentally spread in front of him, he began to analyse. He saw connections and contradictions emerging from this web of data, and by linking these key facts he began to weave a narrative. This narrative, if he did his job properly, would provide clarity about what really happened. He was attempting to tease out the one story that was true.*

It did not take him long to dismiss the Commission's findings. Their narrative claimed that President Kennedy had been shot for unknown reasons by an ex-marine named Lee Harvey Oswald, and that Oswald had acted alone, without the assistance of any other individuals or groups, either foreign or domestic. Garrison could see how they had pulled this story from the mass of data, but he also saw too many errors in their analysis. Too much contradictory information had been ignored, and too many omissions had not been followed through. The Commission's conclusions did not, to his mind, tell the story of what really happened. If anything, it told the story of what people wanted to have happened. It had chosen the most palatable narrative, rather than the true one.

And it was important to know what had happened. Murder is serious and human life is valuable, but JFK's murder had another dimension above and beyond the loss of one man's life. His murder hit people on a symbolic level. Kennedy was not then as universally popular as he is now remembered, but he was young, virile and the figurehead of the nation. The beheading of a king is an ancient and powerful archetype, and when the second bullet removed much of Kennedy's head, that archetype played out in the psyche of the country. The American people, collectively, went into a kind of shock. Like the events of 9/11 and the

---

* We've all been there. Nowadays, Garrison would have a podcast.

death of Princess Diana, it was a tragedy whose impact on the nation's subconscious was greater than anything a rational assessment of the death toll would suggest. The killer shot at one man, but millions were hit. And whoever was responsible, it appeared to Garrison, was getting away with it.

Oswald had spent time in New Orleans, so that gave Garrison an excuse to investigate further. If the true narrative couldn't be identified in the mass of data in front of the Warren Commission, then he would have to get more data. With more and more information, more and more connections would become visible, causing the number of potential narratives to increase exponentially. With enough data, it seemed sensible to assume, the true narrative would eventually emerge. So he began to ask questions.

One individual who soon took his interest was Kerry Thornley. Garrison did not know about Thornley's ideas of Discordianism, or indeed that his key writing had been reproduced on Garrison's own office photocopier. What he did know was that Thornley had enlisted in the Marine Corps in 1959, after graduating from high school with Greg Hill, and had met and become close with Lee Harvey Oswald. 'You might say that I was [Oswald's] best buddy,' he had told the Warren Commission, 'but I don't think he had any close friends. I was a close acquaintance.' Thornley was close with Oswald for just a few months before Thornley was posted to Japan and separated from him.

It was while in Japan that Thornley heard that Oswald had entered the American Embassy in Moscow, handed over his passport, denounced his American citizenship and defected to the Russians.

After leaving the military, Thornley had supported himself by washing dishes in New Orleans while he worked on a novel, *The Idle Warriors*, which featured a main character whom he based on Oswald. At this point Oswald returned from Russia, moved to New Orleans and began hanging out in the same places and with the same people as Thornley. Garrison also knew that Thornley, who at the time was interested in extreme Libertarian politics, had been seen celebrating after JFK's death and was connected to a number of other people he considered suspicious. Garrison had witnesses who claimed to have seen Thornley with Oswald in New Orleans. It was no surprise that Garrison would be interested in Thornley.*

The problem was that Thornley had not known that Oswald was in New Orleans. He had not seen him since his marine days, and was at a loss to explain why Garrison's witnesses claimed otherwise. Unless Thornley was genuinely involved in the JFK assassination, which hardly anyone believes, then some strange coincidences were at

---

* All this JFK assassination stuff looms large in Discordian lore. To contemporary eyes, it seems like ancient history, as far back from modern times as the death of Queen Victoria was to the first Discordians. There's a lot of history in Discordian lore, especially eighteenth-century Enlightenment stories, so it's easy to see it in those historical terms. But to the founders of Discordianism, this was current events.

play. Clearly it must have been a case of mistaken identity, but the accounts which showed that Oswald frequented many of Thornley's hangouts and knew similar people seemed too suspicious to ignore – even to Thornley. As Garrison's investigator Andrew Sciambra told him before Thornley's grand jury testimony, 'If it checks out on the lie detector that you are telling the truth about having no prior knowledge of the Kennedy assassination, you can write another book: because if you aren't lying – and I personally don't think you are – you're a victim of the most fantastic chain of coincidences ever. This is just fantastic!'

He was right, it was fantastic. It was so fantastic that Thornley became fixated on trying to understand just what the truth about those days was. He had to somehow marry his memory of events with the testimonies of others, but try as he might he couldn't find any version of events that could be held up as believable. In time he started to question his own memory, and began seriously entertaining the idea that he was a victim of false memories or mind control. These ideas would eventually lead to the confused and frightening world of paranoid schizophrenia, a fate that would prove to be not unusual for those who immersed themselves in Discordianism. He may have been the first Discordian to start hearing voices in his head, but he would not be the last.

For Garrison, there was the slow realisation that much of the information he was working with was contradictory. Someone somewhere was lying, in other words, and he didn't know who to trust. It was almost as if disinformation was being deliberately manufactured. Clearly some of the facts that he was analysing were wrong, but which ones were they?

In Garrison's narrative Oswald had been a 'patsy', a person set up to appear guilty to allow the real villains to go undetected, just as Oswald had himself claimed in custody before he was killed. Conflicting eyewitness reports stated that Oswald had been in different places at the same time, so Garrison began to theorise that there had been Oswald impersonators planting fake evidence of communist or anti-American activities. Thornley himself was at one point considered to be a possible 'second Oswald'. Once Garrison's theory started entertaining ideas like this, there was little hope that it would produce a narrative of certainty and objective clarity.

Garrison uncovered a lot more information than the Warren Commission had, but this created less clarity, not more. This increased amount of data now suggested many different and contradictory narratives. The list of possible conspirators grew, coming over time to include the Mafia, anti-Castro rebels, Fidel Castro himself, the FBI, the CIA, the Russians, the American Government and Lyndon B. Johnson – and that was before crazy people started adding fictional groups such as The Justified Ancients of Mummu to the list. The number of possible truths increased exponentially, each adding to the atmosphere of confusion and paranoia. Garrison did tease his own preferred narrative out of the chaos, and he eventually tried a local businessman named Clay Shaw for conspiracy to murder the president. Shaw was found not guilty, and the narrative Garrison chose has not convinced many others. Over time the amount of information surrounding the crime has continued to increase, and the real account of what happened in Dallas has long since disappeared under an ever-churning sea of fact and fiction. Confusion has grown as research has accumulated, and there are few who believe that the one true narrative, the only honest account of the assassination, will ever be found.

Sciambra's claim that Thornley was 'a victim of the most fantastic chain of coincidences ever' raises some interesting questions. To choose just one example, what are the odds that Garrison's photocopier would have been previously used to copy the writing of one of his key suspects? At first glance, this seems extremely unlikely. There were 195 million people in America at the time, so the likelihood of two coming together in such a way must be extremely small.

To a mathematician, the issue is not so strange. They would point out that the photocopier link is arbitrary. We artificially assume a greater level of importance to the photocopier link because we know of a connection there, when in fact there are countless other possible connections between any two people. Had it been, for example, that Garrison had once bought a car from Thornley, or perhaps that Thornley had once dated Garrison's niece, then we would have ignored the photocopier and invested these links with the same level of relevance. The true issue is not the photocopier, but whether there is any connection between the two men at all, and the odds of this are considerably smaller than the odds of a specific connection. When you factor in that the two men were both based in New Orleans, and that Garrison's job made him very active in the community, then the odds fall even more. They are still high, of course, but not so high that mathematicians would find them unusual.*

There were many more strange coincidences at play than this, however, and these were what Sciambra was alluding to. These include Oswald moving to New Orleans when Thornley was writing a book about him there, or people who knew them both mistakenly identifying Thornley with Oswald, or the pair never meeting despite frequenting the same places, or Thornley's friendship with people who had discussed the idea of assassinating the president. The odds against all these are individually very high, and, when all such coincidences are considered together, they multiply. A mathematician would see that such high odds are interesting but not inexplicable. The amount of different connections between all the different elements of our

---

* I received a message on Twitter yesterday from someone who called themselves 'Blank'. It said, 'With regards coincidence in your book about The KLF, specifically the photocopier. The odds of [Thornley's work being photocopied in Garrison's workplace] aren't determined by the amount of people in New Orleans, rather the number of photocopiers. Odds slashed.' This is a good point. And also, it is an example of the sort of message I'm still getting about the book a decade after writing it. Long may this continue.

world are so huge, and so many different things happen at any one time, that finding a set of events that have such unimaginable odds is not strange. In fact, when the full enormity of actual events in this world is considered, such unlikely strings of events are guaranteed to happen. Mathematicians such as Persi Diaconis and Frederick Mosteller call this the law of truly large numbers.

Those who find themselves at the centre of such a storm of coincidence rarely find this simple numerical analysis satisfying. They would argue that it does not differentiate between irrelevant coincidence and strange events that seem to possess their own innate meaning. More specifically, there can often appear to be a distinct sense of humour at work, behind the onslaught of coincidence, that mathematics isn't a suitable tool to appreciate.

Thornley would have dismissed the mathematician's claims of coincidence, and instead viewed these events as what Carl Jung called 'synchronicity'. Jung defined synchronicity as a 'meaningful coincidence' or an 'acausal connecting principle', where 'acausal' means a string of events that cannot be fully explained by simple cause and effect. Or, to put it another way, if something is behind these events, then we don't know what. Jung has come to be regarded as one of the giants of modern psychology, comparable to his colleague and rival Freud, but there are many who dismiss his ideas about synchronicity as little more than 'magical thinking'. But for Thornley and many other Discordians who found their lives spiralling out in strange and impossibly unlikely ways, Jung's ideas seemed an accurate description of the world around them. They were being buffeted by events beyond their control, and they thought that something was behind it.

For the early Discordians it was tempting to believe that when Greg Hill used DA Garrison's photocopier to produce the first edition of *Principia Discordia*, something, some spirit of Discord and Chaos, somehow emerged, or returned, or arrived in the world we know. Of course, Greg Hill was an atheist. He intended Discordianism to be a satire of religion, and did not take the idea of goddesses or spirits seriously. By the late 1970s he had become convinced that his Discordian adventures had stirred up something that he was unable to explain. As he told his friend Margot Adler, 'If you do this type of thing well enough, it starts to work. I started out with the idea that all gods are an illusion. By the end I had learnt that it is up to you to decide whether gods exist, and if you take the goddess of confusion seriously enough, it will send you through as profound and valid a metaphysical trip as taking a god like Yahweh [the Jewish/Christian/Muslim God] seriously.' The effects of invoking a made-up god, in other words, were no different from sincerely invoking a 'proper' one.* This was going to be an eventful realisation

---

* Another way of looking at this is to say that when a population does not include a concept like chaos in its collective world view, it is unable to see it. It goes around admiring the order in the world, completely failing to notice all the things that don't fall into that category. To suddenly recognise the category of chaos, then – in this case, by forming a spoof religion around Eris – can make it appear that chaos suddenly arrives out

for those who invoked Eris. As Thornley once remarked to Hill, 'You know, if I had realised that all of this was going to come true, I'd have chosen Venus.'

In the summer of 1983, Bill Drummond walked to Mathew Street and, at the exact time that the Bunnymen went on stage in Reykjavik, he stood on the manhole cover.

Drummond's personal mythology had grown considerably since he saw Echo in the record sleeve. He had come to view the different personalities of his two bands as alchemical opposites. The Bunnymen were cold, aloof and impenetrable, whereas the Teardrops were dangerous, wild and burning. He had come to associate both bands with places that had had a hold on his imagination as a child. The Bunnymen evoked similar feelings to his memory of Iceland, which he had visited as a boy. He had stood on the edge of an immense glacier, and been overawed by the scale and cold grandeur of the place. The thought of the

---

of nowhere. It seems to take over or invade the previous ordered world. When I was growing up in the eighties, to give another example, there was very little meaningful cultural awareness of trans people. I remained oblivious to their nature, even as I was buying their records and going to their concerts. Now that those raised in the twenty-first century have alerted us older, cis-gendered people to their existence, we suddenly see them, which for many has been quite a surprise. As a result, it is fairly common to hear people talk about trans people as if they had just been invented. All this raises the intriguing question of what other blind spots we have, and what else that surrounds us now is going to surprise us when we recognise it and give it a name.

Teardrops, in contrast, conjured up images of Papua New Guinea. He had never been to Papua New Guinea, but he had heard the story of how a great-great uncle of his had gone there as a missionary and been eaten by natives. His childhood mind imagined it as a wild, uncontrollable place, burning hot and dangerous, with thick forests bristling with dreadful things without names. Not too dissimilar, in other words, to how he had come to view Julian Cope.

In Drummond's mind Iceland, Papua New Guinea and Liverpool were linked in a manner that made sense emotionally, if not rationally. He could imagine a great stream of some form of energy flowing through space and powering into the Earth. It poured into Iceland, flowed just under Mathew Street and emerged back out into space again at Papua New Guinea. This was an idea that he entertained, rather than believed. It was a mental folly, in other words, constructed for amusement rather than practical use. But something about it appealed in a way he couldn't dismiss outright, and a plan bubbled up from his subconscious.

His idea was to arrange for the Bunnymen to play a gig in Iceland at exactly the same time as the Teardrops played in Papua New Guinea. He would remain in Liverpool and, at the correct time, he would go and stand on the manhole cover. Quite why he would do this, though, was another matter. He had a vague feeling that something would happen, but exactly what was hard to define. Perhaps he would somehow absorb the energy of the two bands? Perhaps he would gain some form of enlightenment? It was completely mad, of course, he knew that. But that wasn't a good reason not to do it.*

There was one big problem, though. His relationship with Julian Cope had deteriorated to the point where he could no longer influence him. Cope's ego had broken loose following a little fame and a lot of LSD. As Drummond later wrote, 'Cope was careering from being pop pin-up to great acid casualty pop eccentric, somewhere between Sky Saxon and Syd Barrett but with an ego telling him he was Lord Byron, Jim Morrison and the son of a very un-Christian god all at once. Great stuff and I loved it, but how was I to persuade him he should do a concert in the highland jungles of Papua New Guinea when I couldn't even tell him to have a bath?'

The Bunnymen were not as difficult. Drummond had previously arranged a Bunnymen tour which went up and down the country in a seemingly random way, playing unlikely and bizarre venues. It followed the course of his interstellar ley line from Iceland, through the Callanish

---

* This is one of the stories in this book that people ask me about all the time. Who doesn't love it? It wasn't new, though. Drummond had talked and written about it a fair bit over the years, although for some reason few people acknowledged it. Once it was put in the context of the other tales in this book, however, people began to pick up on it to a much greater degree than before. I confess I am a sucker for all those strange stories that sit there in plain sight, oddly ignored, waiting for context to make them visible again. It's one of the reasons why I see writing books about things that have happened and have already been recorded as being worthwhile and necessary.

stone circle on the Isle of Lewis, to Mathew Street and on to the Albert Hall in London. He also organised a cycle ride around Liverpool before Echo & the Bunnymen's 'A Crystal Day' concert at St George's Hall in May 1984, which followed the path of a pair of rabbit ears drawn on a map of Liverpool.* This was all part of Drummond's attempt to evoke Echo, who had been conspicuous in his absence from later Bunnymen record sleeves. Arranging a gig in Reykjavik was fairly normal in comparison.

So as the band took to the stage Drummond duly went down to Mathew Street. It was not the same as it would have been had the Teardrops been involved, but it was the best he could do. He stood on the manhole cover.

A short while later, after he had satisfied himself that absolutely nothing was happening, he wandered off and caught the bus home.

It was time to move on, both from his bands and from Liverpool. He had put a lot into Zoo Records, and he'd remortgaged his house on two occasions to pay for tours and studio time, but the end result had not lived up to his aspirations. He was not proud of the records he made, and he found himself having to make decisions that caused bad feelings among his friends and colleagues. More importantly, it was not fair of him to indulge his inner fantasies at the expense of the careers of these bands. They were just

---

* These incidents are often conflated in the popular imagination, and it is common to hear people say that the Bunnymen played a tour of Scotland in venues that formed a giant pair of rabbit ears when plotted on a map.

not driven by the same forces that he was, and it was not fair to play with their careers for his own internal amusement.

Before long the Teardrops collapsed, the Bunnymen found more professional management and Drummond was offered a job working for a major label. He moved to the Vale of Aylesbury and became an A&R man at WEA.

His inner life, though, still churned.

On 23 July 1973, Robert Anton Wilson began hearing voices in his head. They appeared to him to be communication from an alien life form somewhere in the vicinity of Sirius.

This was not that unusual for heavy drug users in California during the early 1970s. Philip K. Dick, for example, began receiving similar communication from the alien entity that he christened VALIS in February 1975, and Timothy Leary was also channelling aliens at around the same time, to help pass the time while incarcerated in Folsom State Prison. What was significant about Wilson's experience was how he came to interpret it.

Wilson was sane enough to know that just because it appeared as if aliens from Sirius were talking to him, it did not follow that this was what was actually happening. He turned to the medical literature and searched for an explanation. Perhaps there was a known process where a chemical imbalance causes randomly firing neurons to connect in an unusual way, for example, which would explain what he was experiencing? The trouble was, he couldn't find anything. The schizophrenic family of illnesses was very poorly understood back in the 1970s, as indeed it still is now. The illnesses may have been named and described, but a name was not an explanation, nor did it tell him what was going on. Neuroscience has made some remarkable discoveries about the brain, but when it comes down to explaining issues of awareness and the actuality of experience it is still struggling in the dark. Science could slap a label on what was happening to him, Wilson discovered, but it could not explain it.

This being California in the 1970s, Wilson decided to tell a psychic about his experience. She told him that he had it all wrong. He was not hearing voices from aliens from Sirius at all. What was really happening, she explained, was that he was in communication with the spirit of an ancient Chinese philosopher.

Wilson thought about this. It seemed to him to be just as plausible as the Sirius explanation. Either explanation fitted the data just as well as the other. But which explanation should he favour? How could he find out whether he was receiving information from aliens from the star Sirius or an ancient Chinese philosopher? He decided to get another opinion. He asked another psychic. This psychic was adamant that both the Sirius and the Chinese philosopher explanations were nonsense. In actual fact, Wilson was told, he was in touch with the spirit of a medieval Irish bard.

This was getting confusing and lesser men would have

given up and gone quite mad at this point. Wilson, instead, made one the most important philosophical leaps of the twentieth century, although, admittedly, it is not yet generally recognised as such.

As well as undergoing drug-induced schizophrenia, Wilson had been raised as a Catholic and had also been a communist in his earlier years. He had fully accepted these two powerful belief systems before rejecting them both. Thanks to this background, he was able to recognise what he would later call a *self-referential reality tunnel*. This was a philosophy, religion or ideology that was complete and satisfying and which fully explained all the details of the world, assuming that you did not question its central tenet. This central tenet was an idea – and often an appealing one – for which there was a distinct lack of evidence, such as the idea that there was a judgemental patriarchal creator God, or that a propertyless communal utopia would be the final stage of society. The surrounding ideology was an elaborate commentary which developed in order to support the central concept in much the same way that a pearl forms around a piece of grit in an oyster. All the theory and education that is needed to fully understand an '-ism' or religion functioned like a sophisticated defence mechanism which protected this central tenet from crashing and burning on the rocks of reality. The reason these ideological defences were so painstakingly built up over time was because, once inside a self-referential reality tunnel, you had a model that made sense of the rest of the world. This could be an extremely appealing situation, and one that you could happily stay in for the rest of your life.*

The idea that a hyper-evolved intelligence from the stars had selected Wilson to receive great founts of admittedly confusing cosmic wisdom, and hence help mankind evolve into a higher state of being, did seem an appealing notion and one that would explain a great deal. But Wilson could see that it was just another self-referential reality tunnel, like Catholicism or Marxism, and that it was vitally important that he did not come to believe the bugger.†

It was around this time that Wilson watched the Jimmy Stewart movie *Harvey*. In the film, Stewart plays an amiable small-town drunk called Elwood P. Dowd, who stumbles out of a bar and meets an invisible 6' 3½" rabbit named Harvey. 'How are you this evening, Mr Dowd?' asks Harvey. Dowd is not too surprised by this. 'It's a small town, everyone knows my name,' he reasons, and strikes up a friendship with the rabbit. The other characters in the film are more concerned about Dowd's relationship with the giant invisible rabbit, and do not accept Dowd's explanation that Harvey is actually a Pooka, an ancient rabbit spirit from County Derry.

A psychiatrist called Marvin Wilson attempts to treat Dowd, but in doing so cracks up himself. The turning

---

* That's quite a page, isn't it? I reckon you could base an entire book around that page. Perhaps that should be a goal I aspire to – if someone couldn't write an entire book around a page or a section of mine, then I'm slacking and need to up my game.

† At the risk of being horribly smug and self-congratulatory, that's a great paragraph. I wouldn't change a word of that.

point is a scene where he looks up Dowd's word 'Pooka' in a dictionary. He reads aloud: 'Pooka, noun. A Celtic elf or vegetation spirit, wise but mischievous, fond of rum plots, crack pots, and how are you today Mr Wilson?'

'Oh that's all I need,' thought Robert Anton Wilson. 'Now the television is talking to me.'

Still, the idea that an ancient rabbit spirit from Western Europe was communicating with him had a certain appeal, and, now Wilson thought about it, it seemed just as plausible as the other explanations he had. Indeed, it offered something that the aliens and bards and philosophers lacked. There was absolutely no danger that he might take the idea literally.

As Wilson saw it, we all need models in order to deal with the world around us. We need models that fit the existing facts and which have some ability to predict what will happen next. This is what all the best ideologies, religions and philosophies offer us. What we shouldn't do is confuse these models with the real world, for the map is not the territory and the menu is not the meal. Once this is understood, the need to fight to protect the 'truth' of the model falls away and we are free to use different and contradictory models as circumstances change.* So it was that,

_____

* This philosophy is usually called multiple-model agnosticism, and [SPOILERS] we'll return to it at the end of the book. The most common criticism used against it usually takes the form of, 'Actually, there is one complete, true world view, and it is mine.' I'm paraphrasing here, admittedly, but such criticisms do tend to make multiple-model agnosticism seem more convincing.

as Robert Anton Wilson's consciousness kept producing strange and dazzling feats of awareness, Wilson comforted himself with the idea that a giant invisible European rabbit spirit was currently intent on trying to tell him something, and by and large he felt much better about the whole thing.

This is, as no doubt you have noticed, the second time in our story that a giant invisible rabbit spirit has appeared. This is, of course, a coincidence.*

It also has all the hallmarks of what Jung would call synchronicity. Giant invisible rabbit spirits are extremely rare, so when two come along at once it is hard not to sit up and take notice. Indeed, it is hard to think of other occasions where giant invisible rabbit spirits might appear. Cryptozoologists and Forteans do possess accounts of sightings of giant rabbit creatures, but not in any great number. Apart from the film *Harvey*, they make very few appearances in our culture. The only example that springs readily to mind is *Donnie Darko*, a movie made in 2001 by Richard Kelly.

---

* One of the consequences of writing this book is that I am regularly contacted by people who have read it and then been plagued by a storm of synchronicities of their own. These don't always sound as unlikely and implausible to others as they feel to those experiencing them, but I always like to hear them. My favourite, I think, was a woman who wrote to tell me she had been reading this section while her daughter played in the garden. When her daughter came in, she asked her what she had been doing. The daughter explained that she had been 'playing with a giant invisible rabbit'.

What then – if anything – should we make of the fact that the film opens to a montage set to 'The Killing Moon' by Echo & the Bunnymen?

'The Killing Moon' is a song that was written after singer Ian McCulloch woke from a dream with the lyric 'Fate, up against your will' in his head. It was never supposed to appear at the beginning of the film. The director wanted to use 'Never Tear Us Apart' by INXS, but financial and licensing issues got in the way and the Echo & the Bunnymen song somehow barged its way to the front. (The director was later given the chance to make a Director's Cut of the movie, where he was able to shove the song back to a later, Halloween party scene and start with the INXS song as he originally intended.)

What should we make of this? We shouldn't make anything of it. We should forget it and move on. If it makes it any easier, I can assure you that there will be no other appearances in this story by giant invisible rabbit spirits. As our story takes us deeper into the music industry, the rabbit spirit either flees or evolves into something else. Just for now, picture this spirit in your head – tall, powerful, with long ears upright on the top of his head. How does he strike you? Mischievous and lusty? Or something more sinister?

But now – forget him. He's gone.*

---

* What I've just done here is to create an image in the mind of the reader and then instruct them to banish it to their subconscious. I dread to think what my intentions were, or why I thought this was a good idea, but to do

4

Magic and Moore

Bill Drummond, as may already be apparent, is an unusual man.

A good illustration of the odder aspects of his personality can be seen in a May 2012 interview he did with the *Guardian*'s Tim Jonze. Jonze talked to Drummond about

---

so is very different to simply not doing it in the first place. Presumably, I had my reasons, but I suspect it was more instinctual than properly thought through. A lot of chaos magic, for example, assumes that images banished from the conscious mind will have power in the subconscious. This is a good example of why you should never trust writers. You allow them into your head where they start rewiring things, whistling cheerfully as they go. But some of them are right cowboys. Some of them don't take the responsibility and power they wield seriously. And some haven't even realised the power they have, or what they are doing. Those are the ones you really need to keep away from.

his attempts to turn simple acts into art. The example he quoted was how, when walking to and from a fishing spot, Drummond would walk in a route which, if drawn on a map, formed the outline of a fish.

'It may be a form of OCD or just an attempt to give life more meaning than it seems to have,' Drummond replied, 'but as far back as I can remember I have had a habit of trying to create patterns in the games that I played or the things that I was doing. In my childhood this could be climbing ten different trees before the sun passed the spire of the parish church or walking out the shape of a square on the map of our town when going to the shops and back to get the messages for my mum. I was never that interested in organised games or religion because someone else had already worked out what all the patterns were.'

While this does indeed sound like 'a form of OCD', it's worth putting it in the context of his Presbyterian upbringing. Drummond's father was a minister in the Church of Scotland and the strong work ethic of that faith runs through his career. It is particularly evident in the art that he has produced in the twenty-first century. Art for Drummond is not spontaneous, carefree play, but work that needs to be scheduled and completed. The fact that Drummond is a fastidious grafter, by both nature and nurture, made him a potent subject to absorb Ken Campbell's ideas about achieving the impossible.

Drummond also told Jonze that 'using a word such as ritual may be too loaded for my liking, but I guess it is from these motivations in us that ritual is born. In the past dozen or so years, I have tried not to suppress or hide these urges in me and let them openly be the central driving force in my stuff.'

It is this aspect of his behaviour that has led to suggestions that his actions are not art, but magic. '[Bill] Drummond is many things,' the author and music journalist Charles Shaar Murray wrote in the *Independent*, 'and one of those things is a magician. Many of his schemes [. . .] involve symbolically-weighted acts conducted away from the public gaze and documented only by Drummond himself and his participating comrades. Nevertheless, they are intended to have an effect on a world of people unaware that the act in question has taken place. That is magical thinking. Art is magic, and so is pop. Bill Drummond is a cultural magician . . .'*

Does Drummond view himself in this way? He has said that, after he met Mark Manning (aka Zodiac Mind-warp) in 1985, Manning 'taught him about magic', but he doesn't make any claims to be consciously practising

---

* It may be the circles that I move in, or the quirks of my cultural bub-ble, but this way of thinking seems far more common now than when I wrote this. It also seems much less controversial. A decade ago, I think the common image of magic was still quite Harry Potter – wave a wand and somebody turns into a frog. To hear magic defined as art, and to view magic as the manipulation of someone's consciousness, was still some-thing of a counterintuitive jolt. Depending on your point of view, this either downgraded magic with a tacit admission that it didn't exist, or it enchanted the world and empowered art by recognising its everyday reality and impact. The person who I think is most responsible for this cultural shift is about to enter our story . . .

a form of magic, or to have a significant interest in the subject. That said, the location of one screening of the film *Watch The K Foundation Burn A Million Quid* is suggestive.

Most of the venues for these screenings were arts centres or clubs, although there were more unusual locations such as schools, jails and St Michael's Tower on top of Glastonbury Tor. One venue does jump out of the list of tour dates as distinctly different from the others. On 7 March 1996, they screened the film in Alan Moore's house in Northampton.

Alan Moore is a comic-book writer. He has been called the greatest ever comic-book writer so often that it is most probably true. He found fame in the 1980s with works like *V for Vendetta* and *Watchmen* and continues to write prolifically in his native town. Drummond is the same age as Moore, spent two years at art school in Northampton and later worked for six months at a mental hospital in the town. Drummond and Moore went to many of the same clubs, pubs and concerts in Northampton between 1970 and 1972, but they did not meet until the 1990s. Will Sergeant of Echo & the Bunnymen introduced Drummond to Moore's work in the 1980s, starting with *V for Vendetta* and *Swamp Thing*.

Beyond his work, Moore is known for his disdain of Hollywood, his extraordinary beard and for his interest in magic. It is this last point which appears to suggest why Moore was the only individual whom The KLF actively sought out to screen the film, in order to hear his opinion.

If you want to know about magic in the modern era, Moore is the man to ask.*

To understand his take on the burning we first need to grasp what Moore means by the slippery word 'magic'. The place to start is in the early days of his fame, when fans would turn up in droves at conventions and signings and ask him questions. One of the questions that kept coming up was 'Where do you get your ideas from?'.

Most writers hate this question because they can't answer it. Like everyone else, Moore would fudge an answer as best he could. But unlike most writers he recognised that it was actually a very good question and one that he would very much like an answer to. Where did he get his ideas from? By now he had a family to support. Earning money for them depended on the regular arrival of new ideas, over which he seemed to have no control. What would he do if they stopped? Most writers fear even talking about this, seemingly scared that they may offend their muse and be robbed of their talent. If it works, they reason, leave it alone and whatever you do don't ruin it. But this didn't sit well with Moore. His imagination was part of the tools of his craft. A taxi driver, for example, would know how to get under the bonnet of his car and repair it if it broke

---

* Moore made the decision to declare himself a magician on 18 November 1993, his fortieth birthday, so this screening of the film in his front room was around two years later. Bill and Jimmy turning up at his door is a good illustration of how making declarations like that can impact your life.

down.* Shouldn't a working writer be able to do the same to his imagination?

What is imagination? It is the creation of original thought from your own consciousness. But, then, what is thought and what is consciousness? Here he ran into what is known as the 'hard problem' of neuroscience: how the experience of awareness springs from a lump of damp matter like a brain. If the cosmos is just a bunch of inanimate particles flung out of the chaos of a Big Bang, how exactly did it become aware of itself?†

Moore could not find anything approaching an answer to this. The beauty of science is that it strips the subjectivity and bias out of observation and allows us to probe the real world objectively. This is an elegant and extremely useful approach, but not one designed for understanding an intrinsically subjective process such as consciousness. Science can study neurons and brain matter. It can discover how they link together, how they grow and how they fire electrical impulses at each other. But it cannot put a

---

* That's an analogy that has aged badly. The notion that people can and should fix their own cars is dwindling away in this technological age.

† I wish I was better at managing the shift from examining specifics to generalising about broad-stroke, cosmic-level fundamentals. I can feel the reader's eyes roll during a paragraph like this. To do it for no good reason is a terrible crime, but sometimes it is unavoidable and necessary. Context is always important, and you do need it if you want to be true to the story you're telling. Nowadays, I try to elegantly distract the reader as they are led up to the view from the top of the mountain, but it's usually still a little awkward. I'll keep working on this.

thought under the microscope. We can scan the brain and see what regions are active when a person looks at a field of grass, but we cannot isolate the experience of being aware of grass. We cannot find awareness, or store it, or cut it up and find out what it is made of. Many scientists, faced with this, take the view that consciousness doesn't actually exist; it is an illusion. This illusion is an emergent property of the brain. Patterns of activity across the billions of neurons in the brain fool the brain into believing that it is a 'mind', but that 'mind' has no actual existence in any real sense.

This subject was a hot topic in the early 1990s following the publication of Daniel Dennett's remarkable book *Consciousness Explained* in 1991. The book skewered many of our false assumptions about how thought and the mind work. For many people, though, its argument collapsed at the final hurdle – the point when Dennett attempted to show that consciousness doesn't actually exist. The reader could hear Dennett's voice shifting in the book's final sections, becoming hectoring and bullying as his argument seemed to get weaker.* To be fair to Dennett,

---

* This is personal opinion presented as fact, which is never good. When I said, 'The reader could hear . . .', I really meant 'I could hear . . .'. It would have been better if I had owned up to this, not least because that would have given me permission to kick harder. No matter what you are writing, examples of opinions stated as fact always creep in somewhere. Sometimes I do it to avoid getting bogged down in justifications, in order to maintain pace and keep to the main argument. Sometimes I do it for the sake of a good gag. But usually it is done unintentionally, because I confuse the world as I see it with the world as it is. Remain vigilant!

this argument was always going to be a difficult sell. Most people, especially non-neuroscientists, reject the argument instinctively (his book is referred to as *Consciousness Explained Away* in certain circles, or *Consciousness Ignored*). This is especially true of those who have had experience of expanded states of awareness, such as heavy meditators. Moore was one of those who was unconvinced. He was damn sure that his consciousness existed.

His argument went like this: Dennett's arguments were rooted in the impressive work of neurobiology. This in turn sits on some very solid foundations. Biology is supported by chemistry, which itself is supported by physics. We have a good understanding of these fields of study, and their conclusions look secure. But physics itself rests on the smaller-scale world of quantum physics, and in quantum physics the world is affected by an observer – or, in other words, consciousness. The train of logic that claims that consciousness doesn't exist therefore itself requires the existence of consciousness.

We should be slightly cautious about this argument.* Quantum physics is so alien and baffling that it can be trotted out by non-scientists to justify all sorts of freaky claims. In this instance we should be careful about what we mean when we refer to 'the observer'. In quantum physics,

---

* I think of paragraphs like these as 'Yes I know' paragraphs. They don't advance the narrative and slow the story down, so your every instinct is to cut them. But you include them because otherwise you'd get emails from people who assume you aren't aware of these things.

the observer is entangled with the observed in such a way that choices made by the observer can alter the object that is being observed. The passage of information between the pair is the important element here, but does the observer have to be 'conscious' as we understand it? When you put a cold thermometer in a glass of hot water, the thermometer both measures the temperature of the water but it also affects it: it cools it down a little. Here the final measurement produced is a product of both the observer and the observed, but a thermometer is not conscious. Or, if it is, it hides it well.

Ultimately, the need for awareness in an observer is a moot point. If it turns out not to be necessary, consciousness will hardly have been disproved, having instead wriggled out of the picture again. Regardless, Moore was satisfied with his own logic. He took the position that consciousness does actually exist. Ideas are real things. A different type of real, admittedly, but real nonetheless.

Moore was mulling over these issues when he was writing *From Hell* in the early 1990s. *From Hell* – another of his masterpieces – is a dense, multi-layered examination of the Jack the Ripper legend, one which doesn't just concern itself with the crimes, but with the society they emerged from. Victorian London is evoked using psychogeography, a technique based on the *derives* of the Situationists in which the history and associations of places are understood to have an effect on those who visit them. Moore's Ripper is the royal surgeon Sir William Gull, who is murdering prostitutes to cover up a royal scandal but who realises that this 'work' has considerably greater implications and power.

In one scene, Gull is eating with his coach driver. In the course of the conversation Moore gives him the line, 'The one place that Gods unarguably exist is in our minds where they are real beyond refute, in all their grandeur and monstrosity.' Having written the line, Moore later returned to it and thought it over. As far as he could see, if he was being honest with himself, what he had written was true. Try as he might, he wasn't able to produce an argument that honestly refuted the idea. This came as something of a shock.

'The one place that Gods unarguably exist is in our minds where they are real beyond refute.' If the line was true, what were the implications of it?

Moore understood that while we assume we live firmly in the real, physical world, in actuality we live in a mental model of that world.* This model is produced by our minds based on memories and information from the senses. It is a very detailed and convincing model, so much so that it is difficult to accept how unreal it is. If you look at an object, for example, you see colour and assume that the object is

---

* I try to avoid repeating myself too much from book to book, but this idea seems to want to make it into pretty much every book I write. Someday I will write my definitive take on the subject, at which point it will hopefully leave me alone.

that colour. But colour as we experience it is an invention of our minds which does not exist in the real world. It is a mental interpretation of whichever wavelengths of light the object we are looking at cannot absorb and so bounces back to us. This is something that the Buddhists worked out early on. They used to ask students 'What makes the grass green?', and expected them to discover through meditation that the answer was themselves.

But even if we accept that we only know the physical world through a mental approximation, we rarely acknowledge how much of the physical world is actually the product of the mental. For example, consider these words that you are reading – where did they come from? What about the language they are written in? What about the shape of the letters themselves? What about the font? If you are reading them on paper, then how is paper created, and where did the idea to create paper come from in the first place? If you are sitting in a chair, who designed that chair? Or the floor on which it sits? If you are in a room, look at the objects around you. Is there anything there that didn't first appear as an idea in the head of another person? Think about the aims of the job you do or the ideology of your preferred political party. Think about the recipes of the food you eat or the music you listen to. The world we actually live in is made of ideas that have left human minds and entered the physical world. Indeed, the story of our evolution is essentially the story of us retreating from the natural world into the mental one.

The reason we have a hard time understanding this,

Moore realised, is because we lack a model of what the mental world is. The 'I' of awareness is our blind spot, to the extent that the consciousnesses of some of our cleverest and best educated minds, such as Dennett, will deny that consciousness even exists. The first task in getting a grip on the world of ideas, Moore thought, was to create a practical model to describe and understand it.

Moore set out to build a model of the mental world, a place sometimes referred to as the *noosphere* but which Moore calls *Ideaspace*. As the '—space' part of his name implies, he chose a spatial metaphor. This seemed reasonable, he thought, for we naturally talk of ideas being at the *back* of our minds or at the *forefront* of our thinking, we can be *deep* or *high*-minded, and so forth. Ideas, then, were placed in a 'space' in this model. The ideas could be small or large; our most detailed and complicated ideas, such as religions, ideologies or Robert Anton Wilson's self-referential reality tunnels might make up entire continents of Ideaspace. Where this differs from the physical world is that the normal rules of time and space do not apply. Land's End and John O'Groats, for example, are physically very separate in the real world, but very close in Ideaspace because they are so often linked in our thinking. In a similar way, we can just as easily think of something that is happening now, something that happened a few years ago or imagine what will happen in the future. Ideas in this model are connected more like hyperlinks on the internet than geographical locations in the real world. This concept of being linked via connections rather than geography is, of course, similar to how neuroscientists view the storage of memories.

So far, so uncontroversial. But where this becomes interesting is when we consider our own relationship to that world. Moore thought that we each had our own little corner of Ideaspace, our own home in the mental land. Something personal like Drummond's idea of Echo would live in Drummond's own section of Ideaspace. Many ideas, however, are shared, and while we may have our own personal version of them, they are more usefully said to exist in communal space. Concepts such as 'Madonna', 'Sherlock Holmes' or 'Hitler', for example, are shared by almost everybody. For Moore, these communal ideas existed beyond our own personal corners of the mental world.

Could we then wander out of our little territories, go further afield and explore the rest of Ideaspace? Here Moore's model is describing something very similar to Jung's collected unconscious.* Moore thought that, yes, we could open the doors of our individual homes and walk out into this shared landscape beyond. Indeed, he thought that artists had to, for it was their job to wander furthest

---

* Gah! That's embarrassing. This should of course read 'Jung's *collective* unconscious'. Ten years that typo has been in public, and that's the first time I've noticed. Thank you all for being too polite to tell me. It is further proof of that great publishing truism, which is that there is always another typo. I read the audiobook a few years ago and didn't notice. I suspect my mind would have seen the word 'collective', because that is what it expected to see.

from their own patch of the imagination and return with truly rare and exotic ideas which they had to use and make something out of. In this way the world we live in becomes increasingly changed by the mental world.

It is this process – the way thoughts exist and alter the world – that Moore uses the word 'magic' to describe.

What Moore had done was to raise the importance of the mental world of imagination and lower that of the physical. Indeed, you could argue that he has reversed them, claiming more importance for the imagination than the physical to the extent where the physical world is the product of the mental. This approach, in which the material is dependent on events in the immaterial, echoes Charles Fort's belief that 'A tree cannot find out, as it were, how to blossom, until comes blossom-time. A social growth cannot find out the use of steam engines, until comes steam-engine-time.' This was the phenomenon of why, after millennia of inventions such as the electric light, calculus or steam engines not existing, several people would invent the exact same thing at much the same time (at which point there's a mad race down to the patent office, with the winner celebrated by history and the others forgotten). As Moore saw it, the idea had been discovered in a shared area of Ideaspace, and several wanderers had stumbled upon it shortly afterwards.

Moore then took this one stage further, and it is at this stage that the model becomes more controversial. When biological things in the physical world evolve to a certain level of complexity, they become living, conscious, self-determined individuals. Could the same be true for ideas in the non-physical world? Could sufficiently complex ideas evolve into a form of life, and wander Ideaspace as they saw fit? If this was the case, it would explain all those stories of ghosts, aliens, fairies, angels, elves, giant invisible rabbit spirits, the Goddess Eris and all the other unreal creatures that appear throughout cultures and history. This idea would be a leap of faith for most people, but it was a leap that Moore took. Moore has said that he and his friend Steve Moore conjured up a demon in his living room around this time and had a long conversation with it.* First-hand experience such as this would no doubt make that leap easier to make.

Carl Jung had also made a similar leap, although his terminology was different. In 1913 he had been troubled by a recurring dream that was both sinister and disturbing. He dreamt of a terrible flood that covered 'all the northern and low-lying lands between the North Sea and the Alps'. In this flood, which stretched from England to Russia, he saw 'yellow waves, swimming rubble and the death of countless thousands'. When the dream reoccurred, it was accompanied by an 'inner voice' which said, 'Look at it, it is completely real, and it will come to pass. You cannot doubt this.'

---

* To be more specific, this was Asmodeus, a higher-dimensional spider demon. This incident inspired a large section of Alan Moore's epic novel *Jerusalem*.

When the First World War followed and yellow mustard gas started rolling over Europe, Jung had no choice but to see his dream vision as a premonition. For a scientist, this was deeply problematic. It challenged him to come up with a theory or explanation as to how a major event in world history could have been represented in his mind before it had actually happened. This trail of thought would lead, decades later, to his theories on the 'acausal connecting principle' of *synchronicity*. For our purposes, we should note that such an occurrence fits Moore's model of mental phenomena. The contents of Moore's Ideaspace exist outside the physical world's relationship to time. Events that are about to happen – or, rather, the idea of events that are about to happen – could well be discovered in this immaterial realm by deep wanderers such as Jung. Although these events have yet to occur in the physical world, the idea of them may be found forming, like an early warning alarm, in that strange mental landscape that Moore calls Ideaspace and Jung called the collective unconscious.

This was the background to Moore's thinking when he viewed the film of Drummond and Cauty burning a million pounds. 'I thought it was awesome in some ways, very funny in others. It burned well – very clean flames,' he told them.

What was more significant, though, was that the idea of burning the money had been found in their local area of Ideaspace in the first place. The idea had bewitched

Drummond and Cauty so strongly that they had been compelled to act upon it, despite not knowing why they did so. Of course, the theory of Ideaspace means that there was no reason why they should understand what it meant: their reaction to it was largely irrelevant. What was important was that the idea had found them in the first place. Its very violence and its shocking nature indicated that something significant was happening, deep down in the depths of our shared mental world. It was like a volcano that heralds an imminent shift of the tectonic plates. If the physical manifestation of this eruption was anything to go by, it seemed to be linked to one of the most powerful magical ideas we have: money.

'It was a powerful magical event,' Moore told them afterwards. 'I can't see any other explanation for it. You're dealing with a form of language, a conversation – but you're not sure what the conversation is . . . you're waiting for a reply.'

As noted earlier, neither Cauty nor Drummond claim that their actions are magical, nor do they adopt the trappings, clothing or affectations of the occult world. Nevertheless, Drummond's behaviour consistently displays a strong resonance with Moore's belief that the mental world is more important than the physical, that ideas possess validity in themselves and that they can affect the physical world. His visit to the manhole cover and his obsession with Echo are good examples of this.

Moore's opinion of the burning, that it was a conversation and that they were waiting for a reply, also seems to have resonated. As also noted earlier, Drummond still waves away questions about the burning by saying that they are 'still waiting for a response'. So while Moore's ideas about the nature of magic may not help us to understand Cauty and Drummond's personal motivations, they are a valid way to view actions that were the product of *magical thinking*.

Alan Moore would also later say, 'I like Bill Drummond a lot, I really do, but you have to understand that he's totally mad.'

5

The Man and the Mu Mu

Bill Drummond was visiting his parents and went for a walk in the morning. It was New Year's Day 1987. He had left the music industry.*

On 21 July the previous summer, at the symbolic age of thirty-three and a third (or near enough), he had issued a press release to announce that he was quitting his job as A&R man at WEA Records.† It was, he said, 'time for a revolution in my life'. His time would now be dedicated to

---

* Ah, here we go. Ninety-eight pages in and they are about to start making some music.
† This was quite a mad thing to do, wasn't it? What sort of person issues a press release when they quit their job? I can only assume it was intended as a way to drum up attention for his forthcoming solo album. In which case – full marks for originality.

writing, art and climbing mountains. But first, he'd mark both this totemic age and his retirement from the music industry by releasing a solo album.

The album was called *The Man*. It was, somewhat unexpectedly, an album of low-key, acoustic Scottish folk in which Drummond sang songs of love and music in a pronounced Scottish accent over blissful slide guitar.

Recorded in five days and released on Creation, song titles such as 'I Believe In Rock & Roll', 'I'm The King Of Joy' and the opening instrumental 'True To The Trail' reaffirmed his dedication to the potential of music. This was no bitter dismissal of his career or the music industry that he was leaving. Still, it was a deeply odd affair. His voice brought Ivor Cutler to mind, the closing track featured his father reciting a Robert Burns poem and the cover showed Drummond sitting on a Liverpool dock holding his Gibson 330 guitar and wearing blue jeans, white socks and brown shoes. It is remembered mainly for the track 'Julian Cope Is Dead'. After the demise of The Teardrop Explodes, Cope had gone on to have a long, erratic solo career in which he combined moments of visionary genius with a considerable amount of pig-headed noodling.* 'Julian Cope Is Dead' was seen by many as Drummond's response to a song of Cope's called 'Bill Drummond Said', and it gives some insight into Drummond's complicated

---

* I appreciate that fans of Cope at his finest might think this harsh. In my defence, it was written in 2012, after albums like *Citizen Cain'd, Dark Orgasm* and *Rite Bastard*.

relationship with Cope. Its jaunty chorus begins, 'Julian Cope is dead / I shot him in the head'.

With that record made, Drummond was out of the music industry. He sat down and began to work on a book entitled *Why Andy Warhol Is Shite*.

But work on the book did not go well. Two things distracted him. One was listening to Schooly D. The other was his decision to start rereading *Illuminatus!*.

Drummond returned from his New Year's Day walk and phoned Jimmy Cauty. He told Cauty that they should form a hip-hop group called The Justified Ancients of Mu Mu (the misspelling was accidental, for it wasn't until 2007 that Drummond realised that Wilson's spelling was 'Mummu'). Drummond knew that Cauty would understand what he meant by the name. The other reason he called him was because Cauty had recently bought a sampler.

Cauty did indeed instantly understand where Drummond was coming from. The act of taking that name, of adopting the mantle of The Justified Ancients of Mummu, may have seemed a simple, trivial act at the time. That day, 1 January 1987, was the official birth of The JAMs. The Justified Ancients of Mummu had stepped from fiction into reality.

Drummond and Cauty became partners. The fact that this version of their story talks more about Drummond than Cauty should not be taken to imply that Cauty was in any way a junior partner. Had this account been a traditional music biography, filled with details about what track was recorded in what studio and when, then Cauty could have had a more prominent role.* A simplified description of their partnership would portray Cauty as the musician and Drummond as the strategist, but this view doesn't hold up to scrutiny. All the products of their partnership, whether musical or otherwise, came out of mutual agreement. Cauty is just as capable of burning stuff as Drummond.

Any difference in their roles comes down to their individual characters. Cauty is practical and above all curious, quick to get his hands dirty, experiment and see what happens. He is a catalyst. Drummond, on the other hand, is not so much curious but driven. The difficulty of defining exactly how he is driven is what makes this narrative spend more time on him.

Drummond met Cauty in 1985. Cauty played guitar in a band called Brilliant, alongside Youth from Killing Joke and the singer June Montana. Drummond had signed Brilliant to WEA where they had made an album with the pop producer Pete Waterman. 'It was a complete failure,' Drummond has said. 'It was an artistically bankrupt project. And financially deaf. We spent £300,000 on making an album that was useless. Useless artistically, useless . . .

---

* This is another of those 'Yes I know' paragraphs that I mentioned earlier. In this one, I'm basically acknowledging the fact that this isn't really a proper music biography of The KLF. It almost reads like an apology, but it is clearly not a sincere one because I just carry on in the same vein as before.

commercially.' Still, the pair had learnt a lot about making pop records by watching Pete Waterman work. More importantly, they seemed to understand each other. Cauty and Drummond had what the Welsh music writer Richard King describes as 'an almost telepathic way of communicating'.

'We'd never had to discuss anything because we knew we both liked exactly the same thing,' Cauty has said. 'There was never any disagreement on music or anything. It was quite weird, actually.'

So when Drummond mentioned The Justified Ancients of Mu Mu to Cauty, he understood exactly what that meant. Cauty had seen Ken Campbell's production of *Illuminatus!* at the National Theatre. He knew that the name would represent the principle of chaos working against the corporate music industry, a guerrilla band of musical anarchists who existed to disrupt, confuse and destroy. Taking on that name certainly appealed.

In this context, hip-hop was a good fit. This new, emerging form of music had no need for 'proper' bands. It wasn't interested in songs and it wasn't even interested in singing. It certainly had no need for virtuoso musicians. It was quite prepared to take a chunk of someone else's record and use that for its own ends. To many, it almost seemed to be anti-music. Drummond may have been of the opinion that hip-hop was the only music 'fit for these modern times', but this was a minority view at that point. Rap and hip-hop had yet to become the all-conquering commercial and cultural force that we know today. If anything, it seemed like a novelty or a brief fad at best, especially when older white Brits tried their hand at it. Many of the best-selling rap records in the UK were spoofs, such as Roland Rat's 'Rat Rapping' or 'Stutter Rap' by Morris Minor and the Majors. There was still a considerable body of opinion that dismissed rappers as people who talked over a record because they couldn't sing.

But taken together, the ideas of sampling, hip-hop and Discordianism made a strange sort of sense. Drummond could see that. Cauty could see it also. There was no need for further discussion. They got to work.

The Justified Ancients of Mu Mu – The JAMs – existed for one year. They released an album (1987: *What the Fuck is Going On?*) and split exactly twelve months to the day after forming. Or at least that's the official narrative. The actual history is messier, for there was a posthumous album in 1988 (*Who Killed The JAMs?*), a greatest hits compilation (*Shag Times*) and the 'It's Grim Up North' single in 1991. But in broad terms the story of The JAMs, and Drummond and Cauty's interest in hip-hop, took place in 1987.

If and when The JAMs are remembered today, it is usually for their pioneering role in establishing sampling as a legitimate creative act in modern music. In many ways, that misses what it was that they were doing.

Sampling, as we now understand it, consists of taking individual parts of an existing record – a drum beat, perhaps, or a melody line – and making something new out of them. It is about finding a loop or a beat that is good in itself, and using that to build something else. The JAMs, on the other hand, took whole sections of someone else's record and used them as they were. They took things not for how they sounded, but for what they represented. When they took parts of ABBA and The Beatles it was not because of the quality of the sound, but very specifically because they were records by ABBA and The Beatles.

The bluntness of The JAMs musical thefts can be seen as being an unsophisticated, early attempt at sampling. With the art or craft of sampling still being developed, this argument suggests, it is not surprising that these pioneering records have a naive quality. Again, this misses the intention behind what they were doing. A more useful model would be to view them as what the Situationists called *détournements*.

The Situationists were a group of thinkers and critics who were active in the fifties and sixties, mainly in France. At the heart of their thinking was the concept of the *spectacle*. The spectacle can be thought of as the overwhelming representation of all that is real. In the simplest possible terms it can be understood as being mass media, but that simple definition should really be expanded to include our entire culture and our social relations. The spectacle is both the end result of, and the justification for, our consumerist society.

The spectacle draws our attentions away from what is real to what is merely a representation. The Situationists saw in our culture a shift in our focus from *being* to having, and then from *having* to *appearing to have*. This is a process that the users of Facebook will probably grasp immediately. This absorption in the image of things, they felt, was the cause of our modern alienation.* The Situationists were not keen on the spectacle, yet it is the central idea at the heart of their self-referential reality tunnel.

The thinking behind Situationist *détournements* goes like this: every day we are bombarded by adverts, images, songs or videos. They are part of the spectacle of the system, distractions that keep us numb and alienated. Importantly, we get these whether we want them or not, for it is almost impossible to live in the modern world and not be subject to this bombardment. They are a form of psychic pollution, one which is forced on us by capitalists. As we cannot escape from this onslaught, the Situationists argued, our only honourable response is to fuck with it.

Détournement, then, involves taking the cultural images that are forced on us and using them for our own ends. It involves changing the text or context of an image in order to subvert its meaning. The Situationists altered cultural images in the pages of their pamphlets, perhaps by taking a newspaper advert for a consumer product and replacing

---

* This is all very interesting in light of the 'ABBA Voyage' show, which launched in 2022 and features a digital recreation of the band. I've not seen it, but the people I know who have gone seem to have had a great experience. I am now imagining the Situationist Guy Debord going to a virtual ABBA concert and being the only person in the venue having a terrible time, even though he splashed out extra for one of the dance booths.

the text with quotes from Sartre about alienation. These days it is more frequently seen in graffiti, or across the internet on Tumblr blogs and social networks like Facebook, where it is known as 'culture jamming'. Company logos are a frequent target. The idea, as the Situationists put it, is to 'turn the expressions of the capitalist system against itself'. The aim is to break their spell.

In this context, consider the first JAMs single 'All You Need Is Love'. As its title suggests, this begins with a steal from The Beatles' song of the same name. The Beatles, of course, are the highest expression of the 'proper band' model and generally considered to be the unarguable kings of modern pop music. The highest point of The Beatles, many would argue, was their psychedelic explosion in 1967 and the highest point of this was 'All You Need Is Love'. This song was the UK's contribution to *Our World*, the first live global television programme. This event was made possible by the recent invention of communication satellites. For the first time in history, people around the world would come together and watch the same thing at the same time. For such a symbolic event The Beatles boiled down the message of the age into a simple melody and the beautifully sung refrain 'Love, love, love'. Then, surrounded by flowers and the beautiful people of Swingin' London, they sent that message, in the form of pop music, around the entire globe.

So when The JAMs started their first record with fifteen seconds of 'All You Need Is Love', this was no mere sampling. The way they ended the sample, by slowing down the final 'love, love, love' refrain until it collapsed into nothing, can only be seen as a rejection. This was a statement of intent. It was about claiming – and then dismissing – the height of The Beatles and, by extension, pop music as a whole. Such were the ambitions and the acts of the two men who had taken on the name The Justified Ancients of Mu Mu.

That intro was followed by an MC5 sample, the shout of 'Kick out The JAMs, motherfuckers!' which Robert Anton Wilson had discussed in *Illuminatus!*. This was followed by a sampled voice which states 'Sexual intercourse – no known cure', and introduces the lyrical theme of the track. This is a song about AIDS, a disease which had only become known to the general public a few years earlier and which brought an end to the sexual liberation of the 1960s and 1970s. The Beatles' historic expression of the 1967 Summer of Love had been *détourned* and subverted into an opposite, more contemporarily relevant message.*

This basic principle, that you have the right to do what you like with whatever culture is thrust at you, is made explicit in their reworking of The Dave Brubeck Quartet's 'Take Five', which The JAMs retitled 'Don't Take Five (Take What You Want)'. The idea would later take on a more political tone in the internet copyright wars of the early

---

* It's probably worth noting here that they later released a more 'legal' version of the song, with all but a snatch of The Beatles removed. This version, which begins with voices quacking *La Marseillaise*, is the one most commonly heard these days.

twenty-first century. It is the (frequently unspoken) heart of the philosophy behind torrent sites such as The Pirate Bay and related political organisations such as the Pirate Party. It is an argument that is still being digested by our culture.

The finished record was shit, of course. There are very few people who could listen to it today and say, with hand on heart, that *as a record* it has merit.* This is all the more apparent if you play it after listening to The Beatles' 'All You Need Is Love', which retains its innate quality to this day. As Drummond and Cauty's press agent Mick Houghton told Richard King, '[Drummond] came up and played me The JAMs and I thought it was absolute rubbish . . . I just couldn't take it seriously because it was a racket. It was Bill Drummond pretending to be some kind of Glaswegian dock worker over a load of Abba samples, and I thought it was complete tosh, seriously, I really did and I may or may not have said that to him.'

---

* It's rare to read things as negative as this in music biographies. Music book authors know that the only people who have any interest in reading their work are people who love that particular band or artist. Such blunt opinionated negativity, in those circumstances, is not what the readers want. Of course, I know full well that there are people who genuinely love those early JAMs singles, and their view is as valid as mine. You can write in a more nuanced way, starting sentences with phrases such as 'For many people . . .', for example, in an effort to acknowledge this. The problem is, doing so can make the text weasely and a bit insipid. It's rare to have a subject like The KLF where you can be an opinionated oaf and – for some reason – get away with it.

Faced with the difficulty of promoting such a band, Houghton made it clear to the press exactly who The JAMs were. The pair had adopted pseudonyms – King Boy D for Drummond and Rockman Rock for Cauty – and were trying to hide behind the persona of Scottish dock workers, rapping in the pronounced accent that Drummond used on his solo record. The revelation of their true identities was a wise move on Houghton's part, for the press knew of Drummond and Cauty and knew enough to be curious about what they were up to.

The press were intrigued by the mystique that The JAMs were beginning to weave around themselves. Drummond's first lyric on 'All You Need Is Love' was 'We're back again', not a typical opening line for a debut single by a band that had only formed a few months earlier. The rap continues, 'They never kicked us out, 20,000 years of "shout, shout, shout".' Again, it is not usual for rap artists to announce themselves as a continuation of a 20,000-year history. The line 'They never kicked us out' is a clue here. It is a direct reference to *Illuminatus!*, and to the Illuminati's attempts to kick out the Discordian splinter group The Justified Ancients of Mummu.

By 1987, *Illuminatus!* was not widely read. Even those who had heard of it were unlikely to read it, for by then it had the unacceptable air of a hippy text. Yet without knowledge of this book, The JAMs' lyrics appeared to be extraordinarily enigmatic, and certainly unlike anything else around. Even their name was otherworldly – 'Justified?' 'Ancient?' These were not words used in pop music.

Their strange mystique seemed to have an internal logic to it. It wasn't meaningless or surreal nonsense, but it somehow meant something on its own terms. Even when their name was explained as being taken from Wilson and Shea's books, as it was in almost every article written about the band, this didn't reduce the mystery, for very few people went on to read the books. Discordianism was largely unknown then, as indeed it remains to this day. In this context, wherever The JAMs were coming from – wherever that was – seemed to be somewhere new.

For the music press, this was all good. Journalists are, by necessity, more drawn to something that is good to write about rather than something that is good to listen to. And there was much about The JAMs that made good copy. Their habit of publicising themselves using graffiti – another nod to the Situationists – or creating crop circles was something else that the press approved of, for the resulting story would automatically be more interesting than an announcement made by a press release.

It did not hurt, of course, that many of their records quickly became unobtainable. Within a month of the independent release of 'All You Need Is Love', three major record labels had taken out injunctions. The court order they obtained required the record not merely to be withdrawn, but that all existing copies be destroyed. In this instance, they were too late. Only five hundred copies had been pressed, and they had all been sold. All this created great publicity for the release of a subsequent version, which had reworked or rerecorded all the samples in order to make them more or less legal. This legal attention took The JAMs by surprise. 'We just thought that no one was going to take any notice of [the record],' Drummond has said.

The JAMs' legal problems came to a head with the release of their album *1987: What The Fuck Is Going On?*, which included ABBA on the track 'The Queen and I'. 'Included' is probably not the correct word here, for so liberal were The JAMs with their use of long chunks of 'Dancing Queen' that it would be more accurate to call it an ABBA track that featured contributions from The JAMs. ABBA's lawyers were having none of it. Shortly after the album was released, Drummond and Cauty were contacted by the Mechanical Copyright Protection Society, or MCPS. 'One of our members, whose work is used substantially on the 1987 album, is not prepared to grant a licence in respect of their work,' the MCPS wrote. 'We must therefore insist that in respect of this record you (i) cease all manufacture and distribution, (ii) take all possible steps to recover copies of the album which are then to be delivered to MCPS or destroyed under the supervision of the MCPS, and (iii) deliver up the master tape, mothers, stampers, and any other parts commensurate with manufacture of the record.'

Drummond and Cauty took legal advice and were informed that it would cost them £20,000 to fight this in court. And that they would lose.

Publicity-wise, of course, this was terrific. Drummond had initially thought that if he met with ABBA and explained his reasons, then they would be able to come to an agreement as artists. It quickly became clear that no meeting would ever be granted. Nevertheless, Cauty and Drummond headed to Sweden with the *NME* journalist James Brown in tow. Here they played the offending song outside ABBA's publishing company and presented a fake gold disc (marked 'for sales in excess of zero') to a prostitute who, they argued, looked a bit like one of the women from ABBA.* They then destroyed most of the remaining copies of the album by setting fire to them in a field and were promptly shot at by a farmer for their trouble. On the ferry home they threw the remaining copies into the North Sea and performed an improvised set on the ferry, the only known live JAMs performance, in exchange for a large Toblerone.†

---

* In truth she looked nothing like either of the women from ABBA, as I understand it. It's worth noting that Bill and Jimmy's interest in ABBA was unusual at the time. ABBA were not the critical and popular darlings in the 1980s that they are now. Then, they were typically seen as dated and naff. This would all change following their *ABBA Gold* compilation album in 1992, which was released months after Erasure had reached number one with their *Abba-esque* EP. This is another example of The KLF's instincts being out of sync with current thinking, but in sync with a deeper truth.

† As I understand it now, the story of Bill and Jimmy being shot at by a farmer was made up. It was invented by the journalist James Brown, who found Bill and Jimmy a perfect subject for some wild myth making. This is something that Brown talks about in Chris Atkins's 2022 documentary *Who Killed The KLF?* It's interesting that the story does feel wrong. The band had plenty of crazy adventures, yet being shot at by a farmer as if

THE MAN AND THE MU MU

This was the start of Drummond and Cauty's reputations as being masters of the publicity stunt. It is worth noting the gulf between this reputation and how they actually behaved. The traditional role of media manipulator is a scheming, cynical one, where intricate plans are mapped out in advance and followed to the letter. The archetype of the manipulative producer is perhaps best embodied in the Sex Pistols film *The Great Rock 'n' Roll Swindle*. This presents the story of the Sex Pistols as a grand scheme by their manager, Malcolm McLaren, who is shown manipulating the band like a sinister puppet master for his own financial gain.

In contrast, The JAMs, on adventures such as the Swedish trip and others, are simply winging it. The impetus here was that they had to destroy their stock of the album and they wanted to make that act a thing in itself, something symbolic and interesting. Beyond that, they were scrabbling around for ideas and just trying to make *something* happen. Hindsight may fix these events into a narrative that makes them appear symbolic or almost preordained, such as the way the bonfire of their debut album mirrors the later bonfire of their money. But while they are being enacted, they are chaotic. They lack aim and purpose. To

---

they were *Looney Tunes* characters doesn't feel like *their* kind of crazy adventure. It's the sort of thing that would happen to Ozzy Osbourne, not The KLF. This suggests that there is a particular spirit or tone to their capers. I believe the story about the Toblerone, in contrast, to be true. That does feel right for them.

quote one of their press releases, 'The plot has been mis-laid'.*

Drummond now had a band that had the mystique he looked for in Echo & the Bunnymen or The Teardrop Explodes. But there was still something missing from the picture, and that was the very something that had seduced him into the music industry in the first place. This was the magic of a perfect single, the creation of a single slice of plastic containing a song so universally appealing that it speaks to everyone, outlives its creators and makes the world a better place. Critical mystique was nothing to be sniffed at, of course, but it was a shame that their records were so shit.

You can see this lingering love of the great pop single in the second JAMs single, 'Whitney Joins The JAMs'. This begins with the *Mission: Impossible* theme, with the impossible mission presented by the song being persuading Whitney Houston to join their band. During the early parts of the track Drummond pleads with Houston over a bog-standard dance rhythm ('Whitney, please! Please, please join The JAMs. You saw our reviews, didn't you? Please, Whitney, please!') This builds until Houston's biggest pop single, 'I Wanna Dance With Somebody', is

---

* For the best part of a week, I convinced myself that *The Plot Has Been Mislaid* should be the title of this book. As book titles go, it is up there with *This Is a Shit Book*.

dropped into the mix. Again, this is no normal sample, but a wholesale stealing of the track. But that is not how it is presented by the logic of the song. On The JAMs' terms, this is Whitney Houston deciding to join their band, and Drummond sells this angle by whooping 'Whitney Houston has joined The JAMs!' with such excitement that you can't help but feel delighted for him.

It is tempting to see this as a turning point, the moment when the anti-music hip-hop band The Justified Ancients of Mu Mu started to turn towards the pro-music dance band The KLF. Certainly, you can no longer see the Houston sample as an act of *détournement* in the style of the 1987 album. Unlike the Beatles or ABBA samples, this is not subverting the meaning of the spectacle. It is about celebrating how brilliant the song they are stealing is. Many critics viewed this lauding of Houston's single as ironic, but it was nothing of the sort.

It grew out of an attempt to make a credible record that sampled the 'Theme From Shaft'. They booked a studio for five days and Drummond went to the record shop to buy the Isaac Hayes record. 'In the window [of the record shop was] a big cut-out of Whitney Houston,' Drummond has said. 'I love that track, and I loved Whitney Houston then, and I just said "Wow", and bought the album ... We just played that track over and over again, and we just thought, "There's no point us making records when such fantastic records as this have been made." And that's how that track [. . .] grew into a celebration of Whitney Houston.'

And just before 1987 ended and The JAMs were disbanded, they very nearly made a fantastic record of their own. The song was their third and final single of that year, 'Downtown'. Apart from samples from the Petula Clark song of the same name, it had far fewer stolen elements than other JAMs records. It also featured a specially recorded carol sung by the London Gospel Community Choir. Drummond's lyrics revolve around homelessness, to contrast with Petula Clark's romanticising of London ('Neon lights are pretty,' she sings while Drummond snarls 'In Leicester Square, did you do it clean?').

But it is Drummond's interaction with the Gospel Choir that makes 'Downtown' so interesting. The choir start the song with a burst of 'Jesus Christ is born today!', and power through the rest of the song, never appearing fazed or threatened by the blunt drumbeat that keeps everything moving. Drummond starts addressing his lyrics at them in a similar way to his conversation with Whitney Houston, like a drunk shouting a monologue at passers-by. In response to their chant of 'Glory!', for example, he asks 'What glory? In a wine bar world?' Finally he succumbs to their vision and begrudgingly asks 'Okay, let's hear it', just as they shift up a gear, change key and deliver the chorus. And the chorus is pure Christmas Christianity, a song of Hallelujahs, Glory, Angels looking down and Jesus Christ being born. The combination of the single-minded drum machine and the joy in the voices of the London Gospel Community Choir transcends anything else that The JAMs produced. It is hard not to get swept along by the uncynical religious outpouring.*

It was not a hit, nor was it going to be with Drummond's aggressive Scottish rap and the abrupt placing of the samples. But it was a good record and, more importantly, it showed that perhaps they were after all capable of producing the great pop record by which Drummond had for so long been bewitched. But to do so they would have to produce something that matched the religious spirit of the London Gospel Community Choir. How, exactly, could they repeat that transcendence?

---

* When I wrote this, I hoped it would help to raise the profile of this song. 'Downtown' tends to get overlooked in most discussions about Bill and Jimmy's work. I haven't seen any evidence that this has happened, however. I still very rarely – if ever – hear it talked about. Perhaps it is only me who finds some magic in this track after all. Ah well, worth a try.

6

Ford and Fiction

A significant upturn in Cauty and Drummond's financial circumstances occurred in May 1988, when they accidentally produced a hit single. It was called 'Doctorin' The TARDIS' and they released it under the name The Timelords.

It was a novelty record.

It started with a desire to make a credible dance record based around the theme music of the science fiction series *Doctor Who.** Lovers of electronic music consider this

---

* Here's the last piece of our puzzle. Up until now the book has been slowly introducing its five key subjects – Bill Drummond, Robert Anton Wilson, Ken Campbell, Alan Moore and Doctor Who. This is, clearly, a story about a very male kind of madness. I mentioned earlier that, although this story appears wild and rambling and full of tangents, there was a

theme to be something of a classic, and the pioneering work of its creators, the BBC Radiophonic Workshop, is much admired.

The problem was that Cauty couldn't get a standard 4/4 dance beat to work with it. After some experimentation, he came to the conclusion that the only drumbeat that would fit was the glitter beat. As a result, samples of Gary Glitter's 'Rock 'n' Roll (Part Two)', plus the odd bit of 'Blockbuster!' by Sweet, were added to the mix. 'Not until a couple of days into it did we realise how terrible it was,' Cauty admitted to Richard King. Yet by the time they had added samples of Daleks quoting Harry Enfield's Loadsamoney character, it was clear that they had a potential hit on their hands. 'We justified it all by saying to ourselves "We're celebrating a very British thing here … you know",' Drummond told BBC Radio 1, 'something that Timmy Mallett understands.'

Having accidentally created a potentially massive selling novelty record, the question then became how to publicise it. Drummond and Cauty themselves were both

---

strict system in place for deciding what could be included and what was left out. The basic rule was that if something connects to two or more of the five key subjects, it goes in the book. The aim of this is to create the impression that everything is connected in a deeper and more complicated way than common sense would suggest. You'll start seeing a lot of these connections from here on in, now that our five central subjects have been introduced. This approach was of course inspired by the Discordian Law of Fives, which states that everything happens in fives, or is divisible by five, or are multiples of five, or are somehow connected to five, given enough imagination and stubbornness on the part of the observer.

in their mid-thirties and neither were natural frontmen for a mainstream pop record. They decided to claim that the record had been made by Cauty's car. This was a huge American cop car that looked like a beaten-up version of the Blues Brothers' Bluesmobile. It was, if nothing else, an original idea. No car had ever had a hit record before.

Drummond and Cauty thought that this gimmick would make a nice gift for the newspapers, handing them an easy little story on a plate. The press did not agree, by and large, finding the idea idiotic and wondering, perhaps for the first time, if Cauty and Drummond were taking the piss. Regardless, the single sleeve was printed featuring a photograph of the car, now renamed Ford Timelord, complete with a speech bubble saying, 'Hi! I'm Ford Timelord. I'm a car, and I've made a record.' The name 'Ford Timelord' was an echo of Ford Prefect, a character in *The Hitchhiker's Guide to the Galaxy* by the *Doctor Who* script editor Douglas Adams. This was nicely fitting, as Ken Campbell's follow-up to *Illuminatus!* was a production of *The Hitchhiker's Guide to the Galaxy*.*

---

* This is a good example of what I was just talking about – the highlighting of things that connect two or more of the book's five central subjects. This sentence connects Bill Drummond's record with Doctor Who, Ken Campbell and, through mention of the *Illuminatus!*, Robert Anton Wilson. It is a sentence that doesn't need to be there in terms of the narrative, you'll notice. If it was cut, you wouldn't miss it. It is there instead as part of the ongoing scheme to create a woozy, unsettling atmosphere – as if there are forces going on behind the scenes too strange and vast

In three weeks, despite not being playlisted by Radio 1, the record reached the fabled position of number one in the charts. It would go on to sell more than a million copies. A video was shot showing the car driving around locations in Wiltshire, including the Avebury stone circles. It included a couple of home-made Daleks which avoided legal problems by being so poorly constructed that no one could claim with a straight face they contravened copyright.

Another problem was that the producers of *Top Of The Pops* believed that a car sitting by itself on stage for three minutes, flashing its lights in time to the music, would not make an interesting performance. The solution was to recruit Gary Glitter to front the performance, for which he donned a silver cape and hammed it up for all he was worth. His reward was to find himself on the cover of the *NME* for the first time in his career.

The car itself, a 1968 Ford Galaxy, had originally been shipped to England by Pinewood Studios and it had been used as a prop in a number of films, including the first *Superman* movie. It was then bought from Pinewood by a young artist named Gary Mitchell, who painted it to resemble a police car, attached a pirate flag to its aerial

---

for us to understand. Which there may well be, of course, even if they don't always lend themselves to a fun book. After the book was written I kept spotting more connections and wishing that I'd included them. It's a shame that I didn't realise at the time that the then-incumbent Doctor Who, Matt Smith, went to the same grammar school as Alan Moore, for example.

and largely trashed it off-roading and driving dough-nuts in the fields around Godstone in Surrey. Mitchell then sold the battered wreck to Cauty for a few hundred pounds.

Mitchell himself moved to Avebury in Wiltshire, where he worked as a tour guide around the same Neolithic stone circles that his old car had driven past in the video. He met Julian Cope and the pair became close for a short period in the early 1990s. Cope was writing a book about the stone circles of the British Isles and, as he could not drive at that point, Mitchell drove him around the country to research stone circles, and he also accompanied him on his solo Highlands and Islands gigs around Scotland.

Drummond's influence over Cope at this point was complex, to say the least. Cope, who saw no humour in Drummond's 'Julian Cope Is Dead' song, had taken to wearing a 'Julian Cope Is Dead' T-shirt on stage every night, but he wore it inside out so as not to display the slogan to the audience. He also felt the need to make a pilgrimage to Drummond's home town, where he spent a night walking around, thinking about Bill.

Mitchell was with Cope on the Isle of Lewis undertaking research for the stone circles book when Cope received a phone call, and was told that Drummond was planning to flatten Silbury Hill with earth-moving equipment. Silbury Hill is a massive man-made Neolithic mound at Avebury, of intense personal importance to Cope. Mitchell recalls how shaken up by this threat Cope was. 'He went white [after the call], it was a shock to see him like that actually. No one else had that power over Julian. Bill was the only person that he was scared of.'

In the late 1990s Mitchell, now going by the name Flinton Chalk, moved to London and ran the Tom Tom Gallery in New Compton Street, the first gallery to display and sell the works of Banksy. This was opposite the old Ministry of Defence building, which was frequently visited by the Duke of Westminster around the time of the first Iraq war. The billionaire duke, a cousin of the Queen and one of the wealthiest men in Britain, was then the head of the Territorial Army. He would often park outside the Tom Tom Gallery when visiting the Ministry, arriving in full military uniform with a huge SAS-trained chauffeur and bodyguard, only to be confronted by the gallery's window display. It was for this reason that Chalk used to display a large Banksy canvas in the window called *Monkey Queen*, which, as the name suggests, featured the Queen as a monkey.

Around this time, in 2003, Chalk also stocked prints by Jimmy Cauty, including a series of stamps featuring the Queen wearing a gas mask, which was intended as a comment on the Iraq war. These resulted in legal action being taken against Cauty and Chalk by the Royal Mail, and led to Chalk defending Cauty's work in the *Evening Standard*.

All of this is, of course, a string of random coincidences, for there is no reason why the man who sold Ford Timelord to Cauty should go on to have so many KLF related connections. Synchronicities seem to prefer some stories more than others, and this is one that they flock to.* We can see this clearly if we look a little more closely at the use of *Doctor Who* for their novelty record.

From the perspective of the early twenty-first century, making a *Doctor Who* record appears to be an obvious populist choice. It is, after all, one of the most successful and best-loved series on British TV. This was not the case in 1988, when 'Doctorin' The TARDIS' was released. At that time, *Doctor Who* was largely considered an embarrassment, by both the BBC and the viewing public at home. If Drummond and Cauty had been drawn to it for populist reasons, their timing was out.

Doctor Who began way back in 1963. Its first episode was broadcast on the Discordian holy day of 23 November, a date the Discordians honour because it is also Harpo Marx's birthday. The day before, the 22nd, had seen the assassination of JFK and the deaths of C. S. Lewis and Aldous Huxley. Huxley, through his relationship with Timothy Leary and his book *The Doors of Perception*, had been a big influence on Robert Anton Wilson. We have already noted the role of The Justified Ancients of Mummu in Kennedy's assassination in fiction, as well as how the real-world assassination impacted on the growth

---

* Imagine what it would be like if this were not true.

of Discordianism. C. S. Lewis, meanwhile, was a big influence on *Doctor Who* itself, for the wardrobe in his *Narnia* books was a simple wooden box that was also a gateway to another world. Right from the start, then, the programme seems tangled up in many of the threads in this narrative.

For roughly the first twenty years of its life, *Doctor Who* was generally thought of fondly. It could be cheap and it could be daft, but it brought families together and it had imagination, charm and a clear moral centre which made its faults easy to forgive. It had the ability to change all its actors and behind-the-scenes staff every few years, which kept it fresh. But eventually, towards the end of Peter Davison's time in the role of the Doctor, something started to go wrong.

It wasn't just one thing, of course. There were many factors. The *Star Wars* films had upped the bar for special effects so high that the BBC could not compete. The rise of Michael Grade, from Controller of BBC1 to Director of Programmes, effectively turned the BBC against the series. Grade disliked sci-fi in general and *Doctor Who* in particular, and as is usual in hierarchical organisations the boss' prejudices are soon reflected by those they manage. The series' budget, in real terms, was dwindling away into almost nothing.

There were creative problems, too. Peter Davison was replaced by Colin Baker as the Sixth Doctor. Baker was a good actor but he was not someone who possessed the 'kid appeal' necessary for the role. Or, at least, that was the view of Michael Grade, who said that his portrayal of the Doctor was 'utterly unlikeable, absolutely god-awful in fact'. This was an opinion that may have been coloured by Grade's close friendship with Liza Goddard, Baker's ex-wife.*

It didn't help either that Baker's Doctor was dressed in a deranged multicoloured clown outfit. With the benefit of hindsight, some art historians now claim this costume as a postmodern classic, but it did not help the casual viewer take the programme seriously.† The producer's pantomime-esque tastes in casting meant that the likes of the musical theatre star Bonnie Langford joined the cast, while a new script editor moved the show away from the family and kids audience by painting a darker, bleaker, more violent universe at odds with the earlier spirit of the show. The whole thing had become a mess.

As a result the show was put on a very public hiatus for eighteen months in 1986, and ordered to pull itself

---

* Michael Grade has recently given a lengthy interview to the broadcaster Matthew Sweet about his decision to cancel the programme. From the evidence of this interview, it doesn't sound like he was influenced by factors like relationships with Liza Goddard. His motivation appears to be that, in his heart of hearts, he really did think that the programme was shit.

† This opinion about Colin Baker's coat was widely held at the time, and indeed back in 2012 when I wrote this. I have to confess, though, that recently I have come to really like it. Ncuti Gatwa could totally rock a coat like that.

together. When it returned, for its twenty-third series, it was distinctly unimproved. The programme had had its final warning. Michael Grade ordered that Colin Baker be replaced.

It is here that our Discordian threads return to the show. A number of actors were auditioned to replace Baker, but it very quickly came down to a choice between two: our good friend Ken Campbell and Sylvester McCoy (whose big break in showbiz had been sticking ferrets down his trousers in *The Ken Campbell Roadshow*). Campbell auditioned for *Doctor Who* by performing a speech about the nature of time modelled on Alan Moore's Dr Manhattan character, wearing a long coat, sleeveless cartoon T-shirt and wide-brimmed hat.* The producer thought he was too weird, an opinion probably enforced by a message which had been left on his answerphone the previous day believed to have come from Campbell. The message was actually a quote from Charles Fort's book *Lo!*, which begins: 'A naked man in a city street – the track of a horse in volcanic mud – the mystery of the reindeer's ears – a huge, black form, like a whale, in the sky, and it drips red drops as if attacked by celestial swordfishes – an appalling cherub appears in the sea – *Confusions.*'

The production team were unaware that this quote was Campbell's personal mantra, which he would recite

---

* Sadly, this appears to be the one audition for the Seventh Doctor which does not survive on tape. Note how this sentence goes out of its way to link Ken Campbell, Alan Moore and Doctor Who.

in the wings before any performance as a centring exercise. Finding it on the answering machine was deeply unsettling.

As Sylvester McCoy remembers, 'The executive producer of BBC Series and Serials wanted Ken, but the producer of *Doctor Who* wanted me, and his argument was that he thought Ken would frighten the children, and I think he was right. The producer in fact threatened to resign if Ken got the job. So I got it.'

Campbell may have been too weird for *Doctor Who*, but that didn't mean our Discordian synchronicities would leave the show behind. With the money they made from their *Doctor Who* record, Drummond and Cauty made a film called *The White Room*, as we'll soon see. There was one major role in the film that required a 'name' actor, and for this role they cast Paul McGann, then well known for his roles in *The Monocled Mutineer* and *Withnail and I*. A few years after this McGann took over from Sylvester McCoy and became the Eighth Doctor. There was only one person in the entire world who could possibly be cast as the next Doctor, and for Drummond and Cauty to select that very same man for their *Doctor Who*-funded film is . . . well, the odds are pretty high. Clearly this is a story that the synchronicities can't get enough of.

With McCoy cast, the series returned complete with new star, new titles, new music and a new script editor. And it was, if anything, worse than before.* The programme wasn't cancelled immediately, for the BBC did not want to attract the sort of press that would generate. Instead, it was scheduled against the ratings powerhouse of *Coronation Street* for its last two years where its long, painful death was less visible. After the failure of the first McCoy series, it was not going to be given another chance. It was a dead show walking.

It was at this point, between the first and second McCoy seasons when the series' problems looked terminal and the mercurial character of the Doctor was at his lowest point, that Drummond and Cauty called themselves The Timelords and released 'Doctorin' The TARDIS'.

Doctor Who had lost its connection to a wide family audience of young children and amused parents. It was no longer fun. It needed to remind people how good it could be, and what they had once loved about it. Then Drummond and Cauty arrived with a single that was camp, and silly, and ludicrously enjoyable. It was, in the words of critic Peter Paphides, 'the one novelty record that most people admit to liking'. It sold well over a million copies. It was full of energy and anarchy.

It was, in other words, exactly what Doctor Who needed at that point in time.

---

* I know season twenty-four has its defenders now. But from the perspective of the powers that be in the BBC at the time, that was probably a fair summation.

Then the programme returned later that year, and suddenly it was invigorated. McCoy had worked out how to play the role, a new companion created chemistry and the script editor had a clear sense of purpose and direction. Over the next couple of years, as it moved towards cancellation, the character mutated again to become manipulative and mysterious. True, this did not win back the child audience, but it did attract people who would be far more useful for its coming dark ages – writers. Once it was off the air *Doctor Who* continued as a series of novels, and many of the people who wrote Doctor Who fiction in this period – Russell T. Davies, Mark Gatiss, Paul Cornell and Steven Moffat, to name a few – were responsible for resurrecting *Doctor Who* in 2005. Indeed, a number of these people, and many British writers of their generation, have gone on record as saying that they only became writers in the first place because of *Doctor Who*.

When Russell T. Davies brought the series back to television he refreshed the character by using the narrative device of surviving a great 'Time War'. The 'Time War' idea originally came from Alan Moore, who wrote a number of *Doctor Who* comic scripts in 1981 about a '4DWar' which had two time-travelling armies attacking each other at increasingly earlier points in time so that neither side had any idea what the war was about, or who had started it.

If we take Alan Moore's model of Ideaspace seriously – if

only for a moment –* and look at the idea of *Doctor Who*, we see an extremely detailed fiction. The Doctor is one of the great line of British folk heroes; a character in the tradition of Robin Hood, Sherlock Holmes or James Bond. Whereas American folk heroes tend towards cowboys or gangsters who take what they want from the world and end up either rich or winners, British equivalents are very different. They are anti-Establishment figures, even when they work with the Establishment, and they save the day not for personal gain, but because it is the right thing to do. For generations of British school kids, *Doctor Who* was the myth they grew up with. They had only the most superficial knowledge of the likes of Zeus, Odin or Jesus, but they knew all there was to know about Davros, The Master and Cybermen.

The Doctor is the first British folk hero of the TV age, and the nature of his TV origins make him unusual. There is no definitive creator standing behind him, no Arthur Conan Doyle, J. R. R. Tolkien, Ian Fleming or J. K. Rowling. Instead, he popped out from the space

---

* This is a rare appearance of the en dash – not a form of punctuation I used much during my early writing career. During recent books, my current lovely editor (hello Jenny!) started slipping them into my more convoluted paragraphs, and now I've got a real taste for them. If anything, I'm in danger of overdoing en dashes these days. Jenny's attempts to introduce semicolons into my books, in contrast, has been fiercely resisted. The most self-satisfied of all punctuation marks, semicolons are terrible things that only serve to highlight how your paragraph has gone wrong and needs a rewrite. Burn them all.

between many minds. There was a succession of different actors, writers and producers who all invigorated the character for a short while before moving on or burning out. The character is defined by his ability to regenerate and change his personality. He can change all his friends and companions. He can go anywhere, at any time. He is, essentially, the perfect, never-ending story. He will survive long after you, me or anyone currently involved in making the series has died. He adapts, grows, mutates and endures. In this he fulfils much of the standard definitions for a living thing. This is not bad going, for a fiction.

Already, there are untold thousands of *Doctor Who* stories, which, for a character of fiction, is almost unheard of. There have been hundreds of stories on TV, and many, many more available as novels, audio CDs, comic books, films, stage plays, webcasts, fanfics and radio programmes. The growth of the story, compared to any other fiction from the same period, is deeply unusual. Indeed, it has become arguably the most expansive and complex non-religious fiction ever created.

According to Moore's model of Ideaspace, this fiction may be complicated enough to act like a living thing. Note that this is not to say that *Doctor Who* is a living thing, for that would sound crazy. It is to say that it behaves as if it were a living thing, which is a much more reasonable observation. Of course, if you were to then go on to try to define the difference between something that is living and something that behaves like it is living, you would be a brave soul indeed.*

The programme's expansion through all possible media was begun by its first script editor, David Whitaker. Although Doctor Who has no definitive 'creator', Whitaker can be said to be the man who nurtured the heart of the series, sculpting the peculiar mix of humour, morality and wide-eyed imagination that makes the series so unique. He was involved in the creation of most of the iconography of the show, from introducing the Daleks, to making the TARDIS in some way alive and the Doctor able to regenerate into a different actor. He also spread the life of the character beyond television, for he wrote the first novels and annuals and co-wrote the Peter Cushing *Dr Who* movies from the 1960s.

Whitaker's work on *Doctor Who* was particularly influenced by alchemy, a subject that he claimed to be 'very fond of'.† The basic alchemical principle, that a physical object can be affected by the manipulation of a symbol of that

---

* I really like this paragraph. I'm basically marking my own homework here, aren't I?

† This quote from Whitaker about being 'very fond of' the subject of alchemy is taken from a 1978 letter, which was reprinted in *Doctor Who Magazine* issue 98. The writer Simon Guerrier is currently working on a major biography of Whitaker, and he treats the veracity of this letter with some suspicion. Guerrier's book *David Whitaker in an Exciting Adventure with Television* is due to be published by Ten Acre in the second half of 2023, and it should explain why. Even if the letter is fake, however, alchemical themes are still clearly present in Whitaker's work.

object – the idea of it, if you prefer – is used explicitly in his 1967 story *The Evil of the Daleks* (which is also a strong contender for the story that invented steampunk.) *The Evil of the Daleks* is about a pair of Victorian scientists who accidentally build a time machine out of 144 mirrors (the number '144', or 122, being alchemically significant). This basic alchemical principle is still used in the programme today, for example in Steven Moffat's claim about his monsters the Weeping Angels: 'The image of an Angel is an Angel.'

In Whitaker's *Doctor Who*, when the TARDIS broke down because of a problem with the 'mercury in the fluid links', there was specific alchemical symbolism in the choice of mercury. When the First Doctor, William Hartnell, was replaced by the Second, Patrick Troughton, Whitaker gave him a flute and an obsession with hats in order to echo the classical god Mercury (Hermes to the Greeks). All this would have meant little to the children watching in the 1960s. Nevertheless, Whitaker seems to have been consciously shaping the character of the Doctor into a mercurial, Trickster figure.

When the current *Doctor Who* writers claim that they only became writers because of *Doctor Who*, they usually credit the series of novels which Whitaker started and which young boys devoured during the 1970s. There is another explanation, however, which comes from the very format of the programme. In the original series, episodes built towards a climax and ended on a cliff-hanger in which the Doctor or his friends appeared to be in inescapable danger. Of course, the children watching knew that the Doctor would somehow survive. He always did. The question, then, was not would he escape, but how? What could possibly happen to get the Doctor out of that situation? There would be much debate about this in school playgrounds after each episode. And as the kids thought about the problem, their imaginations were being stoked. They were thinking like writers. Indeed, they were trying to write the next episode themselves.

What we have here, then, is a character of fiction, neither created nor 'owned' by any one imagination, who is actively creating the very environment – writers' minds – that it needs to survive into the future. Not only is Doctor Who a fictitious character who acts like a living thing by constantly evolving and surviving, it is also a *self-sustaining* living thing that creates the one thing that it needs to survive. From an evolutionary point of view, that's impressive.*

There is no requirement for those affected by an idea to be aware of any of this. When the media critic Elizabeth Sandifer writes that 'David Whitaker, at once the most important figure in *Doctor Who*'s development and the least understood, created a show that is genuinely magical and this influence cannot be erased from within the show', she

---

* By now you are probably thinking, 'Wow, there is quite a lot of stuff about *Doctor Who* in this chapter, I really wasn't expecting quite so much *Doctor Who*.' Believe me, you got off lightly. There was a lot more in the first draft. I cut pages and pages of the stuff. I got a bit carried away.

does not mean that any of the hundreds of actors and writers who went on to work on the programme saw it in those terms. Or, as Sandifer so clearly puts it, 'I don't actually believe that the writers of *Doctor Who* were consciously designing a sentient metafiction to continually disrupt the social order through a systematic process of *détournement*. Except maybe David Whitaker.'

From Drummond and Cauty's perspective, the story of *Doctor Who* is irrelevant. All that was happening was that they were exploring their mental landscape, and they were fulfilling their duty as artists by doing so more deeply than normal people. This is a landscape with many unseen, unknown areas where who knows what might be found. The KLF explored further than most and, if we were to accept Moore's model, it would perhaps not be surprising that a fiction as complex as *Doctor Who* could encounter them in Ideaspace and, being at its lowest point and in dire need of help, use them for its own ends.

For Moore, and other artists such as the film-maker David Lynch who use similar models, the role of the artist is like that of a fisherman. It is his job to fish in the collective unconscious and use all his skill to best present his catch to an audience. Drummond and Cauty, on the other hand, appear to have been caught by the fish. Lacking any clear sense of what they were doing, they dived in as deeply as Moore and Lynch. They did not have a specific purpose for doing so. They just needed to make something happen – anything really, such is the path of chaos. 'It was supposed to be a proper dance record, but we couldn't fit the four-four beat to it, so we ended up with the glitter beat, which was never really our intention but we had to go with it,' Cauty has said. 'It was like an out-of-control lorry, you know, you're just trying to steer it, and that track took itself over, really, and did what it wanted to do. We were just watching.'

This lack of intention is significant, from a magical point of view. One of the most important aspects of magical practice is the will. Aleister Crowley defined magic as being changes in the world brought about by the exercise of the will, hence his maxim 'Do what thou Will shall be the whole of the Law'. The will or intention of a magical act is important because the magician opens himself up to all sorts of strange powers and influences and he must avoid being controlled by them. Drummond and Cauty were not exerting any control on the process, and so they made themselves vulnerable to the who knows whats that live out of sight in the depths of Ideaspace. For this reason, you could understand why Moore would think that Bill Drummond was 'totally mad'.

All this only applies if you're prepared to accept the notion of magic.*

Nevertheless, it is worth noting because there is another

---

* Sentences like this are cheeky little critters. On the surface, it makes the book appear reassuring. 'Don't worry about all this craziness,' it implies, 'you don't need to accept any of it.' Yet at the same time it is also saying, 'You know the argument the book is making, which seemed so convincing when you were reading it? Don't fall for it.' By appearing comforting and supportive, it manages to further destabilise and wrong-foot you.

fiction that is important in Drummond and Cauty's story. This one is more significant, because this is the fiction that they became, taking on its title and performing their actions in its name. It is also the source of our whirlwind of synchronicities. We are talking, of course, about The Justified Ancients of Mummu. The question then becomes: did Cauty and Drummond choose The JAMs, or did The JAMs choose Cauty and Drummond? A possible clue will come later, when we look at what the founding purpose of The Justified Ancients of Mummu actually was.

7

Writing and Waiting

▲

The huge success of the independently released 'Doctor-in' The TARDIS' gave Drummond and Cauty plenty to chew on. It seemed to them that this was a new stage in the history of music, one where all the previous gatekeepers could be bypassed. For the first time, it was possible for anyone who wanted a hit record to go ahead and make one. This, it seemed clear, was a significant change and one that should be encouraged.

Drummond and Cauty's reaction to this was to write a book. Called *The Manual (How To Have A Number One The Easy Way)*, it contained a set of instructions which promised to allow anyone to repeat their success, regardless of musical talent. It came with a money-back guarantee: anyone who followed their instructions to the letter, and didn't have a number one hit, would get their £5.99 back.

The Manual was a distillation of everything that the pair had learnt about the music industry, filtered through the 'just do it you bastard' approach of Ken Campbell and the anti-pretension pop sensibility they learnt from watching Pete Waterman work. Due to the rapid technological change in music recording, much of the practical information it contains dated very quickly, making it a historical snapshot of a very brief period. The Campbell and Waterman influences, however, have not dated, and it is for this reason that the book is still read by musicians today. Jamie Reynolds of The Klaxons, for example, told the American music journalist Philip Sherburne that they followed the book religiously in order to make their Mercury award-winning first album. 'That's what I did! That's genuinely it. I read that, I noted down the golden rules of pop, and applied that to what we're doing and made sure that that always applies to everything we do.' The Klaxons then went on to drop acid and perform with Rihanna in a laser and neon pyramid at the 2008 Brit Awards, something which suggests that they are a band ideally suited to follow this Discordian-influenced path.

The Manual can best be seen as a modern update of the famous punk-era fanzine illustration that showed the fingering for the chords E, A and B7 with the words, 'This is a chord. This is another. This is a third. Now form a band.' In general, though, that's not how its intentions were perceived. The book gives the false impression that 'Doctorin' The TARDIS' was planned, that Drummond and Cauty knew what they were doing and that they set out deliberately to make a number one record.

Perhaps more than anything they did, *The Manual* led to the pair being perceived as cynical media manipulators rather than random followers of chaos. In a sense, this was always inevitable when they became successful because the public narrative believes that success comes from knowing what you are doing. The equally common phenomenon of stumbling upwards is rarely recognised. Even when it is noticed, it tends to be dismissed as an anomaly, something that 'doesn't count', rather than an example of how things actually work. Few people are comfortable with accepting the extent with which blind chance affects their lives.

The fact that Drummond and Cauty were becoming successful was a clear sign that they knew what they were doing, or so the public narrative went. How, then, should they explain the strangeness of their behaviour? Clearly, it is all part of their plan. It was calculated media manipulation, 'scams' or 'pranks' aimed at generating publicity.

With that narrative in place, Drummond and Cauty were in a unique position where they could follow and enact strong occult currents in full public view without comment. No one took the role of the little boy in 'The Emperor's New Clothes' who stated clearly how odd things had become, not when the entire country was watching and acting like everything was normal.

*

Rave happened.

You only had to look at the crowd to see why rave was different from anything that had come before. At rock concerts and other large-scale musical events, every member of the crowd faced in the same direction. The focus and attention of the entire audience was directed at the stage, where it glorified the musicians who performed there. It can be argued that this was actually the purpose of the event, to focus thousands of minds on a small group of people and in doing so to elevate them, in the words of Robert Plant, to the status of 'Golden Gods'.

Compare that to the early orbital raves of the late 1980s, when first thousands and then tens of thousands of kids found their way to outdoor dance parties on the outskirts of London. The crowd point in any direction they damn well please. That original focus, the band on stage or (later) the 'superstar DJs' on an elevated platform, is absent. Instead, the crowd's focus is turned into itself. It is not on an artist presenting the audience with an experience, but on an audience that is creating its own performance. The crowd are generating, rather than observing. The result is that they were not elevating someone like Robert Plant to the status of Golden Gods, they were elevating themselves.

It helped to be on the right drugs, of course.

Rave emerged spontaneously, neither planned nor designed. It was a genuine grass-roots phenomenon, egalitarian and welcoming. Thousands danced in fields all through the night, out under the moon, in order to achieve a trance-like, ecstatic state. It was a form of communion and it was pagan as fuck.* It couldn't last. The press and the government, appalled by such non-violent having-of-a-good-time, moved quickly to crush it. Ultimately, though, they weren't quick enough. Rave grew too big too quickly, and it attracted the attention of those who felt they could make money from such events. Once this happened and the superstar DJs and the superclubs arrived, the focus shifted from the raw crowd back to the event itself. Rave's spell was broken.

But while it lasted, that spell was powerful and it worked its glamour on Cauty and Drummond.

Once the pair began attending raves and influential nightclubs such as Heaven, hip-hop was quickly dropped. They knew that they weren't very good at it in any case. Clearly, dance music was where it was at. This was evident in their work from a very early point. Even the 'posthumous' JAMs records from 1988 onwards are more dance than hip-hop.

---

* One of the greatest pleasures of being a writer is when someone picks up on some of your words and runs with them. It is as if you have been scattering seeds and, just occasionally, sometimes they germinate. Those words then have a life of their own, beyond you, and this makes you feel like a proud parent – it's a very pure feeling, a glow, which reassures you that you are on the correct track. Some of my words have inspired a Salena Godden poem and become the title of a Black Grape album, and no one can ever take that away from me. The phrase 'pagan as fuck' was another one that a few folk ran with. It now appears on T-shirts. Google should find them for you, if you're tempted.

After the success of their *Doctor Who* record, Drummond and Cauty suddenly had money, and with money came options and possibilities. It allowed them to build a recording studio of their own, in the basement of the south London squat where Cauty had lived for over a decade. The squat, known as Benio, achieved near mythical status in KLF lore, but Cauty was not keen on it. 'I hate the place,' he has said, 'I've no alternative but to live here.' On occasions this squat would become Trancentral. Trancentral was a mythical place that, like King Arthur's Camelot, did not have a set location but instead moved around the country to wherever it was needed. Trancentral was wherever Cauty and Drummond were working together, or any place where things were working well. Trancentral had its own will.*

The pair set themselves a task of releasing a string of club-orientated dance records which were known as the Pure Trance series. The idea was to release one a month for five months, although only the first two, 'What Time Is Love?' and '3am Eternal', saw the light of day. 'This was Jimmy and my response to the urge to make music that had no message other than how it existed on the dance floor,' Drummond said in 2012. 'We wanted to make a minimal masterpiece. "What Time Is Love?" in its original Pure

---

* This is another reference to Bill and Jimmy abandoning intention, in this case during the process of creation. I'd forgotten this was such a prominent theme.

Trance version is the closest we came to it.' The title came when Drummond turned to Cauty at a rave, intending to ask when the MDMA they had taken would kick in, but found himself phrasing the question in the words 'What time is love?' At which point, they both understood that it had started to work.

The Pure Trance records were not expected to be a commercial success but their influence spread slowly through the clubs of Europe, selling continuously, and they brought Cauty and Drummond a great deal of credibility in the dance world, away from the London-based music press.

They were released under the name The KLF. Drummond and Cauty had had this name from the start: the label they had created to release The JAMs' records was called KLF Communications. They had a logo which was known as the 'pyramid blaster'. This was based on the 'eye in the pyramid' symbol which features heavily in *Illuminatus!*. The KLF removed the eye from the top of the pyramid and replaced it with a ghetto blaster; their pyramid no longer observed, it broadcast.

The name The KLF worked well within dance culture. It was minimal and anonymous, offering nothing that might overshadow the music. Stories varied as to whether it stood for anything or not. Sometimes it was claimed that it had no meaning, while other times it was claimed that the meaning was transient and shifted over time.

Drummond and Cauty had first released a record under the name The KLF in March 1988, a few months before they found success with their *Doctor Who*-themed single, although it sounded more like a JAMs track than a KLF one. Its name was prophetic. The first ever KLF record was a 12-inch dance track called 'Burn The Bastards'.

The KLF made a few live appearances at raves during this period. 'Live appearances' may be an exaggeration, as they usually played a tape rather than actually performed. At the 1989 Helter Skelter rave in Chipping Norton, the pair climbed a lighting gantry and emptied out a bin bag containing £1,000 in Scottish one-pound notes – their appearance fee – over the dancing crowd beneath them.

This idea of giving something tangible to the audience runs through many of their live appearances. At an appearance at the Liverpool Festival of Comedy in 1991, the pair distributed ice creams to the crowd from an ice-cream van. At a 1990 appearance at the Paradiso Club in Amsterdam, meanwhile, the pair performed a twenty-three-minute-long version of 'What Time Is Love?', during which they gave most of the instruments and mixing equipment to the crowd. None of this actually belonged to the band. It was the property of the club itself. They were not asked back.

Given Drummond's love of great, euphoric pop and The KLF's later mainstream success, The KLF's initial involvement with rave culture took a surprising turn. Despite the appeal of the dance floor, their attention became focused more on the post-rave come-down. The first KLF album was aimed at the chill-out room. Indeed, it even named it, for that album was called *Chill Out*.

This was Ambient House. Devoid of beats and anything resembling song structure, it owed more to the ambient music created by Brian Eno in the late 1970s and early 1980s than it did to high-bpm music of the raves. Eno, who coined the phrase 'Ambient Music', described his ambient albums as being 'on the cusp between melody and texture' which could be 'actively listened to with attention or as easily ignored, depending on the choice of the listener'. Eno produced a string of such records, in particular four albums entitled *Ambient 1, Ambient 2, Ambient 3* and *Ambient 4*.

Another Ambient House pioneer was Alex Patterson. Inspired by Paul Oakenfold's 'Land of Oz' nights at Heaven nightclub, Cauty formed The Orb with Patterson as a side project. Although their collaboration was short-lived and Cauty soon left The Orb to focus on The KLF, their early experiments married the potential of the sampler to Eno's ambient music and paved the way for a genre that continues to this day.*

For *Chill Out*, Drummond and Cauty added the sound of sheep and slide guitar from Evil Graham Lee (who had

---

* This is a good example of a boring paragraph. I list some facts that I feel should be in the book – for context if nothing else – but I don't have anything interesting to say about them. A good paragraph should be a set-up for a punchy last line, but this one ends in a way that is dutiful and a bit listless. Paragraphs like this find their way into all my books, alas, but I do try to keep them to a minimum.

played on Drummond's solo album *The Man*) to samples of
Elvis Presley, Acker Bilk and Fleetwood Mac. These faded
in and out, as if from far-distant radio stations or as if the
listener was drifting in and out of sleep. It was presented
as a journey through a mythical part of America, with
song titles like 'Pulling Out Of Ricardo And The Dusk Is
Falling Fast' or 'The Lights Of Baton Rouge Pass By'. The
song names were the result of plucking place names out of
an atlas – Drummond always did like his maps. Cauty has
dismissed it recently, saying, 'mostly it's just a list of places.
It was another disaster, really', and many ravers saw it as
unlistenable New Age noodling, boring in the extreme.

The album certainly has its supporters, though. The imagery of the journey across vast spaces in America during
the twilight hours of dawn and dusk, so full of space and
potential, is a perfect fit for this type of music. *Chill Out* is
an album that has aged well.

Ultimately, ambient is an odd genre: it either works or
it doesn't. There may be a critical consensus which rates
Eno's *Ambient 2* and *Ambient 4* above *Ambient 1* and *Ambient 3*, but it would take a brave man to define why. The
KLF were more than aware that this wasn't for everyone.
As they described their work at the time, this was music
that 'loves you even if you don't love it'. Ambient House
was 'the amorphous unconscious', which 'might only make
sense to those who made it to the furthest reaches of dance
music'. After *Chill Out*, they left the genre behind, feeling
that there was little more that needed to be said.

Yet it's tempting to say that the state of mind Ambient

House captured continued to fascinate them. It was all about the end of the rave, when all your energy had been dissipated and all that is left is an unearthly glow, a sense of euphoria that has somehow risen from the worn-out body. It is a feeling of exhaustion where you also feel extraordinarily awake. It's a sense of expanded awareness, the sense that you can see for miles even when you are lying in a dark corner. It is that moment, in the small hours before dawn, that seems to hang outside of time. The lyrics and song titles of their later commercial successes, such as '3am Eternal' or 'The Last Train To Transcentral', continued to echo this state of mind. This mental state seemed to interest them far more than the music it inspired.*

Drummond and Cauty also experimented with ambient video. They took a portable recording studio up to the Isle

---

* This is a great paragraph, in contrast – to my eyes at least. It expresses one self-contained idea sufficiently well that the book can immediately move on and never needs to discuss it again. It gets close to being lyrical without really seeming to try too hard – it's more concerned with the rhythm of the words than with reaching for a thesaurus. And, best of all, it describes something that the reader probably already recognises, but perhaps only unconsciously – something they may already be familiar with, but which they have not before seen framed or brought into focus. The impact is like a light going on inside the reader, and such a paragraph is always worth reading. If you can produce enough paragraphs like that, your book is going to be okay. You probably don't need that many, either. If you can sprinkle enough good paragraphs throughout the book, you'll be forgiven for the pedestrian ones.

of Jura in spring 1990, with the intention of recording a minimalist techno album called *The Gate*. The record never happened, and instead they spent eight days on the island recording sounds and being videotaped by their collaborator Bill Butt. This footage was eventually released as a forty-two-minute 'ambient movie' called *Waiting*. Even among committed and die-hard KLF fans, *Waiting* is considered to be unacceptably boring.*

'Waiting' was what occurred instead of recording. As they later wrote, they were, 'Waiting for the tide to turn on the almost motionless sea. Waiting for the sun to sink beyond the mountains of the Western Isles. Waiting for the stars to stud the darkening sky. Waiting for the dawn to creep in from the East. But maybe more importantly, waiting as emotions within themselves shifted and changed, stirred and settled. Along with this poetic stuff they continued to wait for all the trivial things in life that we seem to spend so much of life waiting for; kettles to boil, phones to ring, baths to run, moods to pass, something to happen, or at least some sort of explanation.'

Towards the end of this period they assembled their speakers on the beach and played music out to sea while they sat in deckchairs at the water's edge, like Canute, and waited for this explanation. It never arrived.

They were waiting to discover what they were going to do next. This is an occupational hazard for those who are

---

* Ha!

not driven by clearly defined goals or a sense of purpose, but instead follow the path of chaos. In the lulls between bursts of energy and action you become purposeless and have no choice but to wait and see what direction you will be pulled in next. So they sat in their deckchairs and waited, until the encroaching sea put an end to their vigil.

Whatever they were waiting for on Jura, they did not find it that time.*

---

* End of Part I. The way the book winds down into a bit of calm seems to work okay, I think, as it means there is a still point in the middle of the book. I realise it appears pretentious to divide such a short book into separate parts, as if it was a mighty epic for the ages, but I do like how the names of the parts gets information across almost subliminally, without it having to be spelled out. To describe something, you can talk at length about it, or you can also just set it down next to something different – at which point its nature immediately stands out. A pair of horns is just a pair of horns, but when they are placed next to some bunny ears they immediately appear harder, more serious, better crafted and less playful. Calling the two parts 'Bunny Ears' and 'Horns', therefore, tells us much about how the second half of Bill and Jimmy's story differs from the first. The shift in chapter titles from two fun alliterative words to a single, focused, vaguely spiritual multisyllable noun is likewise an attempt to, perhaps subliminally, describe the coming change. If nothing else, it helps give the impression that the author has some form of plan and knows what they are doing. That is no bad thing in a deranged narrative like this.

PART II
Horns

8

Ceremonies

At the summer solstice of 1991 a few dozen journalists from across Europe were asked to arrive at Heathrow airport with their passports. Here they boarded a specially chartered plane which would take them, they were told, to a ceremony in the lost kingdom of Mu.*

---

* Just before we head into Part II – how are we all getting on with these footnotes? Are they adding something, or are they interrupting your reading in a way that prevents you from becoming absorbed in the story? When I first thought of doing this, this was my fear – that they would make the experience of reading the book worse. Now I have begun work on them, that fear is of little use and must be discarded. The only way to answer the question it raises is to do it, so I plough on. Now that I have started, the fear has become, what if it works? What if it sells well? That scenario could lead to the publishing industry routinely rereleasing 'author's commentary' fancy gift editions of all sorts of books, causing readers to double-dip and re-buy books that are already successful rather

The plane actually took them up to Scotland, to the Isle of Islay in the Inner Hebrides, and a coach and a ferry took them to the neighbouring island of Jura. The customs officer who greeted them on Jura was Bill Drummond. He sat behind a desk wearing a false moustache and dressed in the uniform of a customs officer, and stamped each of their passports with the 'pyramid blaster' logo.

The journalists were then dressed in robes and led across the island in a silent procession. At the head of this procession was a figure in white with a single horn emerging from his hood. He led them towards their final destination: a sixty-foot tall wicker man, surrounded by a hidden sound system.

They formed a circle around the figure. Here they were addressed by Drummond, although his true identity was masked by the robe and horn. Thanks to a microphone under his hood, his words were being mixed into the trance-like rave music that the sound system was pumping out. The circle of robed journalists chanted while Drummond preached at them in an improvised and meaningless language of his own devising. 'I had a little radio mic on Bill, and I was working the mix,' Cauty told Richard King. 'He was up on a sort of platform in front of the wicker man, dressed with this horn, and did the whole speech in

than taking a chance on books they don't yet know. The hope that I'm clinging to is that commentary like this works well for this specific book, but won't work for others. That's the sweet spot I'm hoping to hit. Wish me luck.

a foreign language he'd just made up. It was totally, totally brilliant, everyone was completely gobsmacked.'

At the finale of what Cauty called 'this whole sort of fake Pagan ceremony', the wicker man was lit. Their wicker man was a powerful-looking figure. It did not stand to attention like the one in the *The Wicker Man* film or those found in historical woodcuts. It had both arms thrust aloft and its legs spaced heroically apart, giving it the aspect of a four-pointed star about to pounce. It didn't smoulder or smoke, but instead blazed straight upwards in a huge column of fire.

Wicker men had been rare in Western culture up until that point. They were first recorded in the writings of Caesar, who claimed that the Gauls used them as part of ritual human sacrifice. They did not really arrive in popular culture until Robin Hardy's 1973 film *The Wicker Man*, starring Edward Woodward and Christopher Lee, which had been filmed around Drummond's home town of Newton Stewart in south-western Scotland. The 1991 summer solstice was marked not only by The KLF's wicker man on Jura, but the first solstice wicker-man burning in Black Rock Desert in Nevada, an event that has grown into the Burning Man Festival. This event, planned by its founders as a 'dadaist temporary autonomous zone', had grown out of solstice burnings on a San Francisco beach which were apparently started spontaneously, rather than inspired by the film. These had been disrupted the previous year by official concerns, resulting in a move out into the desert and the test burning of a figure on Labor Day 1990. As on Jura, these first Burning Man effigies also forwent the traditional stance and stood with arms stretched aloft.

The coincidental arrival of both of these wicker men on the 1991 summer solstice was unusual because, apart from the release of the film nearly twenty years before, there was an absence of any other wicker men in our culture up until that point. Now, of course, they are more common and appear everywhere from Iron Maiden records to the Wickerman Festival in south-west Scotland. For Alan Moore, this would signify the arrival of the wicker man concept in a more accessible area of Ideaspace. Or, to paraphrase Charles Fort, 'wicker men come when it's wicker-men-time'.

The Burning Man Festival's description as being a 'dadaist temporary autonomous zone' is also interesting in light of the glossolalia, or speaking in tongues, that Drummond performed on Jura. Talking in meaningless words like this was common at the birth of Dada. The Cabaret Voltaire in Zurich in 1916 included performances of what they called 'sound poetry'. One such example is Hugo Ball's *Karawane*, the text of which in part reads, 'hollaka hollala / anlogo bung / blago bung / blago bung'. From Ball's perspective, the impulse to stand on stage and address an audience with sounds and gibberish was a reaction against the society that had brought about the First World War. Such a bankrupt society deserved meaningless poetry. What Drummond's impulse was is less clear.

Speaking in tongues is a strange but relatively common aspect of religious practice around the world, and is found in cultures as varied as Haitian voodoo and Indian fakirs. It is best known in the West through Pentecostal Christianity, where it is believed that the possessed speaker has received the Grace of the Holy Spirit and is being controlled by an aspect of the divine. It certainly has a powerful effect on an audience, who suddenly find that all the normal rules of human connection have been dispensed with and that something unknown has taken its place.

Despite Cauty's description of this as a 'sort of fake Pagan ceremony', the trance music, chanting, glossolalia and burning effigy of the Jura ceremony did have an effect on those present, just as the use of the London Gospel Community Choir affected those who listened to 'Downtown'. It was very much a real 'fake Pagan' ceremony, and it had a very real effect on those present.*

The music of The KLF is marked by a noticeable increase in religious imagery compared to the music of The JAMs – or, rather, by a noticeable increase in religious yearning. Certainly the invitations to attend this solstice ritual, called the Rites of Mu, were rich in such imagery: 'The KLF have invited you to join them in a celebration of the Rites of Mu this summer solstice, during which the fall of Mankind may be reversed – returning him to the garden where the rest of Creation awaits.' The problem, the invitations

---

* I should add that there was a large amount of MDMA involved, and that this was quite a significant factor in events.

explained, was that mankind had been distracted from its true nature by the questions Who, Where, Why and What – questions which they described as the 'four beautiful handmaidens of Lucifer'.*

Four graceful, elegant women played the role of these handmaidens of Lucifer. The surviving video images, showing them emerging from the waters around Jura in flowing white gowns as the sun sets, are some of the most powerful images from this ceremony. They are a direct visual reflection of the scene in *Illuminatus!* when angels appear out of Lake Ingolstadt, an event which triggers the grand climax of the book – the beginning of the end of the world.

Of course, the Wicker Man ceremony was preferable to how people were initiated into the 'original' Justified Ancients of Mummu. According to Wilson and Shea's book, initiates had to take part in a satanic black mass that climaxed with a manifestation of the Devil. Satanic black masses were generally considered to be a step too far by musicians in the late twentieth century, even by Bill Drummond.†

---

* Having written a lot about William Blake in recent years, this makes far more sense to me now than it did at the time. I definitely missed a trick by not exploring this more fully.

† Sometimes you have to make a decision between a great line and factual nuance. If I was to be pedantic, I should have included an exception for Scandinavian black metal bands here, who are indeed typically well up for a black mass. To do that, however, would have bogged down the paragraph and robbed it of impact. It's a question of which is the greater crime – making overly broad statements that can be picked apart, or writing a

*

'[The musician Mark Manning] and I realised that we had sold our souls to the Devil,' Bill Drummond wrote in 2005, 'and that if we wanted to retrieve them we should head for darkest Africa, confront Satan and demand our souls back.' This was the impetus for a journey to Zaire that Drummond made with Manning and Alan 'Gimpo' Goodrick in 1996, after he had stopped working with Cauty. It was not the first time Drummond had made reference to the status of his soul. The contract written on the Nissan Bluebird and pushed over Cape Wrath and into the sea, for example, began 'For the sake of our souls'.

These days it is rare to hear anyone state that they have sold their soul to the Devil.

Mark Manning, better known as the rock musician Zodiac Mindwarp, is the author of a number of books including *Get Your Cock Out* (2000) and *Fucked By Rock* (2001). For anyone familiar with his work the idea that he has sold his soul to the Devil seems plausible, but the idea that Drummond has done the same is harder to accept.

Drummond grew up in a religious family and his father was a minister, but it is a stretch to call him religious in the traditional sense. He did burn a million pounds, after all, and there are very few people who view that as a Christian act. Nevertheless, religious, or at least spiritual, themes run

boring book. I suspect that for most authors this conundrum is an endless source of anxiety.

through his work. In 'The Manager's Speech', a spoken-word track from the same period as his solo album *The Man*, he states that the problem with the music industry is not that it is financially broke or artistically spent, but that it is 'spiritually bankrupt'. Drummond then offered his services as manager, not just of bands, but of the entire music industry, in the belief that he could cure it of this affliction.

Generally speaking, no one really believes in the Devil anymore. The idea that you can meet him in person and discuss contracts is far-fetched, even for devout Christians and regular churchgoers. Drummond's claim to have sold his soul to the Devil must be seen, at best, as a metaphor.

Of course, this all does hinge on what is meant by 'the Devil'.

For a Christian, there is a simple definition. The Devil is evil. He's the Big Bad, the one to avoid. You don't need to know anything more than that. If anything, it is better not to know anything more. The Horned One is big on temptation and lies, and keeping as far away as possible is the best possible option. What, though, does the name mean outside the Christian reality tunnel?

Here things get a little more complicated. Whereas Christians are happy to consider various names such as Lucifer, Satan, Beelzebub or Mephistopheles as all the same thing, they often have very specific meanings. Rudolf Steiner, for example, made much of the contrast between two different aspects of the Devil, namely Lucifer and Ahriman. 'Ahriman' is something of an archaic name these days, but we know him better as Mephistopheles.

To Steiner, Lucifer and Mephistopheles are opposite principals. At their simplest, they can be thought of as energy and matter. Lucifer is the light bringer. He represents thought, creativity and spiritual desire. Mephistopheles, meanwhile, represents the physical world. He is matter, solidification, boundaries and limitations. They are both considered to be necessary, for without Lucifer there is no motion, and without Mephistopheles there is no form. Yet they are both considered to be dangerous, and negative. It is necessary to avoid lusting after Lucifer's promise of spiritual bliss, or Mephistopheles' gift of worldly desires. To Steiner, the Christ figure was the mid-point between these two extremes, and this was the state to aspire to. Beyond that mid-point the world would alternate between the negative influences of one or the other.*

This definition of Mephistopheles is the context that explains the satanic associations of the inverted five-pointed star. The five points of a non-inverted star are said to represent the four worldly elements (air, water, earth and fire) as well as the spirit, the fifth element that arises from the

---

* I had completely forgotten all this. You would have thought that I would remember inserting a lecture about the names of Satan into a music book, but apparently not. I wonder now where I got it all from. I know nothing about Rudolf Steiner and have never read him. I suppose all this stuff is a reasonable thing for your mind to ditch – it's interesting, but it's not actually that useful on a day-to-day basis. Ultimately, I agree with Sean Connery in *Indiana Jones and the Last Crusade* – once you've written something down, you no longer have to bother remembering it.

physical world. This star has the 'spirit' point at the top, and if the star is imagined as a human figure with their limbs splayed, like Leonardo's 'Vitruvian Man', then the head is the spirit. Satanists invert this symbol so that this point is down, as if the figure had fallen head-first from above. In this context, the four physical elements are crushing the spirit, trapping it under the physical.

In the medieval Faust legend, the Devil also takes the form of Mephistopheles. It is worldly success and wealth that he is offering to Faust, in return for his immortal soul. The Faust legend is the basis for one of the founding myths of modern music. In this telling, the great Delta bluesman Robert Johnson met the Devil at a crossroads. The Devil tuned Johnson's guitar and gave him mastery of the instrument in return for his soul.

From here, it is possible to trace the influence of the Devil on twentieth-century music, in particular the rock 'n' roll that grew out of the blues. Rock is the 'Devil's music', and proudly so, for the Devil has the best tunes. The connection is, at times, pretty overt. Bands like Black Sabbath, Metallica and the Jimi Hendrix Experience all made use of a musical interval called the tritone, unaware it had for centuries been condemned as 'the Devil's chord' or 'the Devil in music' by the Church. Indeed, even today the shorthand symbol or emoticon for 'this rocks!' is based on hands forming the devil horns symbol, \m/ \m/.

'KLF are gonna rock ya! \m/ \m/.' That sort of thing.

Robert Johnson got a better deal than Faust. His Devil offered him both his Luciferian aspect and his

Mephistophelean side. Johnson was seduced by the creative mastery of music that Lucifer offers, even though that gift attracted the worldly rewards of Mephistopheles. Poor Faust had to make do with understanding and academic knowledge for his Luciferian aspect, which does not sound half as much fun. Faust basically gave his soul for a medieval version of Wikipedia.

Here, then, is the Devil's bargain to musicians. It is Lucifer they crave, but it is Mephistopheles who destroys them.

We can tell this story without the help of the Devil, if it makes you more comfortable. Consider the story of the Greek Titan Prometheus. Prometheus stole fire from the gods and gave it to mankind. As a punishment, Zeus chained him to a rock and he had his liver eaten out by a giant eagle. Then the liver grew back, and the eagle feasted again. In this way Prometheus was tortured for eternity. All of which illustrates a profound truth, which is that gods are bastards.

It seems, at first, to be an odd story. The 'fire' of the gods is spirit, imagination, knowledge, or consciousness itself. It is the spiritual yearning that Lucifer represents. Prometheus gained this, and gifted it to mankind. In return, he was chained to a rock, or trapped by the physical, solid, manifest world of Mephistopheles. The eagle and the liver would have had a symbolic significance that has been lost over the centuries, but we can still understand how they mean pain and torture for Prometheus.

This, then, is the flipside of inspired creativity or the achievement of spiritual ecstasy: a fall from that high state to the base jail of the physical world. This is Prometheus' torture, or the damnation of the soul. Those who glimpse divine wonder will not be able to bear returning to the material world. The simplest way to understand this is to speak to a recovering heroin addict. Alternatively, look at the Romantic poets, or the story of Icarus.

Or consider Led Zeppelin's Jimmy Page. At the peak of his success he was often said to be in league with the Devil, not least because of his obsession with Aleister Crowley. But look at his astonishing creativity in the early seventies, the drugs, the money, the groupies and the fame that followed, and his complete creative impotence afterwards. If we leave aside the Christian associations of the Devil and allow that name to refer to Steiner's two opposing forces, then we have an accurate metaphor for what happened to Page. He lost his soul to the Devil.*

---

* Before this book was first published in paperback, the publishers gave it a legal read to check for libel, privacy and copyright issues. This section was something that was flagged up. The lawyer's comments were, 'I find it difficult to weigh up whether there is any chance that Jimmy Page might complain about the suggestion that he was "in league with the Devil" and that he "sold his soul to the Devil". On the one hand, these statements are plainly defamatory, but the arguments are carefully made, and it might well be thought that Page (with his interest in the Occult) would readily agree with them.' This is still my favourite legal note ever.

In this context, Drummond's claim that he had sold his soul to the Devil makes more sense. As The JAMs, he and Cauty were spontaneous, creative and inspired. They embraced the chaos, ignored rules and were free to do whatever they wanted. But when they became The KLF, they resonated with the world. The world reacted, and embraced them. They accumulated success, fame, critical approval and money. They were no longer above the music industry, subverting it from afar. They were inside it, sinking deeper.

What then of Drummond's trip to the heart of Africa to 'confront Satan' and get his soul back? Drummond and Manning took with them on their journey, of all things, Punch and Judy puppets. There was a symbolic reason for this. In all our literary history and shared culture, Punch is the only figure who triumphs over the Devil.

And if Punch can do it, then it can be done.

So there was hope after all. They were not broken. If Drummond really did think that he had lost his soul to the Devil, he was still seeking a way out. Nothing is impossible. Perhaps if Faust had spent time with Ken Campbell, he wouldn't have given up so easily.

Religious imagery was common within the euphoria of the rave world. 'This is my church,' proclaimed Maxi Jazz in Faithless' 1998 single 'God Is A DJ', and it was clear that he was referring to the rave itself. The religious imagery of The KLF was most pronounced on their post-*Chill Out* album

The White Room, which featured the track 'The Church of The KLF'. The lyrical themes in *The White Room*, however, were subtly different from those used by other rave bands. They were not a recognition of the transcendent aspect of rave. Rather, they concerned seeking and yearning, a journey or a pilgrimage on 'The Last Train To Transcentral' to a place known as the White Room.

In many ways the story of *The White Room* – from its original planned release in 1989 to its eventual release in a radically different form in 1991 – is the story of The KLF. Before we look at it in detail it is worth noting one decision that was made halfway through that project. That was the decision, made in 1990, to make hit singles.

Cauty has linked this decision with the success of Guru Josh's hit 'Infinity', a forgettable rave hit based around a saxophone melody to which the passing of time has not been kind. 'I thought, "It's come to this, we're in competition with Guru Josh",' Cauty told Richard King, 'and I remember saying to Bill, "Well, come on, let's have a hit single then because we know how to do it. We haven't really been trying that hard".'

It was the right moment. 'By the time we'd started becoming The KLF we'd got ourselves together a bit more, we could sort of try and work out a bit more of a long-term strategy,' Cauty has said. 'We were just winging it from day to day, but we could see slightly further into the future and sort of plan things a bit.'

The first step was to go back into the studio and rework 'What Time Is Love?' into a radio-friendly single. The result would be the first of a string of mainstream hit records. It would also be the first of a string of reworked versions of 'What Time Is Love?' and, indeed, reworked versions of much of what they had already recorded.

This was the moment – the point when they consciously decided that The KLF would make hit singles – that the creative flow of the past two years stopped. The continuous outpouring of new material since the formation of The JAMs came to a sudden and abrupt halt. Hereon in, there would be no new songs written. Instead, the fruits of their previous labours would be picked over. Old songs were reversioned, remixed and rereleased. Playful creativity was replaced by hard work, and art was replaced by craft.

In many ways, this was the making of them. Wild, uninhibited creativity is essentially self-indulgent if it is not followed by the hard work involved in manifesting that inspiration into something that connects to other people.* The decision to hone their material into something universal produced work that towered over anything they had done before. It created singles that were as wonderful as the ones Drummond dreamed about back in Liverpool in the 1970s. The material created in their early, mercurial phase was rich indeed, and the skill with which they then distilled and presented it was inspired. But they were entering a different phase at this point, and

---

* Hell yes.

the fire that had marked the initial stages had snuffed itself out.*

---

* I'm pleased with that chapter. As I was reading it back, I wondered whether the discussion about the various names of Satan was necessary, or whether it should have come later, after the band had become huge. Perhaps it works as foreshadowing, I thought to myself. After seeing how the end of the chapter pulled all its ideas together, however, I now see that they were all necessary, and that they lead up to a strong point. Sometimes when you are writing you are drawn to subjects which feel rich, and you explore them trusting that you'll find something fresh and interesting there. Other times, you start with a clear idea or argument, and choose subjects to help explain it. The danger with this approach is that it can make you overly opinionated and preachy, like a Twitter-bore. If the argument is interesting enough, though, you can get away with it, as I think this chapter illustrates. I like that it starts Part II: Horns, making a shift to chapters that are sharper and more focused. Perhaps I should trust my ten-years-earlier self more. He seems to know what he was doing (I totally didn't).

9

Journeys

▲

In 1989 The KLF made a film. It was not released, or even properly finished. But they made it. It was called *The White Room*.

Many successful musicians made films in the 1980s, from Madonna to Prince to The Pet Shop Boys. The KLF's was very different from these. The version that exists is a dialogue-free ambient road movie just under an hour in length.

It starts at a rave in the basement of Cauty's south London squat. Drummond and Cauty leave and get into their car, the 1968 Ford Galaxy of 'Doctorin' The TARDIS' fame. In the back sits a solicitor, played by their real-life solicitor David Franks. He hands them a contract, which they sign without reading. Franks gets out and Drummond and Cauty drive off.

Pretty much most of the rest of the film is them driving.

First, they drive around London at night. Then, they drive around the Sierra Nevada region of Spain. This goes on for some time. Not much happens, although they do find a dead eagle, and at one point they stop for petrol.

Eventually the pair park up for the evening and build a camp fire. This occurs twice in the film. At each point, their solicitor is seen in the smoke from the fire, studying the contract – a distinctly satanic image. Eventually, the solicitor discovers something in one of the contract's clauses. He writes 'liberation loophole!' on the contract.*

At this point, events in the film gain more momentum. Drummond is seen throwing the contract into the air, obviously delighted. He has changed into a pair of plus-fours and is dressed rather like an Edwardian mountaineer. Cauty then paints the car white and they drive, past a

---

* This has reminded me about my complicated relationship with Amazon. On the one hand, I am aware of how little tax they pay, the claims about how they treat their workers and their impact on independent high street shops. I am also aware, however, that if they hadn't established the Kindle Store and allowed me initially to self-publish this book, I would not have written it. I would not then have become a full-time author, able to make a living, of sorts, writing books for the last decade. Who knows what I would have done instead, in that scenario? So, when it comes to Amazon, I have to claim a 'Liberation Loophole' in order to acknowledge the messy, contradictory picture. After I self-published this book, it very quickly took on a life of its own. It was picked up by the publishers Weidenfeld & Nicolson and, seven books later, I am still with them. A major factor in this was the book being praised and supported by the doctor and author Ben Goldacre. This is why, if you ever see him in a pub, you must buy him a drink.

burning bush, up into the snow-peaked mountains. When the car gets stuck in the snow they abandon it and continue on foot. Cauty has not joined Drummond in sporting the Edwardian mountaineer look but instead wears a more sensible white parka. Much of this climbing sequence, it must be said, is particularly beautifully shot. Eventually they reach the summit, where they discover a large white building with a radio telescope. They go in.

They find themselves in a white, smoke-filled void – the White Room. Here there is a pair of fake moustaches on a pedestal, which they attach to their faces. Then they meet the solicitor, sitting at a white table. He shows them the clause he has found in the contract. They nod. The pair then walk away, dissolving into the smoke and vanishing into the void.

The End.

Visually it was terrific. It was a clear step up from the VHS-quality of the *Waiting* ambient film. It had been shot with a professional crew, and it shows. On the downside, it cost them around £250,000.

It was, all in all, an odd way to spend £250,000.

Anyone who has ever had to read record company press releases will know that they contain more unreadable bullshit than any other literary medium. An awkward amalgam of romantic fawning and angry political manifestos, music industry releases are frequently a stream-of-consciousness outpouring of rare and unlikely superlatives, written by people without first-hand knowledge of the music they are referring to. The releases issued by Drummond and Cauty do not, at first glance, appear to be any different.

The statement issued in February 1990, and called 'Information Sheet 8', is a typical example. It begins with a classic summary of their debt to Robert Anton Wilson: 'THE JUSTIFIED ANCIENTS OF MUMU are an organization (or disorganization) who are at least as old as the ILLUMINATI. They represent the primeval power of Chaos. As such they are diametrically opposed to the order that the Illuminati try to oppress on mankind and on mankind's understanding of the Universe.'

It goes on to explain how Drummond and Cauty took on that mantle in order to make records without 'anyone telling them how it should be done. [. . .] But within days of their first record being released,' it continues, 'they began to receive mail and messages from very strange sources. The information they were getting was varied and confusing. They were being warned not to get involved with what they could never understand. They were being threatened. They were being congratulated in taking The War above ground. They were being welcomed on board as "brothers in arms" in the only war that was ever justified, I quote; "To finally separate Time from Space, thus enabling Chaos once again to reign supreme."'

Most readers of music press releases would have skipped over all this. To anyone acquainted with Operation Mindfuck it seems extremely familiar. This raises the question as to whether Discordians were still engaging in those tactics in the 1980s, and whether they were directing them at Cauty and Drummond.

There is good evidence that Discordians did target the pair with hoax letters. In Pete Robinson's well-regarded JAMs history/fanzine *Justified And Ancient History*, he records a 1987 letter from an American called 'Don Lucknowe' who threatened them with 'Deep Shit' if they continued using that name. Drummond and Cauty were worried that they faced legal action from Wilson and they did not reply to the letter because, according to Robinson, they were 'shit scared'.

Robinson made contact on their behalf. The address was that of a now defunct parody news magazine called *Yossarian Universal*. The editor, Paul Fericano, replied to Robinson and told him that 'we now believe' that the *Yossarian Universal* contributing editor James Wallis was responsible for the original letter. Wallis was a big Three Stooges fan, and the name 'Don Lucknowe' is based on a Stooges' catchphrase 'Don't look now'. This interest in Three Stooges-style comedy was a typical Discordian touch, as Discordians are the type of people who consider Harpo Marx's birthday a holy day. According to Fericano, Wallis was 'somewhat of a hoaxer, in our *YU* tradition (it's one of our trademarks – and that's an understatement)'.

Assigning any particular hoax letter to Operation Mindfuck is by definition extremely difficult. Wilson and Shea have explained that no Discordian 'knows for sure who is or who is not involved in any phase of Operation

Mindfuck or what activities they are or are not engaged in as part of that project. Thus, the outsider is immediately trapped in a double-bind: the only safe assumption is that anything a Discordian does is somehow related to Operation Mindfuck, but, since this leads directly to paranoia, this is not a 'safe' assumption after all, and the 'risky' hypothesis that whatever the Discordians are doing is harmless may be 'safer' in the long run'. There is a good reason to consider *Yossarian Universal*'s letter to The JAMs to be part of the Operation Mindfuck, however. 'Yossarian' is the protagonist in Joseph Heller's *Catch-22* and is also, according to *Illuminatus!*, a Discordian Saint.*

Fericano's letter ends, 'Sorry if all this caused anxiety, etc. Tell the members of the KLF that I wish them well, and would love to hear their music. Have never been able to find [music by The JAMs] out here.' All this seems highly plausible. The British music press was widely available in the US, and a story about how ABBA's lawyers demanded the destruction of albums by The Justified Ancients of Mu Mu because of copyright issues was widely reported. The records themselves did not cross the Atlantic in any numbers (indeed, most copies of their debut album

---

* This is all very woolly, isn't it? A heap of stuff that may be vague or mistaken, parts of which are surely entirely invented. But the question is, which parts? I know it's necessary for the story, and it is helpful in putting the bewildered mental states that led to the money burning in context, but I'm finding this to be my least favourite chapter so far. Let's see if it picks up by the end.

were burned in that field in Sweden). All that the American Discordians knew about The JAMs would have been what they saw in the press, and all the adverts that Drummond and Cauty placed in the music press included a PO Box address. It seems likely, then, that American Discordians would have begun sending strange and bewildering letters to Cauty and Drummond, believing that their adoption of the name 'Justified Ancients of Mu Mu' made them clear and deserving targets for Operation Mindfuck.

With that in mind, a further claim in Information Sheet 8 is worth noting. Drummond and Cauty asserted that their solicitor was sent 'A contract with an organization or individual calling themselves "Eternity". The wording of this contract was that of standard music business legal speak, but the terms discussed and the rights required and granted were of a far stranger kind.'

'Whether The Contract was a very clever and intricate prank by a legal minded JAMS fan was of little concern to Drummond and Cauty,' Information Sheet 8 continues. 'For them it was as good a marker as anything as to what direction their free style career should take next. [. . .] In the first term of The Contract they, Drummond and Cauty, were required to make an artistic representation of themselves on a journey to a place called THE WHITE ROOM. The medium they chose to make this representation was up to them. Where or what THE WHITE ROOM was, was never clearly defined. Interpretation was left to their own creativity. The remuneration they are to receive on completion of this work of art was supposed to be access to THE "real"WHITE ROOM.'

The pair claim that they went on to sign this contract, despite the advice of their solicitor to have nothing to do with it. It is worth noting here that Cauty and Drummond were ignorant of Operation Mindfuck. Their sole knowledge of Discordianism comes from *Illuminatus!*, which Cauty had never read and which Drummond had not, at that time, ever finished. By signing any such contract they were not simply 'playing along', for they would have had no context for what the contract was or where it had come from.

In this reading of events, Drummond and Cauty appear to have taken a Discordian Operation Mindfuck prank letter at face value, and spent hundreds of thousands of pounds making a piece of work that would fulfil their part of a hoax contract that they had chosen to sign.

As to what the 'real' White Room the contract alluded to was, Drummond and Cauty were typically candid: 'Your guess is as good as anybody's.' In Discordian terms, the meaning is relatively clear. The White Room refers to illumination, or enlightenment. The word 'room' is interesting. The use of a spatial metaphor to define enlightenment turns it into a place that can be travelled to, or sought on a quest. The search for the White Room becomes a pilgrimage, with the White Room itself taking on the character of the Holy Grail. Drummond and Cauty's film, when seen in this light, becomes a means to an end. The White Room was not intended as a film that would make money or enhance their careers. It was, instead, a step along the path in a search for enlightenment.*

The phrase 'liberation loophole' recurs throughout the work of The KLF, most notably in the lyrics to 'The Last Train To Transcentral'. Drummond defined what he meant by the term in a 2010 interview for *BLOWN* magazine. He talked about the way ideas take shape in his mind, vague and unformed at first but slowly growing and persisting. Should a budding notion be subjected to his objective and critical mind, 'all you learn are all its faults and weaknesses and the reasons why you should not be doing it'. The unformed idea will be riddled with contradictions, and a critical eye will use these contradictions as a reason to kill off the idea.

The liberation loophole, then, is to give yourself permission to accept those contradictions and to allow the idea

---

* I worry now that all the stuff about magic I put in this book has overshadowed the deeper motivations of Drummond and Cauty – as discussed in sections like this. As noted earlier, neither of them claims to be a magician, but because it's such an interesting model to view their work through, it is tempting to project those impulses onto them. There is a difference between magical thinking, which they clearly did, and practising magic or intentionally casting spells, which they didn't. Reading all this back, the pair do seem to have been motivated more by transcendence than magic. One problem with the practice of magic is that it requires you to view the cosmos as 'other', something that you can impose your will upon, wrestle with, and ultimately try and control. From the perspective of transcendence, all that is delusional. There is no other.

to grow under its own logic, protected from the withering scorn of rationality. Drummond has used the phrase 'accept the contradictions' as a form of artistic mantra throughout his career. He wrote about how he came to adopt that approach in his book 17. Although he was not interested in the conspiracy theories that run through *Illuminatus!*, the way they were presented resonated with him. The appeal was in how 'something may appear to be one thing but then turn out to be the opposite, or how something could be what it is and its opposite at the same time. This chimed with a contradiction I had long felt to be at the heart of human existence: that we are totally trapped and totally free at the same time.'

This is the contradiction between the material world of causality and the idea of free will. According to causality, if you put details of all the atoms at the beginning of time into a sufficiently impressive computer, it could calculate all of future history. This does not, instinctively, fit well with our sense of ourselves as independent agents with the ability to make choices. Drummond adopted the mantra 'accept the contradictions' in order not to worry about this. As he wrote in 2007, 'from that moment in June 1973 I decided to accept the total contradiction that everything from the Big Bang to the end of time is preordained in every sense and that we are totally free to do whatever the fuck we want'.*

---

* For those of you who have read my book *William Blake vs the World*, note how well this idea ties in with the different 'left brain' and 'right brain' conceptions of time, and the two definitions of eternity.

*

The first hint that the film was not going to be released came in an information sheet from December 1989. 'As you may already know the film was finished this summer and release was planned for autumn,' it said. 'However, some strange things have happened to the KLF and they have decided to dramatically re-enact these events for inclusion in the film. For this further filming they need to lay their hands on a million pounds.'

The story goes that, following a gig at Heaven, they were accosted by a homeless guy called Mickey McElwee. McElwee told them that, before his life fell apart, he used to do occasional jobs for an international arms dealer called Silverman. Silverman recruited McElwee to follow Drummond and Cauty to Spain during the filming of *The White Room*, he claimed, in order to observe them at a distance. Silverman believed that Drummond and Cauty had been contacted by the actual Justified Ancients of Mummu, a secret organisation who not only existed but whose intention was to bring about nuclear war, just for the fun of it. As McElwee watched the filming from a distance, he realised that a third party was also observing it. This person, whom McElwee believed was working for the British Government and who also knew of the existence of the 'real' Justified Ancients of Mummu, was intending to assassinate Drummond and Cauty with a sniper's rifle. Drummond was apparently nearly shot during the filming of a scene where he walked up to a large Spanish castle.

His life was saved, or so the story went, because McElwee killed the would-be assassin before he could pull the trigger.

When Drummond and Cauty retold this story, they stressed that McElwee was probably a deranged fan who had made the whole thing up, but, nevertheless, the incident had scared the living crap out of them.

A more cynical interpretation, such as the one held by this author, is that they made up this part of the story. The 'ambient road movie' version of *The White Room*, it was acknowledged, was largely perceived as being very boring. It was hard to see why any viewer would care about the two directionless seekers on screen. Weaving a conspiracy-based version of The JAMs' mythology into things allowed them to keep the expensive footage that they had already shot and, at the same time, deliver a more traditional conspiracy thriller about two men who were way out of their depth.

There were a few problems with this approach. The first is that all the Discordian humour had somehow become lost in translation, resulting in the fatal mistake of taking the whole thing seriously. The moment it is supposed that The Justified Ancients of Mummu is a real secret organisation that actually exists, then all that is interesting about them evaporates. In a related problem, the script for this version of the film was terrible. It would have resulted in something far worse than what they already had. The ambient road movie version may have been considered too boring for many to sit through, but it did at least succeed on its own terms.

Nevertheless, the new script, which now included a dramatic recreation of McElwee's story intercut with the existing footage, was budgeted. Paul McGann, as we have already noted, was cast in the role of McElwee (and aficionados of that piece of synchronicity may enjoy the fact that in *24 Hour Party People*, a film about the Manchester music scene during the same period, a similar 'crazed tramp' role was played by Christopher Eccleston, the actor who took over from Paul McGann as the Ninth Doctor Who).

All they had to do was raise the extra million pounds that filming this new script would require.

To do this, they attempted to recreate the success of The Timelords and produce another number one record. Cauty and Drummond emerged from the studio with a cheesy pop single called 'Kylie Said To Jason'. Like 'Whitney Joins The JAMs', it was a product of Drummond's unapologetic love for pure pop and, also like 'Whitney Joins The JAMs', this was completely misinterpreted. Largely perceived as ironic or sarcastic, the single failed even to enter the top 100. The spontaneous creativity of 'Doctorin' The TARDIS', it seemed, had been more effective than deliberate, planned intent. Without the money they had expected 'Kylie Said To Jason' to bring in, they had no way of funding the rest of the film.

A soundtrack album for *The White Room* movie did

finally emerge in 1991. It was a critical* and commercial hit and to this day can still be found in many '100 best albums' lists. It contains versions of their string of hit singles – '3am Eternal', 'What Time Is Love?' and 'The Last Train To Transcentral' – which lifted the duo into a position of global success.

The film, though, was dead. The existing version was never released, and the finished script was never shot. As Drummond once remarked, '[completing] that road movie thing, it can only end in death. We're not ready for that yet.'†

---

* Slightly off topic I know, but this mention of critical approval reminds me of something which happened when I originally self-published this book as an eBook in 2012. Back then, I was still in the habit of checking Amazon reviews to see what people were saying. One day I went online and saw that two new reviews had appeared – one titled 'The best book since the Bible' and the other titled 'Utter rubbish'. I remember staring at these two statements for some time. They are, I am sure you'll agree, quite extreme and polarised. Then I realised that, during the period when I was writing the book, I too had held both those opinions at different times. If I could see the book in those terms, then it was surely fair enough for others to do so as well. At that moment I understood what a review was – just one of thousands of individual perspectives at specific points in time, all valid, all insightful, but which say as much about the reviewer as they do the work in question. Crucially, the work itself was unaffected by them. That might sound like I'm stating the obvious, but I think there are many authors who unconsciously believe that their work is changed by reviews. This realisation has been very helpful to me and I'm profoundly grateful to the authors of those two reviews. They have helped me bypass some of the anxiety that comes with trying to make a living writing books.

† I can see why all this made it into the book – the *White Room* film looms too large in their legend to ignore. Indeed, in some ways their failure to

make the film crystallises their story in a nutshell. But it's hard to write about people trying and failing to do something because that doesn't move the narrative forward. We're still pretty much in the same situation we were when the chapter started, and for a reader that is ultimately unsatisfying. I was probably on the right track by using these incidents as a way to bring their deeper motivations into focus, but I should have done a better job of it. From the evidence of conversations I've had with those who have read this book over the past decade, a lot of people do seem to view their work as the deliberate practice of magic, despite all the remarks about their lack of intent or desire for transcendence. That's a failing of the book, and my fault.

10

Submerging

Drummond and Cauty climbed into the submarine.

They were dressed in hooded, deep-red robes and each of them had a large, fat horn, over a foot long, emerging from their foreheads and pointing upwards at a forty-five-degree angle. They looked pretty damn funny, squashed inside the submarine with only their covered heads and emerging horns poking out of the submarine's turret.*

Behind them was the lost continent of Mu, and on the lost continent of Mu there was a temple. In front of the temple were a troupe of African dancers, another group of six dancers in yellow robes and a scattering of The KLF's

---

* Oh, this is better!

musical collaborators. Near the top of the temple was a throne. Seated around the foot of this throne, dressed in flowing robes of white, sat the Four Handmaidens of Lucifer. On the throne, wearing a golden crown, sat Tammy Wynette.

Tammy Wynette, the Four Handmaidens of Lucifer, the dancers and the musicians all swayed from side to side, waving goodbye to Drummond and Cauty. The pair were journeying onwards in their submarine. They were leaving the lost continent behind them.

It was a hell of a music video.

It was also a hell of a song. The single was 'Justified And Ancient (Stand By The JAMs)'. If you can overlook a limited mail-order 7-inch and the staggered release of their previous American single resulting in a later UK release, then this November 1991 single was the last KLF record. With hindsight, you can read the slogan 'Warning! The Fall of the Empire and the Death of Little Mu are imminent . . .', which was flashed across the screen in the video, as foreshadowing this.

The song 'Justified And Ancient' itself was a thread that ran through their entire career. It was originally planned as the opening track on the debut JAMs album *1987: What The Fuck Is Going On?* and, although that didn't happen, a chunk of the song was used later in that album, towards the end of the track 'Hey Hey (We Are Not The Monkeys)'. A similar snippet drifted into the *Chill Out* album, accompanied by the sound of chirping crickets and running water, in a track called 'Justified And Ancient Seems A

Long Time Ago'. *The White Room* album both opened with a snippet of the song, as a lead-in to 'What Time Is Love?', and closed with their first complete version. With the creation of this single version, the song was finally finished.

It was a record that was entirely of their own creation, and one which seemed to achieve all their musical objectives. On the one hand, it is entirely traditional, the song where Drummond and Cauty finally resort to a chorus verse-chorus structure, and it was built without the theft of major samples from other artists. On the other hand, it is completely detached from reality lyrically, existing only in the realms of its own myth – 'They're justified / And they're ancient / And they drive an ice-cream van.' If The JAMs were an attack on an industry obsessed with authentic songs and authentic groups, then 'Justified And Ancient' can be seen as the conclusion of the project. Looking at it from the outside, not a single line of it makes any sense. Internally, if you allow it to have its own myth on its own terms, then it seems valid and complete. Instead of putting the boot into the classic pop single, Cauty and Drummond absorbed its magic and claimed it as their own. In Situationist terms, it was pure spectacle.*

The most striking thing about the single, of course, is that it features a lead vocal by Tammy Wynette. This is leagues ahead of fantasising about Whitney Houston joining The

---

* In my memory, that paragraph was quite insightful. Looking at it again, it seems pretty vague now. Do you feel you fully understand what I am trying to say here?

JAMs. Wynette, the first lady of country, is as sincere and authentic a vocalist as the twentieth century has produced. There is nothing detached or ironic in Wynette's perform- ance of songs like her biggest hit, 'Stand By Your Man'. When she sings, she means every word. Here, Drummond and Cauty take this voice of authentic honesty and bring it inside their myth, reclaiming the emotional power of modern music for their own ends. 'They're Justified, and they're ancient, and they like to roam the land,' she sings, accepting the lyrics at face value. 'All bound for Mu Mu Land, then someone started screaming, "Turn up the strobe!"'

'I really don't know why they chose me,' Wynette said. 'I was apprehensive at first, but I'm really excited with the way it's all turned out.' The song would do wonders for her career, hitting number one in eighteen countries and number eleven on the Billboard Hot 100 in America. This was Wynette's first top 40 hit in the mainstream, non-country music charts since 1969.

The idea was originally Cauty's. 'What this song needs, Bill, is Tammy Wynette,' he had said as they worked without inspiration on an earlier version. Drummond immediate- ly saw that he was right, adopted his best Ken Campbell attitude and went to find a phone. Twenty minutes later, Drummond was playing the song down the line to Tammy Wynette while she sat backstage in a Tennessee concert hall. She told him she loved it, and suddenly one of the least plausible or likely collaborations in music appeared to be effortless and almost preordained. Drummond flew to Nashville and recorded her vocals, and Cauty somehow made her loose, country vocals work around their rigid dance beat.

A true professional, we can only wonder what she really thought about the lyrics she was given to sing or the imagery of the video. It seems unlikely that she would have interpreted a line like 'We don't want to upset the applecart' as a reference to the Discordian's Golden Apple of Discord, for example. It seems equally unlikely that she was aware that the four white-robed women around her represented the Four Handmaidens of Lucifer. By the time Drummond and Cauty donned their blood-red robes, she had probably given up questioning what was going on. So it was that the pair strapped horns to their heads – a single horn for each man, making The KLF a two-horned beast – and marched up and down in front of her throne while the subliminal message 'Horned Men!' was flashed across them in the video.

A few months later Wynette collapsed while on tour of Australia. She blamed this on overwork caused by all her promotional work on this single. 'Tammy Lays Blame On The KLF', as the headline in the *Sun* newspaper put it.

The finished video incorporated the following scrolling text detailing Wynette's history and many achievements: 'Miss Tammy Wynette: 25 years in the business. 11 consecutive No. 1 albums. 20 No. 1 singles. 5 times voted C.M.A. Female Vocalist of the Year. Stand By Your Man still the biggest-selling country single of all time. 2 Grammies,

5 Marriages, 3 Children. The first lady to sell more than 1 million copies of one album.'

When the video was released, this seemed to be one of the more unusual things about it. Music wasn't judged in terms like that in those days, and musicians did not think to present themselves in such a light. In the early twenty-first century this is exactly how guest performers on TV talent shows such as *The X Factor* are introduced. This modern juxtaposition gives the video a strange quality when viewed today. Everything in it – the music, lyrics, imagery, costumes and personnel – was the result of Drummond and Cauty's idiosyncratic vision. Nothing in it would have survived a committee, or the controlling influence of a manager like Simon Cowell.

Today, *X Factor* contestants are unable to get a haircut without permission. Nothing is left to chance. The approach of total control taken by Simon Cowell and his ilk is the exact opposite of the path pursued by Drummond and Cauty.* Which is preferable is a matter of personal

---

* I think that *X Factor* and similar shows have had a profoundly negative effect on the generation who grew up during their heyday. For them, the idea that a musician needed a panel of judges to validate them was normal – it was just how the world was. The musician was expected to do things right, if they wished to continue, and the judges knew what 'right' was. Of course, if something can be said to be right it must, by definition, have been done before. And if it's been done before, it's debateable as to whether it needs to be done again. The only judge that a musician should attempt to astound is their own higher self. Hopefully the story of The KLF helps remind people of this.

judgement, but you are free to hold up 'Justified And Ancient (Stand By The JAMs)' against any *X Factor*-related record that you choose to see how they compare.

Inside the submarine, Drummond and Cauty turned away from the lost continent of Mu. The submarine was a reference to the *Leif Erickson*, the golden Discordian submarine that featured heavily in *The Illuminatus! Trilogy*. It was named after the Norwegian or Icelandic explorer who had been the first European to discover North America, around five hundred years before Christopher Columbus.

This was relevant because 1992 was the five-hundredth anniversary of Christopher Columbus' 1492 voyage, an event which was widely celebrated in the United States. Drummond and Cauty responded by issuing their final (UK) single in 1992 as a celebration of 'the one-thousandth anniversary of the discovery of North America by the Justified Ancients of Mu Mu'. The JAMs had been searching for the lost continent of Mu, they explained, in the year AD 992. They failed to find Mu, but they discovered America by accident.

That song was yet another reworking of 'What Time Is Love?', which they called 'America: What Time Is Love?'. The video recreated The JAMs' mythical voyage. Shot in black and white and drenched by an ocean storm, it showed The KLF on a Viking longboat of the type used by Leif Ericson. The Handmaidens of Lucifer appear as Sirens on the rocks, pointing the way forward. Glenn Hughes of Deep Purple is also on board.

The video ends with the Viking longboat being burned.

It had been an extraordinary, exhausting couple of years. They had produced a string of hit singles and videos, most notably the 'stadium house trilogy' of 'What Time Is Love?', '3am Eternal' and 'The Last Train To Transcentral'. They had made both the unreleased film and the soundtrack album of *The White Room*. They had burnt a wicker man in a pagan ceremony on the Isle of Jura, recorded Tammy Wynette in Nashville and fulfilled all the promotional duties that come with being one of the bestselling bands in the country. All of this they did independently. There was never a point, Drummond has remarked, when he was not unloading boxes of CDs from the back of vans.

John Dyer of Mute Records told Richard King about negotiations that occurred when Rough Trade Records went into administration. The KLF's records were distributed by Rough Trade and Drummond and Cauty were at one point owed over a million pounds by the company. 'So in the middle of a meeting we'd say, "So you agree to that, Bill? KLF represents 13 per cent of the debt?"' Dyer told King. 'And Bill would say, "Yeah, just a minute," and then he's on the end of the phone going "Yeah, bit more bombastic Jimmy, bit more bombastic," so he's having to do a mixdown with Jimmy Cauty who's in the studio at the other end of the phone. Then he'd ring up Pinewood and would spend a hundred grand on the video. He was hiring the sound stages saying, "No, we don't need the submarine stage today." Incredible, visionary behaviour.' Drummond, in particular, looks noticeably older at the end of his five-year partnership with Cauty than he did before.

And what, in the end, was it for? Drummond and Cauty looked out of the submarine at the waving figures on the lost continent of Mu. They had achieved what they had set out to do. They had made a record – a fantastic record – which satisfied all Drummond's punk-era demands on what a single piece of 7-inch vinyl should be. 'Justified And Ancient (Stand By The JAMs)' is a record that you can play to anyone, from seven-year-old kids to fifty-year-old country music superstars, and they immediately get it. It doesn't need explaining, or placing in a certain context. It is universal. It will still sound great in a hundred years' time. And they did it entirely on their own terms, swimming against the industry instead of with it, creating it out of nothing but their own myth.

So, what now?

The submarine sailed away. It did not sink beneath the waters because it wasn't a real submarine. Nor was it in a real sea, but a sound stage at Pinewood Studios where Cauty's old car had once appeared in the *Superman* movies. Cauty had looked into buying a real submarine but this proved not to be practicable, so he consoled himself with buying a number of armoured vehicles instead. As Drummond said in 1991, 'We want to buy ships, have submarines. They really are stupid things I know, but I feel confident that in the event of us selling ten million albums we would definitely go out and buy a submarine . . . Just to be able to say "Look we've got a submarine and 808 State haven't".'*

In Robert Anton Wilson's book, the Discordians could always travel on to further adventures in their submarine, but Drummond and Cauty could not disappear in this fashion. Their achievement was not physical. It was intangible, playing out in the minds of the audience, becoming part of the Situationists' spectacle and anchoring itself in Moore's Ideaspace. It was very hard, in other words, to see what they had achieved. What, exactly, was all that hard work for?

And what, if 'Justified And Ancient' was everything that they had been aiming to create, could they do now?†

---

* Out of all the KLF quotes, this one is still my favourite.

† I like the way this chapter ends. I think a lot of creative people who have completed significant projects will recognise the feeling it talks about – and the questions 'Was that it?' and 'What do I do now?' Self-care around the end of projects is something of an art in itself. I recommend having a huge backlog of emails to answer, financial accounts, household matters and other tedious chores that you have no choice but to attend to. It's not fun, I admit, but it gets you through. You then need to balance this by making sure you have a lot of fun during the next big project.

11

Endings

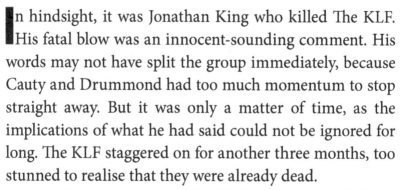

In hindsight, it was Jonathan King who killed The KLF. His fatal blow was an innocent-sounding comment. His words may not have split the group immediately, because Cauty and Drummond had too much momentum to stop straight away. But it was only a matter of time, as the implications of what he had said could not be ignored for long. The KLF staggered on for another three months, too stunned to realise that they were already dead.

It was February 1992 and The KLF had just won the 'Best Band' award at the Brits. Jonathan King was the producer of the awards show, and he had been asked what he thought of The KLF's live performance at the show.

'I enjoyed it,' he said.

He enjoyed it. There was nothing else for it. It had to end.

King was a music producer, TV presenter and a recording

artist who specialised in novelty records. He has sold over forty million records during his career, under various pseudonyms. As he busied himself backstage at the Hammersmith Odeon organising the 1992 Brit Awards, the forty-eight-year-old King was dressed in a garish shell suit and a baseball cap with the word 'KING' stamped in metal across the front. In the coming decade he was named 'Man of the Year' by the BPI, praised by Tony Blair and convicted of multiple sexual offences against under age boys, so in many ways Jonathan King could be said to personify the music industry.* King's acceptance therefore, on a symbolic level, signified the music industry claiming Drummond and Cauty for itself.

Drummond and Cauty's problem with the music industry wasn't the usual adolescent anti-authoritarian posturing that is so common among musicians. It was the result of bitter experience. By that point Cauty and Drummond had spent twenty-five years in the industry between them, from running record labels to producing, working in A&R, being in unsuccessful bands and being pop stars. They knew what the music industry did to people, and they also knew what it had done to them. But by then they also knew how much they had been formed by it. It had shaped their lives and left them feeling corrupted, but it was also an integral part of who they were.

---

* One reason I try to avoid looking back at past work is the fear that it will be full of lines like this – text that should have been handled much better, but which is out in the world, and I am no longer able to rewrite or fix.

It's still surprising that they were asked to provide the opening performance for that year's Brit Awards show. They had been asked to appear the previous year, but negotiations had broken down following their plans to fill a stage with angels and Zulus and arrive on the back of elephants. The deal breaker, with hindsight, was probably their plan to chainsaw the legs off one of the elephants. The elephant, they said, represented the music industry. The organisers understandably walked away at this point, but they should have realised then that they were not dealing with stable individuals.

Cauty and Drummond were never going to stand on stage and entertain an audience of music industry insiders with one of their crowd-pleasing number one hit singles. They did not desire the acclaim of their peers, nor were they focused on using the event as a showcase to further their careers. They were more concerned with the implications of the invitation. The music industry was finally reacting to them, recognising what they had achieved, and attempting to embrace them. It was an invitation that demanded a response, and that response needed to be a summation of their feelings about the industry. In the end they did not quite achieve this, but there is no doubt they tried.

The show began. The audience were seated in rows, dressed as fabulously as their status demanded and looking effortlessly nonchalant whenever a TV camera turned towards them. The KLF were announced as the opening act and the audience cheered and applauded, seemingly delighted. Bill and Jimmy walked out onto the stage. They were accompanied by Extreme Noise Terror, a grindcore band from Ipswich.

At the time, the existence of such extreme metal bands was all but unknown to the mainstream audience. Bands like Extreme Noise Terror and Slayer had been played on John Peel's radio show, and the Midlands band Napalm Death had appeared in a BBC Arena documentary, but beyond a small group of serious music fans most people had no idea that such an extreme type of music even existed. To those unfamiliar with the genre, it did not even appear to be music. It was noise, and it was a shock to realise just how deeply unpleasant noise could be. In an age when speed metal is used to sell energy drinks, it is perhaps hard to appreciate just how incomprehensible bands like Extreme Noise Terror were to a mainstream audience at that time.* With all due respect, they were not how the British music industry wanted to showcase British music to a watching TV audience of nine million people in the UK alone.

The band erupted into a thrash metal version of '3am

---

* This is another example of why timing is important context throughout the KLF story. Timing is important when writing books, also. This book would have been very different if I had written it in 2002, and equally different if I had done it now. I suspect there is a right time when books should be written – a moment when the book that emerges will have a greater impact than one emerging years earlier, or later. Sometimes you have a great idea for a book, but intuitively feel that it's not the right time for it. Although I think there is a lot I could do better now, my feeling is that 2012 was exactly the right time for me to write about The KLF.

Eternal', although there were few in the audience who recognised it. Extreme Noise Terror had two vocalists, each barking lyrics in incomprehensible, atavistic grunts which sounded like a cross between Beelzebub and the Cookie Monster. Between them stood Bill Drummond, leaning on a crutch and smoking a fat cigar. He wore a kilt of Drummond tartan that he had been given for his twenty-first birthday and a battered leather overcoat which was alleged to have been the one worn by Martin Bormann during an escape to Bolivia. He meant business. He spat out new lyrics, full of references to the BPI and the Brits, but the exact words were indecipherable under the volume, speed and sheer presence of the music.

Drummond's interest in Extreme Noise Terror came after he heard them on *The John Peel Show*. He and Cauty had been planning a hard-rock follow-up to *The White Room* called *The Black Room*, and had approached Motörhead about a collaboration. Motörhead declined, knowing full well that their solid metal audience would never forgive them for working with a 'dance music' band. Drummond then called Extreme Noise Terror but the message he left, 'from Bill of The KLF', was initially ignored as it was misheard as 'Bill from the ALF', or the Animal Liberation Front. Extreme Noise Terror were deeply into the animal rights scene and were considerably more likely to be called by the ALF than The KLF. Eventually, though, they connected, and the two bands started working on *The Black Room* sessions.

That album was never finished.

*

Earlier that morning, Drummond had driven to an abattoir in Alan Moore's home town of Northampton and bought a dead sheep and eight gallons of blood. The plan was that he and Cauty would dismember the corpse on stage. The KLF had used sheep imagery throughout their career, ever since they appeared on the cover of *Chill Out*, so destroying one like this had obvious symbolic meaning. They had huge butcher's knives ready, and planned to throw hunks of the carcass into the audience. It was intended to be an act so appalling that they would never have been forgiven for it.

Even this was a compromise. Jimmy had originally goaded Bill by suggesting that Drummond should cut his own hand off during the performance. This was dangerous talk, given how psyched the pair were. They both knew as they suggested ideas that there was a danger they would carry them out.

Cauty's suggestion reminded Drummond of the Red Hand of Ulster. Irish legend told of a race across the sea from the south-west of Scotland, where Drummond had been raised, in which the first competitor to touch Irish land would be declared the King of Ireland. One potential king was lagging behind in the race, so in desperation he cut his hand off and threw it ahead of his rivals, onto the shore, and in doing so claimed the land as his own. When Cauty suggested that Drummond could cut his own hand off and throw it into the audience, the idea interested Drummond because he immediately saw it as in some way claiming the music industry. Drummond's actions were being dictated by his symbolic interpretation of events, as always, but this potent form of internal logic seemed to be pushing them into darker and more dangerous territory. His train of thought was not the normal reaction to being asked to cut off your own hand.

Ultimately, Drummond decided against such drastic action. As an alternative, he considered sacrificing a live sheep on stage. This would make a similar point through the biblical allusions to the Binding of Isaac and the tradition of the sacrificial lamb, in which a lamb's death was offered up to God in order to remove the sins of the tribe. Arranging the live sacrifice of a sheep, however, would be quite problematic on a practical level. This plan was also abandoned, and the compromise solution of dismembering a dead sheep was settled upon. If nothing else it would be easier to transport.

Rumours about the dead sheep had spread during the day, thanks to their publicist Mick Houghton wisely informing the press in order to sabotage their plans. Jonathan King and the BBC were horrified and made it clear that no such act could be allowed, and certainly not televised. Extreme Noise Terror weren't too impressed either, some of them being extreme vegetarians who had been known to vandalise butcher's shops. The sheep remained in the van during the performance, only to reappear later that night dumped on the steps outside the after-show party tagged with a note that read, 'I died for ewe'. The prompt arrival of the police prevented the eight gallons of blood joining the sheep on the hotel steps. Like so many other times, Drummond and Cauty had failed to implement their plans and been left with no choice but to improvise.

Still, while Drummond may not have butchered a sheep on stage, he did have an antique machine gun. As the song ended, he clenched his cigar between his teeth and sprayed bullet after bullet into the audience, the music industry itself. The gun only fired blanks, but it was a cathartic moment.

In a strange way, something about the music industry did die around that point. Music in the twentieth century had shown an incredible ability for invention. New musical genres were constantly created and explored – so much so, in fact, that this was considered normal. The first half of the century had given us such distinctive new genres as blues or jazz. The fifties gave us rock 'n' roll, and the sixties gave us psychedelia and soul. The seventies gave us reggae, heavy metal, disco and punk, and the eighties had delivered hip-hop, techno, acid house and indie.

The assumption was that this level of creativity was normal and would continue indefinitely.

Each of those new genres was a major musical movement, a continent of sound the likes of which had never been heard before. They were usually forged in the crucible of new technology, new drugs or a combination of both. Musicologists have their technical definitions of each of these genres, but non-musicians define them more simply.

Each genre makes us feel differently. We know the mood that a blues record creates in us, and we know that those feelings are different from the ones generated by jazz, heavy metal or reggae. The musical genres, in other words, map out the various moods and states that the human mind is capable of experiencing.

This constant invention of major new genres was believed to be normal in 1994. Those in the Brits audience had personally seen the rise of disco, punk, hip-hop, rave, Madchester and indie in their own lifetimes. The fact that these genres had appeared alongside other creative bursts, such as the invention of video games or street art, also helped to normalise them. Grunge had just happened and, while it may not have staked out as much new territory as its punk or metal parents, it still felt like a distinct and valid invention. It would never have occurred to anyone in those seats, as Drummond fired blanks into the ranks of their peers, that this period of invention had come to an end.

In the years ahead, the journalists and A&R men of the industry would busy themselves seeking the next new thing. Britpop was presented as just such a thing, despite it being a coked-up combination of indie music and nostalgia. Music which sounded like music used to could be a brave new thing, if you were having too much of a good time to think about it. But, as the decade rolled on and the twenty-first century began, it slowly became apparent that major new genres weren't arriving anymore. Sure, genres split into subgenres as they were explored more fully, and the space between different genres were colonised by cross-over artists. Yet these hundreds of subgenres, from drum 'n' bass to black metal, were considerably more limited than the genres being founded just a few decades earlier. They were noticeably less fertile.*

None of this meant that music got *worse*. There were still great songs being written and great performances given. Recording became cheap, the ability to record music and reach an audience became more democratic, and access to the entire history of recorded music became easy. But the idea that there were major new continents of unexplored music slowly faded. The frontier had been colonised. We had discovered the edges of the territory.

Bill Drummond did not know this at the time. Despite machine-gunning the music industry at the point when its engines of creativity died, he did not imagine that he really was killing it. Correlation does not imply causation, after all. But regardless of what he thought he was doing, he was

---

* How does this argument hold up, ten years later? It certainly looks solid when applied to the rock landscape, and probably the dance music world also. The rap world has remained more innovative and 'fertile', however, and genres like grime are evidence of this. That said, grime is a mixing of UK garage, jungle and hip-hop, so it is, by definition, not as sonically distinct and unique a genre as, say, jazz, reggae or heavy metal. I don't think anyone expects to hear a new genre as distinct from other forms of music as those any time soon. The argument, I think, still holds up. The internet is often blamed for this change, but if this were the point in music history when the change occurred, it occurs a good few years before the mass take up of the internet and the online availability of music as MP3s. The old ways were already fizzling out before the new ways arrived.

still the one man in the room whose actions were in sync
with the wider picture.

As the band left the stage a voice declared over the PA: 'The
KLF have left the music industry.' This wasn't intended as
a statement of fact or a premonition, but as a challenge to
themselves.

There were many people in the crowd who were appalled by the performance. Trevor Horn, who was there
to pick up the award for best producer, announced that
the performance was 'disgraceful'. WEA chairman Rob
Dickens said the gesture was 'pathetic, silly and child-
ish'. The classical music conductor Sir Georg Solti tried
to leave the auditorium and had to be persuaded back to
his seat. This was the only reaction from a member of the
audience, Drummond and Cauty felt, that showed any
understanding of what they had done. The press were
deeply unimpressed, and it can be assumed that many of
the watching millions at home were baffled. But there was
something about Jonathan King, and the way he seemed
to personify the entire industry, that made his claim that
he enjoyed the performance so damning. As the *NME* has
noted, the music industry will let you sexually abuse its
grandmother as long as you continue to make it money.
It can absorb any attack, no matter how heartfelt, because
it simply doesn't care about anything except the bottom
line. As the Situationists put it, 'opposition to the spectacle
can produce only the spectacle of opposition'. Or to quote

the philosopher Raoul Vaneigem, 'pissing on the altar is still a way of paying homage to the Church'. In this way the music of the Sex Pistols was eventually played to the Queen at the opening ceremony of the London 2012 Olympics, and the music of Kurt Cobain was eventually covered by The Muppets.

To add to the insult, The KLF then picked up the Best Band award, but they were awarded it jointly with Simply Red. Simply Red were at the time at the height of their commercial success, following their multi-platinum *Stars* album. It was not a good time for the industry to tell Drummond and Cauty that it considered them to be the best that they could possibly be, which was just as good as Simply Red. Such an accolade is easy to misinterpret.

Drummond and Cauty had left immediately after their performance, so a motorcycle courier collected the award on their behalf. The statue was later discovered by a farmer in Wiltshire, buried in a field near Stonehenge. The farmer returned the statue, so Cauty and Drummond had to go back to Wiltshire and bury it even deeper.

At that point, Jonathan King was not known to be a paedophile: only in 2001 was he jailed for the sexual assault of five teenage boys. This makes him the third person in this story to have been sent to prison for sexual offences related to minors. Gary Glitter, who appeared with Cauty and Drummond on *Top Of The Pops*, was jailed for possessing thousands of images of child pornography and charged with having sexual relations with a fourteen-year-old child. Chris Langham, the *Thick Of It* actor and co-author with Ken Campbell of the *Illuminatus!* stage play, was jailed in 2007 for possessing child pornography.

You might think this a remarkably high instance of such crimes for one story, and you would be correct. It becomes more uncomfortable in light of a character in *Illuminatus!* called Padre Pederastia, a paedophile priest who initiates new recruits into The Justified Ancients of Mummu by leading a satanic black mass. Not all the coincidences that circle this story are light and funny.

After the Brit Awards, the actions of The KLF were quickly rationalised by journalists as 'pranks' or 'scams'. They were nothing of the sort. They were an honest expression from the very core of Drummond and Cauty. As Drummond told the journalist Danny Kelly the next day, 'There is humour in what we do,* and in the records, but I really

---

* There was indeed humour in what they did, but it was significantly less central to their work than with Ken Campbell, Robert Anton Wilson or Alan Moore. Those men all managed to hit that magnificent sweet spot where they took themselves seriously and didn't take themselves seriously at the same time. To read interviews with Bill and Jimmy from this period, it's hard to imagine that they were the same people who made 'Doctorin' The TARDIS'. It is also pretty evident that they will never make a record like that again. Perhaps if they had had a heightened sense of humour during this period things wouldn't have turned out as dark. A healthy sense of your own absurdity offers significant protection against many dangers.

hate it when people go on about us being "schemers" and "scammers". We do all this stuff from the very depths of our soul and people make out it's some sort of game. It depresses me.' Once again they had reacted instinctively on the deepest level they knew, and found their actions misinterpreted as some sophisticated Machiavellian media manipulation.

They could not wound the industry, and they could not fight it. When they first decided to take on the mantle of The Justified Ancients of Mummu their intention had been to claim the music industry for themselves. Instead, it had swallowed them up.

They had failed.

They were in a very dark place. As Drummond told Danny Kelly, 'Looking back, we realise we don't really know what our motivation was. All we know is we've got, as well as everything else, this dark side to our personality. We looked into our souls and entered into the same area that [Charles] Manson must have entered . . . and that bloke who shot up Hungerford.' Here Drummond was referring to the mass shooting in 1987 by a lone gunman called Michael Ryan, which led to the tightening up of Britain's gun laws. Kelly challenged him on this because, if it was hyperbole, then it was in terrible taste. He asked Drummond if he really meant it. 'I do actually. Yes I do,' Drummond said. 'It is the same area. Somebody recently used the phrase "corporate rebels" – about The Manic Street Preachers, I think – and both Jimmy and I didn't want to be just corporate rebels because there's just so much of that, shameless, in the music business. We felt we were head butting . . . head butting . . . trying to push at what's acceptable. It was completely pointless and you don't know why you're doing it but it has to be done. And that's what Michael Ryan did; he just woke up one morning and thought "right, today's the day I go out and get the bastards" and went out and shot the bastards . . .' A number of journalists from this period came away from interviews speculating as to whether or not Drummond was on the edge of a breakdown.

What next? Where could they go from there? They had been on a journey deep into the very heart of the beast. They had failed, and they might never feel clean again. They had to get away, but was it possible for a group that successful to escape from the industry? In 1992, The KLF were massive. The previous year they had sold more singles than any other act in the world. They had had a string of global number one records. They had hits in America. The critics adored them. How could they escape from the industry? How could they become forgotten?

How could they reclaim their souls?

The first step was to stop. *The Black Room* sessions were ended and Extreme Noise Terror paid off. Then they killed The KLF. A full-page advert announced the fact in the press (and was largely considered to be a clever marketing ploy to promote the forthcoming *The Black Room*). They left the country, spending time in Mexico. Still this wasn't enough, so they took an even more drastic step. They deleted all their records.

Being completely independent, they were one of the few acts to be in a position to do this. True, they couldn't do anything about the records that had already been sold, and they were unable to delete their catalogue in non-UK territories where they had licensed their work. But in the UK, at least, there would be no KLF records in shops, no special edition reissues, no songs licensed to compilation albums, adverts or video games. This act, in many ways, was far more brutal than the later money burning. In pure financial terms, it has been estimated that this would have cost them something like five million pounds in future earnings.

They were removing their body of work, the result of extraordinary risks and effort, from the public sphere. This was a cost that went far beyond the financial. Yet they thought it necessary, for what they wanted to get back was far more valuable.

12

Undercurrents

▲

The K Foundation, as Drummond and Cauty called themselves when they stopped being The KLF, burnt their money in August 1994. The period of the early to mid-1990s is frequently overlooked in our cultural histories, yet it was far more potent and strange than it is usually given credit for. In order to understand why it is significant that Cauty and Drummond's bonfire took place in this period, it is necessary to recognise what was so odd about those years.

Our mental landscape was very different a century or so earlier. Victorian England had been, on the surface at least, a bastion of certainty. The Victorians had three immoveable beacons by which they could orientate themselves and their society: the pillars of Church, Empire and Crown. This, of course, was not to last. Charles Darwin had developed a scientific model that was ingenious and ground-breaking, but which had *implications*. Perhaps wisely, he kept it hidden away in a drawer for twenty years. But in 1859 he published.*

Mainstream scientists and philosophers in the nine-teenth century believed that they understood how things were organised, and where the human race belonged, in the natural order of things. But Darwin's work, in com-bination with breakthroughs made in the field of geology regarding the age of the planet, caused one of the unshak-able pillars of Victorian certainty to crack. The teachings of the Church about the origins of life on this planet had been shown to be wrong. This was a severe failing for an organisation which exists to proclaim an infallible under-standing of truth.

The great Churches of the world didn't react to the new understanding well. In 1870, eleven years after the

---

* Here I randomly spend a few pages outlining my next book, *Stranger Than We Can Imagine*. I didn't realise I was doing that at the time, of course, but that's what it is. After this KLF book was released and hit a nerve, I could very easily have found myself becoming the 'strange mu-sic book guy'. People would have expected books just like this one from me and been confused or disappointed if I did not deliver. I would have staked a claim on my own territory, as all branding experts advise, but the result would have quickly become one of diminishing returns. With hindsight, following *The KLF* with something as different and ambitious as *Stranger Than We Can Imagine* was probably the closest I've ever come to a good career move. I'm now in a fortunate position where the territory I'm allowed to explore as a writer is wide and expansive. As long as every new book isn't quite what people were expecting, then they seem happy.

publication of *On the Origin of Species*, the Vatican formalised the doctrine of papal infallibility. This dogma asserted that the action of the Holy Spirit can remove even the possibility of error from the Pope. The Pope was right, in other words, because he was the Pope, who was right. This was clearly a form of circular logic, another of Robert Anton Wilson's self-referential reality tunnels, and once that had been recognised the Darwinists found themselves outside the Church's logic. They could no longer submerge themselves inside the Church and unquestioningly accept what it had to say. Calls for the need to have 'faith' could no longer be met with reverent acceptance. Indeed, they were increasingly met with knowing smirks. Nietzsche was one who was brave enough to articulate publicly this change in the world. 'God is dead,' he wrote in 1882, 'and we have killed him.'

This change in understanding may have been unsettling, but it was just a warm-up for the goodies that the twentieth century had in store. New ideas came thick and fast from the likes of Einstein, Planck, Freud, Picasso and Joyce. Every breakthrough seemed to be pulling in the same direction, that of undermining certainty. Things were no longer anywhere near as simple as they had been. Our most fundamental bedrocks – time, space, matter, the rational mind –were discovered to be nothing like as dependable as they appeared. We were steaming ahead into uncharted territory.

The First World War erupted, and shattered any notion that there was glory in Empire. As the value of Church and

Crown eroded in contemporary thought, the public's need for an unarguable authority gave momentum to politicians, who quickly offered up the state as a candidate. They differed in the details, or course – the fascists thought the population should serve the state while the communists thought that the state was the servant of the people – but the methods used to enforce the centralisation of power were essentially the same. These ideas played themselves out to their horrendous conclusions during the Second World War. The notion that the state should be the central authority in our lives has never seemed credible since.*

As the decades rolled on, the search for an unarguable touchstone to replace Church, Crown or Empire in our lives took on ever more urgency. For populations still traumatised by the conflict of the 1940s, enforcing social conformity in the 1950s made a lot of sense, yet this was stifling for the generation coming of age after the war. In the 1960s they sought liberation, but the philosophies that

---

* I wish now that I had realised this was all stuff for the next book. Here again is the problem with zooming out to the big picture for some broad-strokes background – it's very hard to do without sounding like a Substack blogger proclaiming their new take on how the world has got it wrong. One reason this doesn't work here is because we had become invested in Bill and Jimmy and the dark night of the soul they were entering. That was much more interesting. Instead, we get a history of the twentieth century in five minutes, just when we're not in the mood for it. Brief, broad overviews like this lack human characters to interest us and, without that, all you have is a lecture. It's not that what is being said is uninteresting, but some subjects do need space and a cast of characters to do them justice.

made so much sense on a personal level did not scale up well to the level of society. In the 1970s the attention shifted to the self, but the hedonistic self-indulgence grew to such unbearable levels that punk was needed to tear it down. In the 1980s they believed that money and the pursuit of material possessions was the answer. Wealth was pursued, but it did not have the power to satisfy us properly, and that, too, was soon discarded as a candidate for our unassailable personal omphalos.*

So what next? By the time we reached 1990 all options had been tried and found wanting. We could return to the Church, the state, politics, material greed, personal liberation or hedonism if we wished, but we could no longer see them without being aware of their faults. They were damaged goods, still significant but no longer permanent and secure. But what other options did we have? Did we have any? It appeared not. We were out of ideas.

And so there was heard a global, existential gasp of generational fear. There was nothing to believe in. This awful period was brief, and we can date it quite precisely. It arrived in mainstream culture in 1991, fully formed and simultaneously emanating from many different art forms. Douglas Coupland's debut novel *Generation X* was published in March that year, and the generation it described suddenly found themselves with a name. Another label arrived in July, when Richard Linklater's no-budget indie

---

* An omphalos! I really was developing the next book, wasn't I?

movie *Slacker* reached cinemas. The American comedian Bill Hicks' career started taking off in the UK, and the generation found their philosopher. Then, in September, their anthem arrived. Nirvana released the single 'Smells Like Teen Spirit', and the story of alternative music was changed forever.*

Slackers were not well dressed, because there was no reason to dress smartly. Their uniform was old jeans, Converse trainers and warm, practical lumberjack shirts. They were not career-minded, for there was no reason to pursue the corporate dream. They were seen largely as apathetic, but it was an apathy born of a logical assessment of the options rather than just innate laziness. They were often well-educated and creative, and were usually portrayed as being talkative and self-obsessed. If they had a mission, of sorts, it was to work out how to move forward from where they were.

With the Berlin Wall down and Thatcher and Reagan out of office, there was a clear sense that the old order had finished. Modern historians also draw a line at this point. The historian Eric Hobsbawm coined the phrase 'the short twentieth century' to cover the period 1914 to 1991, from the start of the First World War to the end of the Cold

---

* This is better. I should have cut the last century and just started talking about the 1990s. The popular idea of the 1990s is sanitised, I think – it's seen as all Tony Blair and Spice Girls. But something far darker and more interesting was occurring under the surface. Perhaps these paragraphs are an outline for a book I've yet to write – an elegy for the twilight of the analogue world.

War. This is a useful time frame for a historian because it works as a complete narrative. Francis Fukuyama's hugely influential 1992 book *The End of History and the Last Man* also recognised that a change of great historical significance had occurred. Fukuyama argued that an era of great political upheaval had ended and that Western liberal democracy was the final stage of human government. He was essentially unable to imagine what could possibly happen next.

For that was the question that needed to be answered: 'What next?'. Looking to the past didn't help; it didn't have any answers and it was all out of ideas. The past shrugged as if to say, 'Good luck. You're on your own.'

At first, Generation X was linked to a sense of relief and a feeling that they had recognised the blind spots of the past and were now facing up to things with a refreshing honesty. But as 1991 rolled into 1992 and 1993, this honesty became less invigorating and increasingly unbearable. It started to become apparent that they were not going to find a focus for their narrative, or a way to repair the damage to their mental landscape. The sense of mounting horror came closer and closer to the surface. The nihilism reached its peak in 1994, the period of Kurt Cobain's suicide, the burning of the million pounds and the year Bill Hicks died. This was the point when the constant creation of new musical genres that had characterised the twentieth century came to an end. That era was over. By this point there was a desperate need for a way out. Any way out.

*

The changes that signified the arrival of the next era began towards the end of 1994. In Britain, Tony Blair and Gordon Brown had taken control of the Labour Party and had launched New Labour. John Major wrote in his memoirs that his victory in the 1992 general election 'killed socialism in Britain'. Margaret Thatcher was of a similar opinion, as was, it seems, Tony Blair, whose first act upon gaining the leadership of the Labour Party was to remove the social-ist 'Clause IV' from the party's constitution. After Blair, politics would no longer be led by ideology, but by opin-ion polls. This was the 'Third Way', a political discourse dominated by spin, where it was not what you did that was important, but how that played out in the press.*

In Europe, the Maastricht Treaty paved the way for the modern European Union and, ultimately, the euro. In the United States, George W. Bush entered political life in 1994 as Governor of Texas. Netscape released the first version of their Navigator software that year, the first popular web browser, and Microsoft followed with a high-profile launch of their Windows 95 operating system the following year. The modern digital era began. The world of Google, Wiki-pedia and Facebook was coming into being. The old order was being ripped up. The new era was being born, and it was the Age of Networks.

---

* That bit still holds up well, unfortunately.

As the blogger Neuroskeptic notes, during the period from 1945 to 1990 new cults, religions and sects were springing up all over the place. This period gave us the likes of Scientology, the Hare Krishnas, Transcendental Meditation, the Moonies, Jesus Freaks, the Manson Family, Heaven's Gate, Jonestown, the Kabbalah Centre, the Nation of Islam, the New Age, Neopaganism and Wicca. Why, he asks, did that outpouring of new religious groups dry up so abruptly and decisively, with hardly any popularly known groups forming after the Waco siege of 1993? The question points to a deep change in our culture, and once again marks the early years of the 1990s as the end of an era. It was not just new musical genres, it seems, that stopped appearing at that point in time.

We can date the end of that era, what Hobsbawm called the 'Age of Extremes', to the end of the Cold War in 1991, and we can date the start of the information era to the first popular web browser in 1994. What, then, should we make of those years in between? They are boundary years, comparable to what anthropologists call a liminal state. They were a period when the old rules were gone, but before the new order was formed. They were a period, in other words, when normal certainties did not apply, when anything was possible and the strange was commonplace. As John C. Calhoun, the seventh vice-president of the United States once wrote, 'The interval between the decay of the old and the formation and the establishment of the new, constitutes a period of transition which must always necessarily be one of uncertainty, confusion, error, and wild and fierce fanaticism.'

Being innate storytellers, we neglect this brief, confusing period and prefer instead the clearer narratives that surround it. If you Google each year in the last quarter of the twentieth century, you'll find that each successive one has an increasing number of mentions online, as you would expect given the growth of the internet during this period. The only exception to this upward trend is the period between 1991 and 1994, when the number of mentions declines. The age of John Major and George Bush Sr, it seems, does not attract our attention. Our cultural narrative skips from the Stock, Aitken and Waterman late eighties to the Britpop and The Spice Girls mid-nineties quite happily. Even the Adrian Mole diaries skip these years. This boundary period is a cultural blind spot; we choose not to look at it.

But there is much that can be learnt from such a time, and great art can be found there. In The KLF's field of music, for example, this brief period brought albums such as *Loveless* by My Bloody Valentine, Primal Scream's *Screamadelica*, Nirvana's *Nevermind, Automatic For The People* by REM, *Peggy Suicide* by Julian Cope, U2's *Achtung Baby* and Oasis' *Definitely Maybe* – all records that are considered the career best, or thereabouts, for those musicians.* Considering the long careers of many of those bands, the fact that their highest achievements all fall within that narrow

---

* This is an embarrassingly rock- and indie-based collection of examples, isn't it? No mention of *Enter the Wu-Tang (36 Chambers), Selected Ambient Works 85–92* or *The Chronic*? More shame to bear.

period does suggest that there was something in the water at that time, so to speak.

In the moments that followed the withdrawal of one wave of history you could see, if you chose to look, a brief glimpse of the undercurrents at work in the late twentieth century. It did not last long, for the next grand wave arrived and drowned out these subtle workings with energy and noise. And that next wave was noisy.*

The escape route from the nihilism of the early 1990s was, in the end, mindless optimism. Things could only get better. Adopting this belief entailed not worrying about the details. And it was fun! This, then, became the 1990s that we choose to remember, a time of Cool Britannia, the Millennium Dome and the dotcom bubble. Ego-fuelling cocaine became the drug of choice, BritPop and The Spice Girls were on hand to entertain us, and the modern digital world created itself anew. Times were exciting again. We could not help but be swept along with that tide, and we found that it supported us to the extent that we no longer felt the need to worry about our foundations.

How does the death of that era compare to its birth? Hobsbawm pinpointed the beginning of that era, the 'short twentieth century' of 1914–91, as the beginning of the First World War. This was when the age of empires collapsed

---

* A+ paragraph – would read again.

upon itself and the political realities of the twentieth century began. It coincides roughly with what the American
author and lecturer Susan Cain calls a shift from a culture
of character to a culture of personality.

This era's birth couldn't have been more different from
its death in the 1990s when, having exhausted itself, it qui-
etly laid down and died. The period of the First World War
was a brutal, violent explosion, when the collapse of the
Victorian system engulfed the whole world in sheer bloody
horror. Everything – from our social structures to our relationship with technology and the nature of the human
condition – was shredded before the unstoppable firestorm.
Nothing survived. A time of mud, gas and unimagined
mechanised slaughter, it is no exaggeration to call this
exactly what it was: the darkest point in human history.
True, the death toll was higher in the Second World War,
but that war had been psychologically understandable in
the context of the time. No one was in any way prepared
for the actuality of The Great War, and there is no horror
greater than the arrival of the unthinkable.

This was the period that spawned the Cabaret Voltaire.
As we have seen, the six members of this group share with
Cauty and Drummond a sense of being haunted by what
they did and an inability to explain or come to terms with
their actions. This makes a strange sort of sense when we
view this period as the liminal gap between eras. There was
no narrative context at that point to explain their actions,
because the old story had ended and the new one had not
begun. If Cauty and Drummond had burnt their money

earlier in the twentieth century, it would have been seen as a Surrealist act, or perhaps a Situationist one. If they had done it ten years later, it would have been understood in terms of the global anti-capitalist movement. Doing it in the period between eras made it incomprehensible, for there was no surrounding context that could make sense of what they had done. Nothing is really explainable in liminal periods, as anyone who has attempted to understand the First World War using the Victorian world view will have discovered. How can you explain an act, except as part of an ongoing narrative?

The movement that the Cabaret Voltaire created is known as 'Dada' – a meaningless, idiotic word which showed their contempt for art itself. Art, as they saw it, was the product of the society that gave birth to it. It was the finest aspect of that society, its highest expression, and by the nature of its transcendent qualities it could glorify and even justify that society. What, though, if that society was rotten to the core? What if you lived in a world so misguided, flawed and terrible that it could create the unthinkable slaughter of the Somme? Any art it produced would have to be treated with contempt. Any beautiful expression that could in some way redeem the society that formed it would be unacceptable. It had to go, all of it. The sensual Art Nouveau style that had so defined the preceding decades collapsed almost overnight.

Dada was anti-art. It was negation, a creation that saw itself as destruction. Its very nature makes it seem impossible to define or pin down, but its echoes can be heard throughout the twentieth century in movements such as Situationism, Discordianism and punk. The word itself oscillates between being a verb and a noun, between having meaning and no meaning, between being an established movement of many years' standing to being a spent force the moment the Cabaret Voltaire closed. It cloaks itself in gnomic pronouncements that make it appear more of a disembodied conscious presence than an art style. 'Before there was Dada, Dada was there . . .' the painter and sculpture Hans Arp, one of the founders of Dada, has said. This is usually about as clear as it gets.

The more you look at the Dadaists' attempts to define Dada, the more you are reminded of Daoists' attempts to define the concept of the Dao. The Dao is the central concept in ancient Chinese thought, usually translated as the 'way' or the 'path'. It also oscillates between being a verb and a noun, between having meaning and having no meaning. *The Dao De Jing*, the Daoist central text, begins by declaring that the Dao that can be named is not the Dao. As first lines go, this can throw the reader a little. What it means by this is that the Dao is everything and, because a name or definition is a small part of everything, that name therefore cannot be the thing itself. The all cannot be accurately defined, as any definition is limiting. Dao is, by definition, beyond definition, beyond 'is' and 'is not'.

When Arp said, 'Before there was Dada, Dada was there', he echoed *The Dao De Jing* which states that the Dao is all heaven and earth, and that the Dao existed before heaven and earth. In light of these comparisons, the Dadaists' attempts to describe Dada appear as if they are describing something fundamentally similar to the Dao. This may initially appear counter-intuitive, of course, because the Dao is associated with peaceful acceptance whereas Dada is violent negation. But Dada emerged during the First World War. The Dao, at that point, would also have been violent negation.

One point that many commentators make about Dada is that, while its intention is to destroy or negate, it is still the product of the very thing that it is fighting against. It is a creation of the society that it rejects, and can only exist alongside that society. In the words of Greil Marcus, 'Dada was a protest against its time; it was also the bird on the rhinoceros, peeping and chirping, but along for the ride.' Marcus also discusses the philosopher Henri Lefebvre, '. . . an old man, whose life's work had been the investigation of "modernity," he said so queerly that what was truly modern about modernity, what was actually new, what was really interesting, was not its works – technology, abundance, the welfare state, mass communication, and so on – but the peculiar character of the opposition modernity created against itself: an opposition he still called "Dada."'

A Daoist would be amused by Lefebvre's observation, for a thing to carry its own opposition is anything but modern. This is one of their most fundamental principles and it is depicted in the best-known Daoist symbol, the Yin-Yang. This icon shows a circle, half white and half black and seemingly rotating as if the black and white elements were continually replacing each other. This constant flow between opposites is, in Daoist thought, the fundamental nature of the world. In the centre of the black there is a white dot, and in the centre of the white there is a black dot. This symbolises that each state carries the seed of its opposite – that the Yin always contains the birth of the Yang that replaces it, and vice versa, just as Robert Anton Wilson's Illuminati carried the seed of the Discordians and the music industry gave birth to The Justified Ancients of Mu Mu. Mathematicians also recognised this truth, once they gained a grasp of the nature of chaos. Whenever they looked inside chaos, they found order, and wherever they looked closely at order they found it to be riddled with chaos.

Dada can be thought of as a form of Dark Dao, a path that was as sick and feverish as the era that formed it. Dao is an ungraspable concept that contains both the very nature of the world and also the way the world will unfurl. In this context it is no wonder that Dadaists could not define what they had done, as Dao both contains and is more than any single definition. In this liminal period, in this time between eras as the old ways destroyed themselves and before the new order emerged, there was only this fundamental nature of the world remaining, an unnameable Dao that could only be implied by the meaningless noise 'dada'.

The subsequent shift of eras during the early 1990s was a mirror opposite, a small, quiet death that has almost disappeared from history. It was here that The K Foundation, with their meaningless name, performed the act that they could never explain or get over. How different, then, was the fundamental nature of their act of destruction? How close to the underlying nature of the world were they working? The undercurrents that were so briefly visible in the gap between two eras were still exposed. And because the money was burnt in this liminal space between two waves of history, the meaning of the act was not absorbed or dissipated by either of them. The timing, in other words, was perfect. The subconscious was fully exposed when the deed was done.*

---

* I like the ending. It's nice and ominous. I doubt all the long-winded discourse in this chapter amounts to anything more than the poetic conceit it builds to. But that's fine. A good poetic conceit is always worth having. Still, that was an odd time in the book to throw in a chapter that had nothing at all to do with the KLF story. For all that it set the scene, it didn't advance the narrative. Having the wisdom to put aside material you are excited by for another day is a tricky discipline to master when you start out as a writer, I fear.

13

Foundations

'**A**bandon All Art Now,' proclaimed the adverts in the broadsheet press, 'Major rethink in progress. Await further announcements.' It was August 1993, more than a year since the end of The KLF. The adverts were placed by Drummond and Cauty's latest alias, The K Foundation. After they stopped making music, Drummond and Cauty formed an art foundation.*

This in itself is unusual. There is no precedent for

---

* I wish I had included in this chapter, for balance, some advice Julian Cope once gave about the art world. I can't remember now where he said this, but in my memory it was written all in capitals. His advice was this: NEV-ER FALL FOR THE ART TRIP. There may have been an exclamation mark. This sentiment is something I've been thinking about quite a lot recently.

musicians working together in a non-music-related capacity after their band has split up. At best, you can point to members of bands who have later married. Cauty and Drummond's continued working relationship may even be unique in musical history.* It suggests that their work was not actually about music, and that the music was a means to an end rather than the ultimate goal of their partnership. Even when the music stopped, the work continued.

In general, the art world took a dim view of The K Foundation. Their activities began shortly after The KLF split, when a series of adverts was placed in the press complete with *Illuminatus!*-style pyramid symbols and cryptic slogans such as 'Time Is Running In' or 'Divide and Kreate'. They were initially concerned with the nature of time, and promised a move away from our current understanding of time into a more 'eternal' state.† These adverts have been described as being Situationist-inspired, but The K Foundation were not *détourning* existing advertisements.

---

* Ten years later and I'm still unaware of any other comparable examples. I think this might be because, although there are artistic collaborators who include music in their work, that music never resonates with a sizeable audience in the way that Bill and Jimmy's music did. It takes a lot of focus and hard work for music, and indeed all forms of creative expression, to go from being 'good enough' to becoming something that people genuinely care about and remember.

† These initial K Foundation statements are often overlooked and usually overshadowed by what was to follow, but they are another example of how upfront the pair were about being focused on transcendence.

They were paying many thousands of pounds to create new advertisements. They may not have been advertising anything other than themselves, but it was a noticeably different approach from the one the Situationists took.

The 'Abandon All Art Now' advert of August 1993 was the first that concerned itself with the subject of art rather than time. It was followed two weeks later by another, which read, 'It has come to our attention that you did not abandon all art now. Further direct action is thus necessary.' They went on to announce a shortlist of four artists for their 'worst artist of the year prize', whose work would be exhibited at the Tate. As that shortlist was the same as that year's Turner Prize, which was the reason for their work appearing at the Tate, this was first assumed to be nothing more than a joke.

It soon became apparent that this was not the end of it. The K Foundation prize was £40,000, exactly twice that awarded to the winner of the Turner Prize. On the day of the Turner award, 23 November, they bought TV advertisements around the broadcast of the ceremony on Channel 4. They announced that their 'winner' was the artist Rachel Whiteread, seemingly before it was announced that Whiteread had also won the Turner Prize. Their forty-grand prize was nailed to a board and chained to the railings outside the Tate. Whiteread refused to come and collect it, and was informed that if she didn't claim it by 11 p.m. it would be burnt.

Eleven o'clock arrived and Whiteread still hadn't shown. The money was doused in petrol. Gimpo fumbled with the matches. It was just about to be torched when Whiteread appeared, deeply irritated, and said that she would donate the money to young artists.

If she had not turned up, Drummond and Cauty's futures might have been very different. Burning money on the steps of the Tate would have had a far greater impact on the art world than anything else the pair had planned, and the later burning of the million pounds would probably never have happened. As it was, their actions produced a lot of comment and discussion, but also a deeper sense of annoyance and dismissal.

The art world assumed an air of polite remove from the activities of The K Foundation from then on, and it soon became apparent that no suitable gallery was going to host their inaugural exhibition. This was called *Money: A Major Body of Cash*, and it largely consisted of what money the pair still had from The KLF years nailed to things. The key piece was called *Nailed To The Wall*, and consisted of a million pounds in fifty-pound notes nailed to a board. The reserve price for this was going to be half a million pounds. The purchaser could therefore double their money by simply taking it apart. If they hung it on the wall the value of the notes would decrease over time, but the value of the art might increase. The exhibition, then, raised many thorny issues about the relationship between art and money. Or at least it would have done if a gallery had been found to put it on.

The art world is a very different place from the music industry. It is considerably less sure of itself. The music industry knows that the power of a perfect song is universal and that there is no way to deny it. This is why, as previously noted, it can absorb any attack. The art world is on far shakier ground. To generalise, the validity of the products of the art world is often much easier to deny. The importance of the strange magical glamours of context and reputation are paramount, for it is only with *context* and *reputation* that careers are built. The attack on the Turner Prize came dangerously close to damaging these vital spells with an 'Emperor's New Clothes' moment, so the art world had no choice but to close ranks and keep them out.*

A crucial tool in this respect is the art world's ability to declare who is or is not an artist. In their view, The K Foundation were not artists. As a gallery owner put it in the BBC documentary about the burning, 'I just don't think you can want to be an artist, you're either an artist or you're not an artist.' The remains of the burnt money,

---

* One factor in this is what I think of as the 'art defence'. It is not unusual for otherwise worthless work, which only engages people on the most superficial level, to be defended on the grounds that it is 'art'. Here 'art' is agreed to be something powerful and of deep importance to the human condition, so it follows that if it's 'art', then it's important. Unengaging books, films or albums, in contrast, are not excused on the grounds that literature, cinema or music are important. No bored audience would be fooled by that trick. This art defence is one of the reasons why the need to police what is or isn't art is of great importance to the industry. It is also why the current state of AI-generated images, which is going to be a real challenge to working painters and illustrators, may be less of a threat to the art world's powers that be.

in this context, 'would have been art – if they had been made by an artist'. To be accepted as an artist, it is usual to be young, dedicated and fresh from a good art school. It is not acceptable to have done a different job and become an artist later in life. True, galleries can usually be found to put on exhibitions by 'dabbling' musicians, but the art world sees these much the same way as the music world sees novelty singles. They're not what it's about, basically, and while they can be a bit of fun and can bring in useful foot traffic to a gallery, they are not worth risking context or reputation over.

Lacking a gallery or art world acceptance, The K Foundation did what they could. They exhibited the work to the press in a field near Heston Service Station, while armoured cars painted orange drove around blasting out ABBA's 'Money, Money, Money'. But lacking a gallery called for a rethink, and that rethink led to the decision to simply take the million pounds and burn it.

That was how this was always going to end, wasn't it? From the first KLF record 'Burn The Bastards' onwards, it was always going to end in flames.

There was some thought about staging this burning at a gallery but that was quickly dismissed. If it was done at a gallery, people would look at it as art. It might be bad art or good art, but it would definitely be art. And that felt wrong, somehow, even to an art foundation. That wasn't what this was about.

*

Was it Art? That was the key question on the adverts to promote screenings of *Watch The K Foundation Burn A Million Quid*. The K Foundation was, after all, an art foundation. Cauty and Drummond may not have been actively working in the art world after The KLF, but they were certainly hectoring and bothering it from the side-lines. Even for those who felt that what they did didn't cut it as art, it still appeared that they were *trying* to make art.

The question 'was it art?' is complicated by the general lack of agreement about what 'art' actually is.

It is interesting to remember what Charles Shaar Murray wrote when he reviewed Drummond's book *45* for the *Independent*. 'Drummond is many things, and one of those things is a magician. Many of his schemes [. . .] involve symbolically-weighted acts conducted away from the public gaze and documented only by Drummond himself and his participating comrades. Nevertheless, they are intended to have an effect on a world of people unaware that the act in question has taken place. That is magical thinking. Art is magic, and so is pop. Bill Drummond is a cultural magician . . .'

'Art is magic . . .' This is also a quote from *Illuminatus!*, as those are words used by a Discordian called Mavis in the first volume of the book. It is Alan Moore's view as well. He does not mean this as a vague generalisation or a touchy-feely feel-good slogan. He means it literally. Magic is not a science and it is not a religion, despite the efforts of people to define it as such. Magic is art – or the Art, if you prefer. Writing a book or painting a picture is like pulling a rabbit out of a hat – you are producing something out of nothing. A thing now exists in the world that was not there before.

Viewed in this context, the history of magic suddenly starts to make a lot more sense. A grimoire was a grammar. A spell is to spell. In the beginning was the Word. The trappings of magic can be read equally as the trappings of the creative spirit. Song, dance, performance, recitals, music and pantomime can all be seen to have their roots in the magical practices of tribal shamen. Opera itself was the creation of alchemical thinking, an art form that included all other art forms within it.

After all, what is magic for, exactly? It doesn't produce any useful scientific discoveries. For all its talk of great power, those who dedicate their lives to it have a notable tendency to end up alone and in dire poverty. On the other hand, there is an abundance of great art that has been produced by those with magical interests, be they Mozart, Yeats, Blake, Dalí, Elgar or Mondrian.

As everyone from magicians like Moore to the most rational scientist will tell you, magic is only in the mind. But the mind is also the realm of art – it's the role of art to explore and illuminate and express this very territory. In Moore's view, re-establishing and clarifying the association between art and magic would be beneficial in two main aspects. Firstly, it would give the practice of magic a purpose. And, secondly, it would give the art world a shot in the arm and produce art of greater wonder and illumination than the half-arsed fumblings it has been content with of late.*

The question 'Is it art?', then, should more meaningfully be looked as 'Is it magic?'. And in this respect, Moore was very clear. The answer was 'yes'. The money burning 'was a powerful magical event,' he said. 'I can't see any other explanation for it. You're dealing with a form of language, a conversation – but you're not sure what the conversation is . . . you're waiting for a reply.'

The negation of the money, in this context, can be seen as a sacrifice. A sacrifice is a statement of intent. It serves to focus the mind and the more valuable the object sacrificed is, the greater the focus. You are offering up something of worth in the hope of receiving or achieving something different.†

Of all the unsettling questions you can wrestle with, the question of what modern money actually is is a real humdinger. We know money is a token of value that can be used as a medium of exchange, but that tells us what money does, not what it is.

Modern money is no longer a representation of some

---

* Those interested in this argument are advised to read Alan Moore's essay 'Fossil Angels', which Google will find for you.

† Modern-day money burners, such as Jon Harris and the Church of Burn, point out that money burning is the only moral form of sacrifice. If you choose to sacrifice a goat, for example, then that's hardly fair on the goat. If you burn the notes in your wallet, on the other hand, then the only person to suffer is the one doing the sacrifice.

physical value such as an amount of gold or silver. Some of it has a physical form, such as pieces of paper or small, round pieces of metal, but the vast majority does not. Most of the money supply is virtual, existing only as a pattern of bits inside a computer. Our money system is known as 'fiat money', which means that it is created out of thin air. But if money is created out of nothing, then how can it have value?

To answer that, it is more useful to look at Alan Moore's definition of magic than to study economics textbooks. Money is a perfect example of something that doesn't exist, but acts as if it does. Money has value only because we say it has. This is an agreed illusion shared by people and governments alike, and surrounded by institutions and laws in the same way that theology surrounds a central idea in one of Robert Anton Wilson's self-justifying reality tunnels. It is an extremely useful belief, which is why it endures. Believing in the value of money is necessary for almost all our modern society and culture. Nevertheless, there isn't anything underpinning the value of our money system other than the fact that the other guy believes in it, too.

Money is also designed to move. It does not matter to what ends the movement of money is used, for there is no inherent morality to the system. The only important factor is that it keeps sloshing around, being used and reused. From the point of view of money there is only one perversion, which is to permanently remove money from circulation.

The reason for this goes to the very core of the financial economy, and the practice of charging interest. Today, all money is loaned into existence. A central bank will only physically create money, in other words, if some individual or organisation has asked to borrow it. If you take out a mortgage for a house from a bank, it is your signature on the deeds that creates that money out of thin air. The bank will then loan you the money, and charge a small percentage – the interest rate – for its efforts.

This system is so widely accepted that it sounds perfectly normal, but it does raise the question of where the money to pay the interest charge comes from.

This is best illustrated with an example. Imagine that a new bank opens in a new country, and imagine that it produces a currency that we'll call shillings. Now imagine that this bank then attracts ten customers, all of whom wish to borrow ten shillings. The bank charges interest at 10 per cent, so that everyone has to return eleven shillings to the bank. But how can these ten people all return eleven shillings when they not only do not have that amount, but there aren't enough shillings in existence? The debtors will have to find a way to get the extra money from each other. Competition, therefore, suddenly becomes necessary. Should one debtor have all his money taken from him by the rest, then nine people will be able to return the eleven shillings to the bank, while the losing debtor will have no option but to borrow more money from the bank. More money is thus created, and the economy grows.

It was not always like this. For most of history such a

system was utterly forbidden. The word 'usury' is now used to mean the charging of excessive interest for loans, but the original use of the word meant making any charge at all for lending money. Writing developed after money, so it is not possible to know how far back into history this taboo goes, or why our Bronze Age ancestors were so set against the idea. What we do know is that the earliest recorded laws explicitly forbid usury. In the New Testament, when Jesus overturned the tables at the temple, his anger grew from the fact that the moneylenders were engaging in usury. Jesus, it is generally accepted, was a pretty non-violent type of guy, so when you note how all the other sins, cruelties and injustices of the world failed to tip him over into anger you get a glimpse at just how taboo usury was. Others who denounced usury include Plato, Moses, the Prophet Muhammad, Aristotle and Buddha. When a line-up like that is in agreement, it is perhaps worth thinking twice about our acceptance of it.

Why was making money from financial loans so unacceptable in the ancient world? This is open to interpretation, but one possibility is that it appeared to go against the natural order of things. Work created wealth, so wealth accumulating without work was unnatural. It was seen as a form of tyranny, or theft. Usury was a corruption, a financial cancer, and one that could throw economies off balance and bring them crashing down.

But if usury, in the original meaning of the word, was so taboo, how did it become acceptable and establish itself as a cornerstone of modern economics? Much of the answer to this question involves the behaviour of different religions. Usury is still forbidden under Islamic law, but a complicated system of Islamic banking was developed that does not include interest, but instead has many charges. In doing so it manages to remain true to the letter of the anti-usury law, if perhaps not the spirit. In Judaism, they took the approach that usury was only forbidden between Jews, so charging interest on loans to non-Jews was religiously acceptable. Jews were then able to travel to non-Jewish communities and act as moneylenders, a trade that brought them wealth but also a great deal of historical resentment. In Christianity, usury was banned by papal decree, but when Henry VIII split with Rome and established the Church of England in 1534, he took a different view. Henry made usury religiously acceptable, a move which some economists view as key to the Elizabethan Golden Age that followed.

Technically speaking, the charging of interest on loans is still forbidden in the Catholic Church, but in practice no one pays a blind bit of notice to this.

In *The Eye in the Pyramid*, the first volume of *The Illuminatus! Trilogy*, the character of Joseph Malick is told the history of the formation of The Justified Ancients of Mummu. The story stretches back to a time when a series of stones called The Seven Tablets of Creation were carved, around 2500 BC, at which time the chief deity was called Marduk and 'the official religion of Marduk [. . .] was based on usury. The priests monopolized the medium of exchange and were able to extract interest for lending it. They also monopolized the land, and extracted tribute for renting it. It was the beginning of what we laughingly call civilisation, which has always rested on rent and interest.'

It is at this point that The JAMs were formed. 'When the first anarchist group arose, they called themselves Justified Ancients of Mummu. Like Lao-Tse and the Daoists in China, they wanted to get rid of usury and monopoly and all the other pigshit of civilization.' Here, then, is the *raison d'être* of The JAMs. They are anarchists, representing the forces of chaos in the war against order. That order is civilisation and civilisation is based on usury, or the system of interest on loans. The Justified Ancients of Mummu, then, were formed to destroy usury.

This is not something that has been widely noted. Should you talk to even the most obsessive KLF fan, one who has gone to the lengths of reading Robert Anton Wilson's eight hundred-plus-page novel a number of times, they will probably be unaware that the destruction of usury is the reason that The Justified Ancients of Mummu were established. It is stated clearly, as the quotes above show, but the book is such a torrent of information that, unless you are looking for it, a detail like that is unlikely to stick in your mind. Nevertheless, the fact remains that the fictitious organisation The Justified Ancients of Mummu, who became a physical group when Drummond and Cauty took on their name and philosophy, exist to bring about the destruction of the usury that is at the heart of our system of money.

*

Interest is not a fundamental quality of economies. It is an idea that has been projected onto the work and wealth of the physical world. The reason our economic system incorporates concepts such as interest and usury is nothing more than historical choice. There have been eras when negative-interest economies have been tried instead, for example. In these systems, your money depreciated over time, slowly losing value. This concept is similar in practice to stockpiling grain over winter because, thanks to the action of mice and other pests, the amount of grain you had come spring would be less than you started with. Negative-interest currencies have the advantage of encouraging the use of money. Instead of hoarding it, it makes more sense to use it in a productive way, such as repairing buildings or starting businesses. Under this model the currency circulates more readily and freely, and saving is discouraged.

The reason why a positive-interest currency has been favoured is because it encourages economic growth. Indeed, it demands it, for the system would collapse if there was no growth to pay the interest charges to the bank. Bankers are very keen on economic growth because, without having to do anything else, it automatically translates into more wealth for them. For this reason, a steady-state economy is unacceptable. It may seem reasonable for a tradesman to wish to perform a regular amount of work each year, enough to pay them sufficient money to live on, but our system cannot work like that. The existence of interest charges – usury, by the original definition – requires that the economy must continually grow, which means that more work must be undertaken, year in, year out.

The belief that endless growth is natural, inevitable and possible has become universally accepted. It has done so by building around itself one of Wilson's self-referential reality tunnels to protect itself, a reality tunnel built out of laws, self-interest and economic experts. But there is a problem here, and it's a significant one. Perpetual growth is in no way possible, regardless of what economists say.

This issue is often couched in environmental terms, such as the statement that perpetual growth is not possible in a finite world of non-renewable resources. This argument was made strongly as far back as 1972 in *The Limits to Growth*, a book produced by the think tank The Club of Rome. *The Limits to Growth* has been roundly attacked over the years by politicians and economists inside the 'perpetual growth' reality tunnel, usually with arguments about the inexhaustible supply of human ingenuity and so forth.*

In fact, the basic point does not even need the environmental focus. Growth is exponential, so even small rates such as 2 or 3 per cent a year cause doubling in a generation and soon become absurd. The physicist Tom Murphy

---

* It's worth noting that recent academic analysis of this fifty-year-old work shows that its conclusions are still proving to be pretty damn accurate. Unfortunately.

has calculated that projected rates of energy growth, for example, have the Earth using the same amount of energy as the Sun in about 1,400 years, and more than the entire galaxy of 100 billion suns in 2,500 years. In human terms, 2,500 years isn't that long. We are still reading books that were written 2,500 years ago.

This, of course, is not going to happen.

For a more fundamental example of why this is, consider a particle being accelerated through space. As we know from Einstein, energy and matter are intimately linked. As the particle gains energy to move faster, its mass increases. This increase in mass means that it requires more energy to keep accelerating, which further increases its mass and further increases the amount of energy needed for it to accelerate, and so on. It is for this reason that the speed of light is fixed and finite. Photons can't accelerate indefinitely.*

Put more simply, the increase in a quantity affects the ability of the forces acting on an object to create a further increase. This simple law seems to affect everything. This is perhaps the main reason why economies can't grow indefinitely, any more than photons can go faster than the speed of light.

---

* Physics is full of examples like this, which make useful analogies when talking about how things outside the world of science work. The problem is, the moment you start using words like 'mass' and 'energy', you can feel your reader's eyes glaze over. It would have been better to have added an extra layer of metaphor in this example.

In the late twentieth century, such an argument was heresy. Global economic collapse was unthinkable. The global economy was believed to be solid, healthy and self-repairing. A magical 'invisible hand' protected the markets and ensured that they would forever continue to function. With one eye on the short term and the other on the self-referential reality tunnel that claims perpetual growth is both possible and normal, economists and politicians could see no flaws in their economic model. This was apparent in the somewhat stunned testimony of Alan Greenspan, the former chair of the Federal Reserve, when he appeared before a US House of Representatives committee to be questioned about the great economic collapse of the early twenty-first century. 'I made a mistake in presuming that the self-interests of organizations, specifically banks and others, were such that they were best capable of protecting their own shareholders and their equity in the firms,' he said. When the chair of the committee, Henry Waxman, suggested to Greenspan that 'you found that your view of the world, your ideology, was not right, it was not working?' he replied, 'Absolutely, precisely. You know, that's precisely the reason I was shocked, because I have been going for forty years or more with very considerable evidence that it was working exceptionally well.'

The absurdity of perpetual growth was unaffected by our leaders' inability to consider or discuss it. It lurked hidden, somewhere in the depths of the collective unconscious or the unexplored wild spaces of Alan Moore's Ideaspace.

Eventually, some unwary explorer would stumble too close, and actualise it.

A couple of years after The K Foundation ended, Drummond had a flash of insight. 'Most of the people who wrote about what we did, and the TV programme that was made about it, made a mistake,' he said. 'I was only able to articulate it to myself afterwards with hindsight. They thought we were using our money to make a statement about art, and really what we were doing was using our art to make a statement about money.'

This tallies with comments made by Cauty at the time. 'We nail [the money] to a bit of wood so that it can't function as it wants to. It's to do with controlling the money. Money tends to control you if you've got it, it dictates what you have to do with it, you either spend it, give it away, invest it . . . We just wanted to be in control of it.'

The K Foundation had been set up to dispose of the money that remained from the KLF days. Drummond and Cauty behaved as if this money was tainted in some way, and that it had to be disposed of in a safe, artistically pure way. The aim of The K Foundation, then, was to cleanse it. In doing so, we can surmise, they might recover the souls they had lost in the music industry.

Cauty and Drummond described The K Foundation as an 'art foundation', which led to their actions being viewed from the perspective of the art world. With hindsight, it is easy to see how they fell into this position. With The KLF over, they knew they still had work to do together but they did not have a framework with which to define what that work was. It was not music, that was clear, for those days were behind them. But if not music, then what? There is no established tradition of *tainted money cleansing and dispersal foundations*. 'Art', meanwhile, was a vague enough term with which to hide all sorts of strange behaviour. What else could they call themselves, then, but an art foundation?

And how else could they do it? They couldn't give it away or spend it, because that's what money wants. It wants to circulate. That's what gives it power. Even if you nail it to a piece of wood, someone will come along sooner or later to steal it and set it free. Physically destroying it is the only way to stop it. But before it can be stopped there first needs to be the idea that it can be stopped, and that it is not invincible. Up until then, this was largely unthinkable.

The burning of the million quid should not be seen from the perspective of art. It was never about art. It was much more than that, and much more obvious. It was about the destruction of money.

It was about the idea that money could be defeated.*

---

* On the surface, this looks like another chapter with very little to do with the story of The KLF, but for me it was more successful than the last one. The issues of art and money are clearly fundamental to the story of Bill and Jimmy and the burning, so it feels relevant. A lot of the ideas in there were interesting, too. There's a lot of stuff that should be common knowledge, but frequently isn't. It certainly helps that, ten years later, those ideas still hold up well. Yes, I enjoyed that one – good work me-in-the-past.

14

Unthinkable

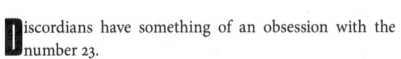

Discordians have something of an obsession with the number 23.

Robert Anton Wilson first heard about the strangeness of the number from William Burroughs. Burroughs met a sea captain named Captain Clark, in Algiers in 1960, who boasted to him that he had never had an accident in 23 years. Later that day Clark's boat sank, killing him and everyone on board. Burroughs was thinking about this and reflecting on the nature of fate when he heard a radio report about a plane crash in Florida. The plane's pilot was called Captain Clark and the plane was flight 23.

Burroughs began noting down incidents relating to the number 23, and soon Wilson was doing the same. It seemed that wherever there was a significant event, frequently linked to birth or death, the number 23 would appear. Babies get 23 chromosomes from each parent, for example. In the *I-Ching*, 23 means 'breaking apart'. The most popular psalm at funerals is Psalm 23. An unnatural number of anarchists seemed to have died on the 23rd of the month. There was nothing too unusual about any individual occurrence of the number, but the way they kept turning up was unsettling. There was a certain unnerving quality about the places in which they tended to appear. Wilson filled the *Illuminatus!* books with the 23 Enigma, as it became known. It fitted in well with a Discordian principle called the Law of Fives, because 2+3=5. The Law of Fives states that everything is related to the number five, if you look hard enough.

As an example of how the 23s mount up, and deliberately limiting ourselves only to things discussed in this book, we can make a list like the following:

Bill Drummond was 23 when he worked on the *Illuminatus!* play, which had 23 cast members. Jung's dream about Liverpool that inspired O'Halligan and Campbell was on page 223 of Carl Jung's *Memories, Dreams, Reflections* (Jung was the man who coined the word 'synchronicity'). Robert Anton Wilson's oldest daughters were born on 23 August and 23 February, and he first started hearing voices in his head on 23 July. Drummond and Cauty burnt the million pounds on 23 August 1994 (1+9+9+4 = 23). 'Doctorin' The TARDIS' was released on 23 May, the car had 23 painted on its roof and the Turner Prize incident occurred on 23 November. November the 23rd was also a Discordian holy day (being Harpo Marx's birthday), the date when Ken

Campbell's *Illuminatus!* was first performed, the date this book was first published and, in 1963, the date that *Doctor Who* was first broadcast. That first episode of *Doctor Who* was 23 minutes long and had a budget of £2,300, and it would be the disastrous 23rd series of *Doctor Who* that resulted in Ken Campbell and his protégé Sylvester McCoy auditioning for the role.

There were 23 years between 'Stand By Your Man' and 'Justified And Ancient (Stand By The JAMs)'. The devil horns hand symbol has 2 digits up and 3 clenched, while 2 divided by 3 is 0.666 recurring. The catalogue number of Drummond and Cauty's first record was JAMS23, and their rare live performances usually lasted for 23 minutes. The final KLF Communications info sheet was number 23. The video for 'It's Grim Up North' was filmed on the M23.The agreement that Drummond and Cauty signed on the Nissan Bluebird was to not discuss the burning for 23 years. The name 'Justified Ancients of Mu Mu' (as we have noted, accidentally misspelled by Cauty and Drummond from Wilson's 'Mummu') has 23 letters.

And so on.

All this is magical thinking. There is no physical link between any of the dates or incidents mentioned. The link is a mental one. A recognition that the number is somehow significant leads to a connection between unrelated occurrences of the number.

Magical thinking is also the level on which Drummond works. This has been clear from the very start, with his preoccupation with the rabbit spirit of Echo. Magical thinking is a universal practice – it is, essentially, how our brains work – but it is usually tempered with a practical materialism. What makes Drummond remarkable is that this seems to be his overriding working level, something he achieves by applying his 'liberation loophole' and accepting the contradictions. The actions of The KLF are best understood as magical thinking being manifest by punk bloody-mindedness.

If you look at the 23s associated with Drummond and Cauty, they fall into two distinct types. The first are 'genuine' occurrences, where the number spontaneously manifests itself in unexpected ways. Examples of this would include the Turner Prize being announced on 23 November, Drummond being 23 when he first read *Illuminatus!*, or the 23 you'll inevitably notice shortly after putting this book down.* The second category is 'forced' occurrences. These are a deliberate use of the number by someone who is aware of the 23 Enigma and feels drawn somehow to further it. Examples of these are the 23 painted on the roof of the cop car, or using it in a catalogue number. There is nothing mysterious or supernatural about these occurrences, but what they do reveal is a desire for synchronicities and magical events. They are a form of sympathetic magic, which acts out the synchronicity on a ritual level in the hope it will conjure up the actual thing.

---

* Thanks to everyone who has contacted me over the past decade to tell me about the 23 they noticed after they put this book down.

Drummond and Cauty did this. They did this a lot. They hammered away at it, trying to generate a response. Alan Moore said that the money burning was 'a form of language, a conversation – but you're not sure what the conversation is . . . you're waiting for a reply', and this was no different from what they had done in The KLF. They were kicking off on a magical level. They were demanding attention. From a magical perspective they were a pair of attention-seeking arseholes, demanding to get fucked.*

The 23 Enigma is the best-known aspect of Discordianism, and Cauty and Drummond used it very deliberately. As should be clear by now, the myth they wrapped around themselves was taken very blatantly from the *Illuminatus!* books. Taking the name The Justified Ancients of Mu Mu is the most obvious example of this, but there are many more. Their first album included a song called 'The Porpoise Song', after Howard the Porpoise in the books. The use of lines such as 'Kick out the jams motherfuckers', 'immanentized the Eschaton' and 'everybody lie down on the floor and keep calm' are all taken from the book.

But how well did they know Wilson's work? In his 2008 book *17*, Drummond writes about being asked to appear at an event at the Southbank Centre in London to

---

* We're heading towards the finale now, picking up pace and energy and abandoning humour, hence the appearance of spikey sentences like that. That was a blunt way to end a section, wasn't it?

commemorate Robert Anton Wilson's death the previous year. Drummond agreed after hearing that Alan Moore would also be appearing, but he was unsure about what he should do at the event. For inspiration, he decided to read *Illuminatus!*.

He claims that he had never read the whole thing before. When Campbell gave him a copy to help him design sets, he read little more than the first volume because that was where most of the play was taken from. He was not particularly impressed by what he read. He was more impressed in 1986 when he picked it up again and it inspired him to form The JAMs with Jimmy Cauty, but even then he only read as far as page 138 in a trilogy of over eight hundred pages. Cauty, although he had seen the play, had never read the book at all.

Reading the whole thing, in 2007, was something of a shock.

Because it was in there, all of it – rabbit spirits, Lucifer, submarines, the angels in the lake, even, to his horror, the burning of money. It seemed as if his life had been mapped out in this one book. It went far beyond the obvious stuff he stole from the first volume. At the time he was involved in a choir called The17, for example, but had not realised that the number 17 kept appearing in the book at the same places as the number 23.

This was a similar situation to how he learnt about the Situationists, for he only really learnt what they were about, and why his actions kept being described as Situationist, in 1995.

Seeing his own history sketched out in the book was deeply unsettling.

Rationally, you can argue that he must have seen later sections back in 1976 and, while he may have had no conscious memory of them, they could have hung around in his subconscious somehow. Those familiar with the book, however, may wonder if there is more to it than that. I had written 90 per cent of this book before I finally got round to reading *Illuminatus!* myself, despite having a copy on my shelf for twenty years. Upon reading it, I was startled to discover that it contained a number of subjects which I had already been writing about, unaware of their inclusion in *Illuminatus!* and unsure if I could justify their inclusion in this book. I had written about usury unaware that the founding reason for The JAMs was to destroy usury, and I had written about Lucifer unaware that a satanic mass was the initiation into The JAMs. I had noted the surprising number of paedophiles in this story while being unaware of the character of Padre Pederastia. Such is the way with this particular novel. Reading it almost seems superfluous; it is possible to be swept along just by the idea of it. It is a novel that is content to sit on a shelf for decades and wait for you to be ready for it.

When The K Foundation were burning their money, Alan Moore was at work in Northampton finishing his version of the Jack the Ripper myth, *From Hell.* Moore's Ripper, the insane royal surgeon Sir William

Gull, viewed his Whitechapel murders as a magical act. He, like Drummond and Cauty, had no sense of exactly what he was doing. It didn't matter to him. He was just aware of how powerful his actions were, and how deeply they would affect the world. Moore's Ripper, of course, is a fictional creation. While he may not have known the reasons for his actions, his creator had a very clear idea.

In *From Hell*, Moore claimed that the Ripper murders were a magical act that gave birth to the twentieth century itself – a century with all the horror and violence of the world wars, but also a century of fame and celebrity. And, indeed, in this Moore may have a point – the public fascination with the Ripper murders was such that it is frequently claimed to have started our current tabloid culture. It is plausible to view the Ripper murders as a microcosm of the brutal century that followed.

There have been many serial killers since then. The deliberate killing of five poor women by one individual now would not have the impact it had then, in that it would not be remembered or talked about more than a hundred years later. Recent UK serial killers with a similar number of victims include Stephen Akinmurele, Kenneth Erskine and Steve Wright, and their names or crimes are not generally remembered by the public. But back in 1888, it was an extraordinarily powerful and shocking series of events. It negated everything that was accepted about what Victorian culture was capable of creating. Now, it would be a depressingly familiar item on the news, but one forgotten in weeks. Our children calmly channel-hop past descriptions of events on the news that would make the people of earlier ages faint.

What, in the modern age, would be equally unthinkable? Not horrible or evil or sick, but unthinkable?

What, other than the negation of money? Not manipulating the symbols of money, but actually negating money itself. Making money itself cease to exist is, if viewed as a sacrificial offering in the modern age, an extraordinarily potent act.

We have a choice now. We can either look at these events rationally, or use magical thinking.*

If we look at these events using magical thinking, and in particular the style of magical thinking that we've borrowed from Alan Moore, then a story emerges. It goes like this:

Once upon a time, in the late 1950s, Greg Hill and Kerry Thornley had a conversation in a California bowling alley. From that conversation, the idea of Eris, the Goddess of Chaos, arrived in the twentieth century.

The idea of Eris led to the creation of the religion of

---

* Ah, here we go. We're building towards the 'reader's choice' bit. If memory serves, I was very pleased with this. It's rare for a book to offer the reader a choice. I think a lot of readers have been a bit shocked by this – they had been assuming they were a passive observer along for the ride and were quite unprepared to have their views included in this way.

Discordianism, and to the mass disinformation campaign known as Operation Mindfuck.

The spirit of Eris entered a trilogy of books called *Illuminatus!*, and via a play based on those books it reached Bill Drummond.

Bill Drummond was particularly receptive. He did not have a detailed conscious understanding of Eris or Discordianism, but that doesn't matter. What was more important was that not only were Drummond's actions dominated by thinking on a magical level, but that Ken Campbell had taught him that the trick of doing the impossible was just to go ahead and do it.

Drummond's magical thinking was dominated by a pure, unarguable love of pop music. This turned him towards the music industry, even though it was always the power of music, the effect it had on people, which interested him more than the making of music itself.

The corporate music industry was perhaps no place for someone like Drummond, but it did allow him to meet Jimmy Cauty. Drummond and Cauty understood each other, even if nobody else understood them. Cauty was more deeply involved in the actual creation of music than Drummond was. He was also someone you could rely on to get things done. The pairing was a positive feedback loop. With each justifying the other, they would go far further together than they would apart. Sometimes all you need is for someone to see what you are planning and not look bemused.

At this point the spirit of Eris offered the pair a direction.

Drummond and Cauty took on the name and objectives of The Justified Ancients of Mummu. True, they weren't aware of what those objectives are. They were distracted by the throwaway line which linked The JAMs to the music industry to the extent that they missed their founding principle, namely the destruction of order by an attack on the very heart of the economic system.

The Justified Ancients of Mu Mu launched a suicide attack on the music industry. They were defeated by the forces of order and control, in the form of ABBA's lawyers. This defeat led to a bonfire of vinyl in a Scandinavian field.

The KLF rose from the ashes of the bonfire, with their first record, 'Burn The Bastards', being a direct reference to the incident. This act of burning became a constant thread in The KLF, from the wicker man on Jura to the Viking longboat that failed to reach Mu.

News of the Scandinavian bonfire reached the Discordian heartland of Northern California. The disciples of Eris responded by spreading confusion and paranoia to Drummond and Cauty through the tried and tested means of Operation Mindfuck. Cauty and Drummond started to become nicely unbalanced.

Open as they were to non-material influences, Drummond and Cauty provided a life-saving service to the fictional character of *Doctor Who*. They had no knowledge of this, of course. In return they received the freedom of money and the taste of success. Clearly, this could be a double-edged sword. To their credit, they did not fall for the glamour of money and pissed it away on a road movie, as suggested by the followers of Eris. They were 'True To The Trail'. Although they did not know that The JAMs' original aim was to attack our current money system, their actions here revealed themselves to be remarkably suited to that task. They had not been seduced by the bullshit glamour of wealth. If the thought of Eris, hidden away in Moore's Ideaspace, could be pleased, then Eris was pleased.

The KLF got serious. They entered the belly of the beast. Drummond and Cauty collided with the music industry. It was hardly a fair fight. They lost their souls. They gained a large amount of money.

Drummond and Cauty would much rather have had their souls than a large amount of money.

Regaining your soul from the Devil is supposed to be impossible, but Ken Campbell had taught them how you do the impossible. You take the first step. Then you take the second, and you don't stop until you've done it.

They stopped being The KLF. They did all they could to remove themselves from music history.

That just left a pile of money. That, too, was part of The KLF and if they wanted their souls back, it would have to go. But money is tricky. Spending it or giving it away wouldn't destroy it. Rather, that would allow it to escape. How could it be destroyed? There was no precedent for such an act. There was no precedent for such a thought. That money might not be invulnerable was unthinkable. To defeat it was impossible.

Nevertheless, that is what they did. They took it to a

boathouse on Jura in the liminal period between eras and torched it. The money burnt, like it was nothing more than pieces of paper.

Whatever quality it had that made it more than paper was also burnt.

Did this save Cauty and Drummond's souls? That is really a question for them, but between you and me the answer is yes, it did.

Did it achieve the aims of The Justified Ancients of Mummu, to destroy the usury-based money system? On a magical, rather than a practical, level it was the toppling of the first domino. The idea that the economy was not invulnerable was established in Ideaspace.

Drummond and Cauty had done well. They had now finished what they set out to do and could remove the name Justified Ancients of Mu Mu from their shoulders and retire with honour.

A new era began, the age of networks, and the dotcom world it created immediately announced its arrival by creating a massive economic bubble. Thus, the guiding narrative of this era was declared. The global economic collapse began in earnest in 2008. It was always going to, because continuous economic expansion is not possible. And it is still in the process of collapsing, in no way pre-pared for the energy crisis and the climate crisis that are gathering speed. When Drummond and Cauty started work, the idea of such a collapse was unthinkable in our culture. It resided in the darkest corner of human thought, unvisited and ignored. It needed to come to light. It needed to be actualised. And, in its purest form, that is what Cauty and Drummond did.

They may have intended to save their souls from the Devil of the music industry. They may have been in the process of a mental breakdown and making a last cry for help. They may have been attention-seeking arseholes after all. But, in burning a million pounds, Drummond and Cauty performed the magical act which set the scene for a global economic collapse and, in doing so, created the twenty-first century.*

---

* How does this notion sound ten years later? It was written in the aftermath of the 2008 crash, which made it then seem a little more plausible than it might otherwise have done. Returning to it in 2022, it does seem disturbingly prescient, especially with the reference to the energy crisis and the climate crisis. For the past forty years our economic system has been tweaked and shaped so that people go to work and create wealth, but that wealth doesn't go to those who did the work. It goes instead to those who own stuff, such as landlords, shareholders and landowners. For journalists and politicians, their career depends on not saying this out loud, and pretending that more of the same will sort our problems out. Since the book was written, we've had the rise and normalisation of food banks and the 'working poor'. We've had the inflating and bursting of cryptocurrency bubbles, in which the notion of value is completely detached from the physical world. We're not yet at the stage where billionaires or even landlords are being attacked in the street, but who is confident that this isn't coming, sooner or later? The notion that Bill and Jimmy heralded all this is, of course, just a poetic conceit. The challenge of writing the book was to move the reader from a position where the idea would have sounded absurd, to one where they are really not sure. In the last ten years, I think, that idea of coming economic collapse has become more disturbing and troubling. I suspect that this is one reason why the book is still being read and talked about, while 99.9 per cent of books have been forgotten a decade after release.

That, then, is our story for those who are prepared to entertain magical thinking. If you liked this explanation, and found the narrative in this book satisfying, you should skip to page 277 and continue by reading the epilogue.

If you are unwilling to entertain magical thinking, or found this narrative unsatisfying, you should continue with this chapter.*

---

* When this book first appeared, as a self-published eBook, this bit was presented as a 'choose your own adventure'-style multiple-choice question. The reader physically had to decide which option to click in order to proceed. I heard from people who stared at this page for hours, trying to work out exactly what it was they thought. This book was written because eBooks and the Amazon Kindle Store had just been launched, which gave me a way to reach an audience, so it felt natural to play around with that new medium. EBooks are basically html, so it was not hard to do. That version of the eBook is still the one available outside the UK – the one with the red cover. The choice doesn't work quite so well in a physical book, alas, because it is apparent that the 'magical thinking' option is just skipping a chunk of the book, which the reader has paid to read. The new UK eBook is a straight port of the paperback, so it also doesn't force you to make a decision and click on one of two options. If my memory is

That was the story for those who allow themselves the luxury of magical thinking. It is tempting to do so, for our minds work that way and completely denying the irrational is very diffcult. Concepts as diverse as marriage, the monarchy or the Olympic torch can only be understood in this light, and training your brain not to use magical thinking is both extremely difficult and no fun at all. The fact that our thoughts and the world of matter operate under completely different rules is basically something that we have to put up with.

If we stay rational, however, the idea that Drummond and Cauty performed a magical act that kindled the modern world is total bullshit.

That idea, rather than a 'truth', is the central tenet of the self-referential reality tunnel created by this book, and the rest of this narrative exists to support, protect and justify it.

From the rational perspective, there is no material connection between the events in the Jura boathouse and the larger changes in the world, and this lack of causality means that anyone who suggests otherwise is the worst kind of fool. Even exploring the idea for entertainment's sake is suspect these days. From the rational materialist perspective, all we can really say about the money burning is that it occurred because Cauty and Drummond are a

---

right, this was because to do so would be 'a bit tricky'. I would love to play around more with multiple-choice, non-linear narratives like this. Maybe one day!

pair of attention-seeking arseholes, and note that the path of chaos is always going to lead to a meaningless ending.

This divide between the rational and the irrational exposes something of a fault line in our current culture wars, and with good reason. As we have seen, the mind essentially runs on a form of magical thinking which processes things in a manner unlike the way in which the material world behaves. Concepts such as time, space, connection and energy work in fundamentally different ways in the mental and physical realms. This has been something of a sore point for philosophers over the centuries. Much effort has been expended by people trying to convince themselves that, because only one of these contradictory models can be valid, the other is invalid. Rationalists have attempted to train their minds to work in a whole new way, one that permits as little magical thinking as possible. Others have claimed that the material world is basically a plaything of God and only behaves as it does because that is the sort of thing he is into.

Alan Moore has a nice little dodge to avoid this problem. He claims that magic is not real, if we define 'real' as meaning something that unarguably exists in time and space. Magic, he points out, only exists in the mind. But this does not mean that it cannot explain the larger world, for there is an established tradition of things which are best explained with things that don't exist.

The mathematical concept of imaginary numbers is a useful example here. As the laws of maths make explicit, imaginary numbers not only don't exist, they can't exist.

The basic imaginary number, known as *i*, is defined as the square root of minus one. This cannot exist because there is no possible number, minus or positive, which will produce a minus answer when multiplied by itself. Regardless, mathematicians in the eighteenth century played around with imaginary numbers for the fun of it and found them to be surprisingly useful. Over time their properties became understood and they became an important tool for engineers. Our understanding of phenomena such as radio waves or electricity is reliant on them.

This is not to say that electricity behaves as it does because of something that doesn't exist. Rather, it says that our most practical and useful models for understanding electricity rely on something that doesn't exist. Likewise magic (or art, if you prefer) doesn't exist but, then again, it doesn't need to. In a narrative driven by people who practise magical thinking, magical thinking is a tool for following that story.

This still leaves us stuck with a question, though – which is the best model by which to view these events, the magical thinking perspective which offers a descent into nonsense or a rational perspective which shrugs and gives up? For an answer to this we will return to Robert Anton Wilson, and plunge back into the heart of Discordianism. For such a Discordian-influenced story, it is fitting that we should make sense of it using Old Bob's eyes.

*

Many people have been asked to explain quantum physics over the years, but Robert Anton Wilson had perhaps the best answer. He described how, after he left LA, he moved into a little apartment in Santa Cruz. After something was stolen from his car he called the police, and they told him that he didn't live in Santa Cruz after all, but in a place called Capitola. The post office disagreed, and assured him that he did live in Santa Cruz. Wilson then spoke to a reporter on the local paper to see if he could shed any light on this, and the reporter explained that he did not live in either Santa Cruz or Capitola, but in an unincorporated area known as Live Oak.

Wilson was delighted to discover that he lived in three different places at the same time. His apartment didn't move, of course. What happened was that different authorities had drawn different lines on their maps. Each authority had a system that worked well enough for their own purposes, so they had no reason to change it. The problem with quantum physics, Wilson argued, is that many people fail to realise that it is we who draw the lines on the map. 'It seems hard to understand how a particle can be in three places at the same time without being anywhere at all,' he said, 'but when you remember that we invented all the boundaries [. . .], then quantum mechanics is no more mysterious than the fact that I live in three places at the same time.'

Hence we have experiments that show that light travels as a wave, and we have experiments that show that light travels as a particle. This strange dual nature of light, where it behaves as a wave when treated as a wave but like a particle when treated as a particle, baffled many of our greatest physicists for many years. Wilson's point is that both the 'wave model' and the 'particle model' are our own inventions, the lines that we have drawn on the map. Both models are elegant and useful, but they are not light itself. Light is not affected by our attempts to understand it. Like Wilson's apartment, it remains its own thing, removed from the models we use.

This recognition, that we habitually confuse our models with what they describe, is central to Wilson's thinking. Instinctively, we feel it is possible to know the nature of things themselves, so there is a natural resistance to accepting that we can only know our models. Wilson's work was dedicated to wearing down that resistance. His philosophy was one of *multiple-model agnosticism* – not simply agnosticism about the existence of God, but agnosticism about everything. With *multiple-model agnosticism* there is no point getting hung up on the models themselves, because that's all they are – models. Models are by definition smaller and simpler facsimiles of whatever it is that they are trying to describe. The models are not 'true', but they do vary in usefulness depending on how accurate they are in different cultures and circumstances. Once this is recognised, we no longer attach our sense of personal identity to the models we use, and we lose our resistance to swapping between different models when necessary.

Personally identifying with models that we don't realise are models is the cause of much discord. An obvious example of this is the furious arguments that erupt on the internet between people who, although they don't realise it, are largely in agreement. These nasty, vitriolic clashes occur between people who both agree that people should try to be nice to each other, that the economy is important, that freedom is a good thing and that family should be protected. What is happening is that both sides in the argument are using different models (typically, different political models) and that those models are clashing in much the same way that the particle and wave models of light clash. These internet ranters fail to realise that they are confusing their models with the actuality, or that their arguments are about their models, not about the thing-in-itself. No true communication can occur in such instances. As Wilson wrote in *Illuminatus!*, 'You cannot understand a man's actions unless you understand his beliefs.'

The twentieth century was a continuous retreat from the notions of certainty and absolute truth. Einstein, Joyce, Heisenberg, Jung, Edward Lorenz, Timothy Leary and Kurt Gödel repeatedly demonstrated that what had once been ordered was actually uncertain and what had once been true was really only true from a particular point of view. Our culture made a brave stab at absorbing this new perspective but its response – postmodernism – left a lot to be desired. Postmodernism was the collision of unrelated forms, all of which were given equal validity. This, clearly, was something of a dead end. Postmodern theorists may have convinced themselves that the statement 'the sun will rise tomorrow' was as valid as the statement 'the sun will not rise tomorrow', but they would have bankrupted themselves trying to prove it to a bookmaker.*

The result was a retreat away from postmodernism and a return to models that promised certainty. This, unfortunately, ignored what we learnt in the twentieth century and the reasons why these certainties had been discredited in the first place. The resulting cultural battleground forced people even deeper into their self-referential reality tunnels, and those who believed in one great self-evident truth were forced into long, bitter warfare with others who favoured a slightly different great self-evident truth.

This is a great shame, because there was another option. The other option was Wilson's multiple-model agnosticism, where neither 'the sun will rise tomorrow' nor 'the sun will not rise tomorrow' would be confused with reality, the thing-in-itself, but both would be seen as models that could be assessed to see which was preferable in the current situation. In this example, the 'sun will rise tomorrow' model appears to be pretty useful, while the alternative appears to be rubbish and should probably be put into storage. This is the reason why I earlier described Wilson's decision to adopt a 'giant invisible rabbit' model to explain why he was hearing voices in his head as 'one of the most important philosophical leaps of the twentieth century, if, admittedly, it is not yet generally recognised as such'.

---

* That description of postmodernism is essentially how it is portrayed by its enemies. Postmodernists would be shaking their heads at that. Let's hope they chose the 'magical thinking' option and skipped this bit.

Multiple-model agnosticism, then, is a way out of postmodernism which doesn't lead to the belief that, out of all the billions of people in the world, you are the only one who really gets it and everyone else is an idiot. The problem is, however, that our models are too damned convincing, and it is a struggle to remember that they are models and not reality. Hence much of the work of the Discordians – bar the stuff included purely for shits and giggles – is aimed at shocking people into realising the extent to which they confuse their models with the actuality. The 23 Enigma is a good case in point. Wilson was basically training his readers to notice 23s everywhere and, as any Discordian will tell you, he did this very well indeed. There is nothing special about the number in itself. It is the fact that it has been singled out and had meaning applied to it, and that Discordians have been trained to recognise it, which is significant. Had it been the number 47, or 18, or 65, the effect would have been the same. Indeed, in his later years Wilson admitted that it would have been much better if he had trained his readers to spot quarters on the ground instead of number 23s.

Of course, multiple-model agnosticism also allows you to consider the model which states that the above paragraph is mistaken, and that the number 23 is significant. Many Discordians have explored this model at length. As I understand it, that model doesn't lead to anywhere pleasant, but the curious are encouraged to explore it for themselves to see if that's true.

The reason the 23 Enigma is useful is because it

demonstrates the amount of information that our models filter out. In actuality, the coincidental and synchronistic appearances of the number 23 are matched by coincidental and synchronistic appearances of every other number, even though our models fail to react to these. They are just models, after all, and models are significantly less detailed than what they represent. Reality itself is ablaze with infinite connections: every particle in the cosmos affects every other particle. It's Too Much, it really is, and seeing reality in all its innate finery would be so overpowering that you'd be in no state to nip down to the shops when you need a pint of milk.

Understanding just how simplified and restrictive our personal models are is a useful tool to prevent you from confusing them with reality. A narrative, such as the one presented in this book, is a perfect example of this. From the near-infinite set of data points that were created by Cauty and Drummond's activities, one particular path was selected by this author to serve as a model for what occurred. The decisions that dictated which data points were ignored and which were presented as significant were made in an attempt to create a narrative that was (a) a good yarn, and (b) something that would mess with the reader's head on as deep a level as possible. Neither of those reasons is concerned with uncovering some profound and unarguable 'truth' about what happened, even if all the actual facts they reference are true.

There are many other possible narratives that could have been presented and which would have been equally valid.* The idea that this chosen narrative is the 'correct' one is only plausible if you forget that this narrative is just a simplified model of what happened back in the 1990s, and confuse it with the thing itself.

Wilson put it better. As he used to say, 'All statements are true in some sense, false in some sense, meaningless in some sense, true and false in some sense, true and meaningless in some sense, false and meaningless in some sense, and true and false and meaningless in some sense.' The statement 'Cauty and Drummond's burning of a million pounds was a magical act that created the twenty-first century' is a perfect example of this.

Alan Moore's magical thinking and the materialist rational perspective, we must remember, are both models. They're both pretty interesting models, to be fair, and there are a lot of good things about both of them. Artists couldn't create without magical thinking, just as engineers couldn't work without rational materialism. It is easy to see how both artists and engineers could confuse their models with the real world, knowing as they do how useful and reliable they are. But neither of these perspectives gives a complete picture. A musician is not going to be able to create a sampler using magical thinking. Or to demonstrate the blind spot of materialism, find a photograph of Johnny Rotten in 1976 and look into his eyes: as a human being, you will know that there is something extraordinary going on,

---

* If I were a more honest writer, I would include a version of these last two paragraphs in every book I write.

something that the rational materialist model cannot even hope to explain.

When you are dealing with models, it is necessary to remember that they have limits. Even the best only work at certain times and on certain scales. Newton's laws are so reliable and accurate on human scales that we trust our lives to them when we climb into aeroplanes, yet they break down at larger or smaller scales. They are unable to predict the orbit of Mercury, for example, for which we need the models created by Einstein, and they are little use on a subatomic scale. Communism, some have claimed, is the most effective model for social order, but only in tribes of around thirty people or less. Alan Greenspan's economic model, likewise, was unfortunately only useful under specific conditions. Magical and objective materialism are both models, even if this is often forgotten. And, being models, they too have limits beyond which they are little use.

The magical thinking of the mind fails, more often than not, when it tries to move beyond the immaterial and affect the material world. Likewise, objective materialism has proved to be a fat lot of good at explaining or predicting the mental worlds that we inhabit. Once we are aware of those limits, the idea that these two models are incompatible falls away. Using multiple-model agnosticism, we no longer have to take sides and nail our colours to one or the other. We simply have to remember which model works in which circumstances and ensure that we apply the correct model for the projects we undertake, be they writing love poems or predicting earthquakes. The need to use multiple models comes about because we do not possess one perfect, unarguable model that works in all situations and which everyone agrees is functionally perfect. If one is discovered it will be a cause for much celebration, but that day has yet to come and it seems optimistic to assume that it is around the corner. As a result we make do with a variety of competing explanations which we need to hop between and assess in order to see which is the most useful, on either practical or aesthetic levels. This is more work, but it keeps things interesting.

From a multiple-model perspective, the burning of a million quid in the boathouse in Jura can be said to be both a meaningless act by two attention-seeking arseholes which was in no way connected to the wider changes in the world at large, and also a magical act that forged the twenty-first century. This makes it far more interesting than if it was just one or the other, for when the irrational magical world and the unconnected real-world dovetail, when they tell much the same story from incompatible viewpoints, there is a rush of insight and aesthetic harmony. We become like Picasso during his Cubist period, seeing his subject from multiple perspectives and producing a single image that is both nonsensical and also full of understanding.*

---

* So there we have it. The book builds and builds until it is revealed to be . . . an argument in favour of multiple-model agnosticism. And not,

Bill Drummond, it seems, was clearly on to something when he advises that we *accept the contradictions.*

That is this author's preferred take on the situation, anyway. You are free to consider other models. Perhaps this chapter was intended as an elaborate 'banishing ritual', intended to dispel any troublesome energies that the writing of this book may have stirred up?

Multiple-model agnosticism does challenge you to work these things out yourself.

To quote *Illuminatus!* for the last time: 'Think for yourself, schmuck!'*

---

as you may be forgiven for thinking, a book just about The KLF. Or, at least, it is for all the people who didn't skip this bit. What a cheek! I'm still amazed that so many people have been so accepting and positive about this situation. I like to think this was because it was in the spirit of what The KLF were – the deception seems to tell you more about them than a straight biography would. I hope you can see why this feint was necessary. Would you have heard about, or decided to read, a book that pitched itself honestly as one about multiple-model agnosticism? This is still the most useful and most fun philosophy I have encountered. I hope that you, too, will find it a useful tool in your mental toolbox. I also hope you realise that the writers you let into your head can be tricksy critters with strange motives. Or at least, they should be. Find the ones that have your best interests at heart!

* There are not many books that can get away by ending with the author saying to the reader, 'Don't ask me. You work it out!' It's presented as if it's the reader's fault for asking a question, even though it was the author who raised the question in the first place. This book does so many things shamelessly wrong that you almost have to admire it.

EPILOGUE

▲

A few years ago I visited the primary school of one of my children. She has since moved up to secondary school, where a teacher told her that the father of a recent pupil had been a pop star who burnt a million pounds yet 'was a really nice guy'.*

But enough of coincidences about The KLF. Cauty and Drummond have moved on from those days. Both have worked as artists in the years since The K Foundation. Drummond's art has focused on simple, meaningful work, such as making soup or building beds. Cauty's work has retained more of The KLF's anti-authoritarian attitude, which now fits more comfortably into the post-Banksy

---

* Here we welcome back the magically minded who skipped the last bit. Hi folks! After finishing this book, I had a lot of strange synchronicities and weirdness in my life. It turned out that, unbeknown to me as I was writing this, one of my children was in the same school and in the same year as one of Jimmy's. That led to an awkward parent–teacher evening.

art world. Both have made music, but noticeably not for profit. Cauty's Black Smoke project gave away all its music free online. Drummond created a conceptual choir called The17 which will never be recorded, because he believes that recorded music belongs in the twentieth century. Both have kept to the contract they signed on a Nissan Bluebird and pushed over the edge of Cape Wrath, and have largely avoided discussing or continuing their work together.

That, at least, is the situation at the time of writing. That contract will expire in November 2018. The pair are still in regular contact. Who can say what will happen then?*

At the primary school I was looking at a poster of the solar system on the wall of a classroom when a teacher came up and spoke to me. 'I get so many parents complaining about that poster,' he said, as if fearful that I was going to do the same and hoping to confront me before I had the chance.

'Why's that?' I asked. The poster showed nine planets and their relative sizes, complete with other information such as number of moons and so forth. It seemed uncontroversial to me. The planets went, from left to right, Mercury, Venus, Earth, Mars, Jupiter, Saturn, Uranus, Neptune and Pluto.

The teacher tapped at the blue circle on the right, the ninth planet. 'Pluto isn't a planet anymore,' he said. This was true. In 2006, an international body reclassified Pluto

---

* I, for one, wasn't expecting Spotify.

as not a planet, but a dwarf planet. Pluto has many defenders, however, and this has proved to be a controversial decision.* The poster, clearly, was printed before any of this happened. From the teacher's comments, it appeared that some smart-arsed parents had been showing off their knowledge of astronomy at the poor poster's expense.

'It's a dwarf planet,' the teacher continued, 'so it makes sense to include it on a poster showing all the proper planets.'

'What about Eris?' I asked.

He looked blankly at me. 'Eris?' he questioned.

'Eris is also a dwarf planet,' I explained. 'It's the biggest actually, bigger than Pluto. It's the ninth biggest thing in the solar system. If you're going to have Pluto on there, shouldn't you have Eris?'

There was a pause. 'I've never heard of it,' he said, and walked off to find a less irritating parent to talk to.

There's no reason he should have heard of it, of course. It's big enough to have a moon of its own, Dysnomia, but it is a very distant thing. It was only discovered in 2005, and it has a wantonly elongated orbit that usually places it much further from the Sun than Pluto. It has recently been remeasured and found to be almost identical in size

---

* That's putting it mildly. A lot of people are still fighting about the status of Pluto. I wish now that I'd noted in the original text how this is a great example of what Robert Anton Wilson was talking about – how we project our maps and models out onto the physical world, confuse them with reality, and then fight over them as if they were real.

to Pluto, so my claim that it was the ninth biggest thing in the solar system was actually wrong.* The arguments that it generated in the astronomical community following its discovery led to the controversial classification of what was and wasn't a planet, and this led to poor Pluto being demoted. It was these arguments and the discord that they generated which resulted in it being given the name Eris. That, and the fact that Eris was the 'favourite goddess' of its discoverer, Mike Brown.

I wonder what Hill and Thornley would have made of this? They invoked Eris, and brought her into the twentieth century after being forgotten for a couple of thousand years. The concept of chaos then spread through academia and the counter-culture, those being the two places where new ideas are explored, and the results range from the chaos mathematics that drive our climate models, to chaos magic and the events in this story. Then Eris is discovered in the heavens, circling our Sun, bringing argument and upset. 'As above, so below', as the saying goes.

Eris is out there, somewhere, following her messy orbit. She may be ignored by those who simplify the solar system into a neat, orderly model. She may not be taught at school. She may never be well known, or discussed in everyday conversation.

But she is out there. Synchronicities are only synchronicities if you choose to notice them. Paying attention to them

---

* Our most recent measurements show that Eris is slightly smaller than Pluto, although it does have a higher mass.

is entirely optional, and it makes no difference to dwarf planets like Eris.

Regardless of if or how you think about her, she remains out there.*

---

* The end. We made it! Thanks for keeping me company through this. I don't usually go back to old work and, if I'm honest, I'm not feeling drawn to doing it again. Looking at the book now with the benefit of distance, I would have to describe it as . . . patchy. That's the word that comes to mind. There are some really nice bits of writing, and I still enjoy its willingness not to follow the rules. It's hard for me to judge what reading about some of the ideas in here is like, as they have now become so internalised in me, they appear unremarkable. A lot of the enthusiasm for this book seems to come from people who are being introduced to these ideas for the first time, so the impact of that is hard for me to judge. I can only assume that, as I was enthusiastic enough about them at the time, then they will still have an effect on some people. What I have learnt from this exercise is that, as long as there are some really good bits in the mix, people are happy to overlook the flaws, and ultimately only remember the highs. As in books, so in life. For all the horrors, it is the good bits that stay with you.

NOTES AND SOURCES

PROLOGUE: The Fuckers Burned The Lot

The account of the money burning on Jura is based on Jim Reid's article in the *Observer* ('Money to Burn', 25 September 1994), Gimpo's account published in *K Foundation Burn a Million Quid* (Goodrick and Brook, 1997) and the BBC *Omnibus* documentary *A Foundation Course In Art* (6 November 1995, director Kevin Hull). Drummond and Cauty's quotes to the BBC are also taken from this documentary.

The '100 Coolest People' list that Drummond topped was published in the September 1993 issue of *Select*. It described him thus: 'What has this giant of coolness not achieved? Like the Monolith in *2001: A Space Odyssey*, Drummond has always been a step ahead of human evolution, guiding us on [. . .] Deranged, inspired, intensely cool.'

The quote from Greil Marcus regarding Dada is taken

from his superb *Lipstick Traces* (2001). Details of the tour of the film *Watch The K Foundation Burn A Million Quid* are taken from the book *K Foundation Burn A Million Quid* (Goodrick and Brook, 1997).

The account of the Cape Wrath incident comes from *A Real Cliff-Hanger*, Craig McLean's article in *Blah Blah Blah* (March 1996) and an 8 December 1995 advert placed by The K Foundation in the *Guardian*.

The quote from Andrew Smith comes from his 13 February 2000 *Observer* article 'Burning Question'.

The online sources of unofficial KLF material referred to are too numerous and transient to list, but for those armed with curiosity and Google, searching for the KLF FAQ or libraryofmu.org is a good way to start.

1. Eris and Echo

Details about Julian Cope and Bill Drummond in Liverpool come from Cope's autobiography *Head On* and Drummond's short book *From the Shores of Lake Placid and Other Stories* (a modified version of which was later reprinted in his book *45*).

Accounts of the early days of Thornley, Hill and Discordianism, plus Thornley's links to the JFK investigation, come from Adam Gorightly's 2003 book *The Prankster and the Conspiracy*. The *Principia Discordia*, together with its many and varied introductions and forewords, was also a useful if untrustworthy source.

The Charles Fort quote comes from his 1932 book *Wild*

Talents. Drummond's 1998 quotes regarding Echo come from *From the Shores of Lake Placid and Other Stories.*

2. Illuminations and Illuminatus

Details of Carl Jung's dream, and the position of import-ance it played in his life, are recounted in his 1963 book *Memories, Dreams, Reflections.* Drummond's quote about Peter O'Halligan is taken from *From the Shores of Lake Placid and Other Stories.* More details about O'Halligan (and the Liverpool/Discordian crossover in general) come from the essay 'Illuminatus! Amazing Adventures in Put-ting Science Fiction on the Stage' by Jeff Merrifield, which is based on his doctoral paper and can be found online at http://www.playbackarts.co.uk/meryfela/merypage.htm. Michael Coveney's book *Ken Campbell: The Great Caper* was also an invaluable source for much of the material about Ken Campbell and the *Illuminatus!* stage play, and the source of the quotes from cast members Bill Nighy, Jim Broadbent and Chris Langham. Robert Anton Wilson wrote about his introduction to Discordianism and his time working at *Playboy* in *Cosmic Trigger* Volume 1: *The Final Secret of the Illuminati* (1977).

The April 1969 *Playboy* letters page quoted was scanned and put online by Jesse Walker.

3. Sirius and Synchronicity

Jim Garrison's investigations into the assassination of JFK

are detailed in his 1988 book *On the Trail of the Assassins*. The account of Thornley's unwitting involvement in these events, including his quote to the Warren Commission and the quote from Andrew Sciambra, comes from Adam Gorightly's *The Prankster and the Conspiracy* (2003).

Jung's thoughts about synchronicity are taken from his 1951 essay 'On Synchronicity', which was republished in 1960 in the book *Synchronicity*. Bill Drummond's account of his trip to the Mathew Street manhole cover appears in *45* (2000) and *From the Shores of Lake Placid and Other Stories* (1998).

Robert Anton Wilson's experience of hearing voices that appeared to be from Sirius is discussed in much of his work, especially the *Cosmic Trigger* series, but a good source of the events discussed here would be the 2002 audiobook collection *Robert Anton Wilson Explains Everything (Or Old Bob Exposes His Ignorance)*.

I am indebted to the Fortean scientist Ian Simmons for alerting me to the fact that cryptozoologists do indeed record occasional accounts of sightings of giant rabbit-like creatures.

4. Magic and Moore

Bill Drummond's quote to Tim Jonze appears in both Jonze's 28 May 2012 *Guardian* article 'Bill Drummond: The Creative Urge Is in Us All' and also Drummond's book *100* (2012).

The reference to Mark Manning teaching Bill Drummond about magic comes from Drummond's own biography (long version) on his website www.penkilnburn. com.

Alan Moore discusses his take on magic and his concept of Ideaspace in countless interviews, but his conversation with Eddie Campbell in their book *A Disease of Language* (Moore and Campbell, 2005) is as good an account as you will find. Moore's comments on the money burning are taken from *K Foundation Burn A Million Quid* (Goodrick and Brook, 1997).

5. The Man and the Mu Mu

Details about Drummond leaving the music industry and releasing his solo album *The Man* can be found throughout his writing, most notably in his books *45* (2000) and *17* (2008). His relationship with and rereading of *Illuminatus!* is discussed in his book *17* (2008).

Details of Cauty and Drummond's working relationship, plus the quotes from Cauty to Richard King, come from King's 2012 book *How Soon Is Now? The Madmen and Mavericks Who Made Independent Music 1975–2005*. The later quote from Mick Houghton is from the same source.

Drummond's quote about Brilliant is taken from a transcript of his interview on the Norwegian radio programme *Bomlagadafshipoing* in 1991, which is archived at www.libraryofmu.org. Drummond's later quote regarding his reaction to the Whitney Houston record is from the same source. The description of Situationism is based on Guy Debord's 1967 copyright-free text *The Society of the Spectacle*, and Drummond discussed his awareness of Situationism in *17* (2008).

Details of the release of 'All You Need Is Love' and the resulting legal issues are taken from Jeremy J. Beadle's book *Will Pop Eat Itself?* (1993). Drummond's quote about how he didn't think that anyone would take any notice of the record comes from Pete Robinson's *Justified And Ancient History* (1992). James Brown's account of the trip to Sweden was published in the *NME* on 17 October 1987.

6. Ford and Fiction

Cauty's quotes to Richard King come from King's book *How Soon Is Now? The Madmen and Mavericks Who Made Independent Music 1975–2005*. Drummond's quote to BBC Radio 1 is from an interview with Richard Skinner for *Saturday Sequence*, broadcast in December 1990. Background information regarding the 'Doctorin' The TARDIS' record can be found in Drummond and Cauty's 1989 book *The Manual (How To Have A Number One The Easy Way)*. Details of the synchronicites surrounding the car and its previous owner come from conversations between the author and Flinton Chalk.

Michael Grade's comments about Colin Baker come from his 2003 interview with the *Daily Telegraph*, and the reference to Grade's relationship with Liza Goddard comes from William Langley's 11 March 2007 article in the same paper, 'He eats, sleeps and breathes television – and at last he's got round to watching some.' The details of Ken Campbell's audition and the casting of Sylvester McCoy, including McCoy's quote, come from Andrew Cartmel's 2005 book *Script Doctor: The Inside Story of Doctor Who 1986–89.*

Peter Paphides' quote about novelty records comes from the *Observer Music Monthly,* 22 February 2004. Information about David Whitaker, including the quote about alchemy, comes from *Doctor Who Magazine* No. 98 (March 1985). Discussion of Whitaker's mercurial influence, and his influence on *The Evil of the Daleks* in particular, is based on the arguments of Elizabeth Sandifer in her 2018 book *TARDIS Eruditorum – An Unauthorized Critical History of Doctor Who, Volume 2: Patrick Troughton.* The later quotes from Sandifer are taken from her excellent blog, http:// tardiseruditorum.blogspot.co.uk.

Reference to David Lynch's creative process was inspired by his 2006 book, *Catching The Big Fish: Meditation, Consciousness and Creativity.*

7. Writing and Waiting

The illustration which included the words 'This is a chord. This is another. This is a third. Now form a band' appeared in the January 1977 edition of the fanzine *Sideburns.* The description of rave culture is inspired by a conversation with the late Fraser Clark. Robert Plant shouted out, 'I am a Golden God!' while being photographed by Peter Simon on a balcony overlooking Sunset Strip in LA in 1975.

The description of Trancentral comes from an email from Cally, Bill Drummond's manager, to this author in February 2013. Drummond's quote regarding the original 'Pure Trance' version of 'What Time Is Love?' comes from his 17 April 2012 article in *The Quietus*, 'At the Age of 59'. Cauty's dismissal of *Chill Out* comes from Richard King's *How Soon Is Now? The Madmen and Mavericks Who Made Independent Music 1975–2005* (2012). The KLF's descriptions of ambient music come from their 1990 press release entitled *Ambient House – The Facts?*, and their description of the ambient video *Waiting* comes from the 1990 press release *KLF Infosheet 10*.

8. Ceremonies

Cauty's quotes to Richard King come from King's book *How Soon Is Now? The Madmen and Mavericks Who Made Independent Music 1975–2005*. Details of the history of the Burning Man Festival come from the festival's own website, www.burningman.com, and The KLF's invitation to Jura and their description of the Four Handmaidens of Lucifer were reprinted in their 1991 press release *KLF Infosheet 13*.

Drummond's quote regarding his soul comes from his book *The Wild Highway* (2005, co-written with Mark

Manning). For an introduction to the ideas of Rudolf Steiner, see Gary Lachman's *Rudolf Steiner: An Introduction to His Life and Work* (2007).

9. Journeys

The existing edit of the unfinished *White Room* movie can usually be found on video streaming websites such as YouTube or Vimeo, and the script to the final version of the film is also widely available on KLF fansites. Further details about *The White Room* movie come from Pete Robinson's *Justified And Ancient History* – where Robinson's letter from Paul Fericano was republished – and the many and various *KLF Infosheets*, particularly *Infosheet 8*.

The quote from Wilson and Shea regarding Operation Mindfuck is taken from the appendixes in *The Illuminatus! Trilogy*. Bill Drummond's comments to *BLOWN* magazine are reprinted in his 2012 book *100*.

10. Submerging

Bill Drummond writes about the circumstances that led to the collaboration with Tammy Wynette in his book *45* (2000). Jim Dyer's quotes to Richard King regarding Rough Trade come from King's book *How Soon Is Now? The Madmen and Mavericks Who Made Independent Music 1975–2005*. Bill Drummond's quote about wanting a submarine comes from Roger Morton's *NME* article

'One Coronation Under a Groove', published 12 January 1991.

11. Endings

Much of the details surrounding The KLF at the Brits, including references to their plan to chainsaw the legs off an elephant, the quotes in reaction to their performance and the quotes from Drummond, come from Danny Kelly's 29 February 1992 *NME* article 'Welcome to the Sheep Seats'. Further information about the thinking behind the plan to sacrifice a live sheep come from a February 2013 email to this author from Bill Drummond's manager Cally. This stresses that the idea behind Drummond throwing his severed hand into the audience was not to claim the music business for himself, but to claim it 'for a Higher Master'.

The Raoul Vaneigem quote is taken from Greil Marcus' 1989 book *Lipstick Traces: A Secret History of the Twentieth Century*. The Situationist quote is from Guy Debord's *The Society of the Spectacle* (1967).

12. Undercurrents

Eric Hobsbawm discusses the 'Short Twentieth Century' in his 1994 book *The Age of Extremes: 1914–1991*. The blogger Neuroskeptic discusses the lack of modern cults in his 16 August 2012 posting *Where Have All The Cults Gone?*, at http://neuroskeptic.blogspot.co.uk/2012/08/where-have-all-cults-gone.html.

The quotes from Greil Marcus regarding Dada come from his 1989 book *Lipstick Traces: A Secret History of the Twentieth Century*. The quotes about Daoism are based on *The Dao De Jing* by Lao Tzu.

13. Foundations

A number of The K Foundation adverts or announcements are reproduced in Goodrick and Brook's 1997 book *K Foundation Burn A Million Quid*. The quotes from the art gallery owner, and Cauty's later quote about controlling money, are taken from the BBC *Omnibus* documentary *A Foundation Course In Art* (directed by Kevin Hull, broadcast on 5 November 1996). Charles Shaar Murray's quote comes from his book review in 26 February 2000 edition of the *Independent*. Alan Moore's argument that Art is Magic is detailed in his essay 'Fossil Angels', which can be found online at http://glycon.livejournal.com/13888.html.

The Limits to Growth, by The Club of Rome, was first published in 1972 by Universe Books, and has been updated a number of times since. The physicist Tom Murphy discusses the impossibility of perpetual economic growth in his essay 'Exponential Economist Meets Finite Physicist' on his blog at http://physics.ucsd.edu/do-the-math/2012/04/economist-meets-physicist. Alan Greenspan's 2008 comments to the House Committee were widely reported; see, for example, George Packer writing for the *New Yorker* on 23 October 2008, 'End of an era (2): Greenspan's world view fails him'. Drummond's quote about using art to make a statement about money comes from his March 1997 interview in *The Wire*.

14. Unthinkable

For more on the 23 Enigma, see Robert Anton Wilson's 1977 article 'The 23 Phenomenon' in issue 23 of *Fortean Times*. Drummond writes about his exposure to Situationism, as well as his experience of rereading *Illuminatus!*, in his 2007 book *17*. Wilson's discussion about quantum physics and the fact that he lived in three places at the same time can be found on the 2002 audiobook collection *Robert Anton Wilson Explains Everything (Or Old Bob Exposes His Ignorance)*.

Epilogue

Details of the discovery of Eris by Mike Brown and his team can be found in the 10 December 2005 issue of *The Astrophysical Journal Letters*.

TIMELINE OF EVENTS IN THIS STORY
(1916–2000)

1916 *5 February* – The Cabaret Voltaire nightclub opens in Zurich, Switzerland.

1927 Carl Jung dreams about a tree of light in Liverpool.

1932 *18 January* – Robert Anton Wilson born (Robert Edward Wilson, Brooklyn, New York, USA).

1938 *17 April* – Kerry Thornley born (Kerry Wendell Thornley, California, USA).

1941 *21 May* – Greg Hill born (Gregory Hill, California, USA).
10 December – Ken Campbell born (Kenneth Victor Campbell, Ilford, England).

1953 *29 April* – Bill Drummond born (William Ernest Drummond, Butterworth, South Africa).

18 November – Alan Moore born (Northampton, England).

1956 Greg Hill and Kerry Thornley meet at California High School in East Whittier, California.
19 December – Jimmy Cauty born (James Francis Cauty, Liverpool, England).

1957 Discordianism born in a California bowling alley, following an argument between Hill and Thornley.

1959 Kerry Thornley enlists in the Marine Corps and meets Lee Harvey Oswald.

1961 *9 February* – The Beatles play the Cavern Club, Mathew Street, Liverpool.

1963 *22 November* – JFK assassinated. Aldous Huxley and C. S. Lewis die of natural causes.
23 November – First episode of *Doctor Who* broadcast.

1965 The manuscript now known as the *Principia Discordia* is first published, in an edition of five copies, via the mimeograph machine in DA Garrison's office, New Orleans.

1967 Guy Debord publishes *The Society of the Spectacle*.

1968 *January* – Thornley subpoenaed to appear before Jim Garrison's investigation into the assassination of President Kennedy.
Late 1968 – Operation Mindfuck begins.

1969 Robert Anton Wilson and Robert Shea start work on *Illuminatus!*.

1971 Robert Anton Wilson and Robert Shea finish *Illuminatus!* and begin searching for a publisher.

1973 *June* – Bill Drummond accepts the contradictions inherent in the problem of free will versus causality.
23 July – Robert Anton Wilson receives mental communication that claims to originate from the star Sirius.

1975 *September* – *The Illuminatus! Trilogy* finally published.

1976 Bill Drummond meets Peter O'Halligan, founder of the Liverpool School of Language, Music, Dream and Pun.
Bill Drummond meets Ken Campbell, who has just formed the Science Fiction Theatre Company of Liverpool.
Ken Campbell reads *Illuminatus!*.
Drummond designs sets for Campbell's *Illuminatus!* stage play.

28 November – The *Illuminatus!* stage play premieres at Mathew Street, Liverpool.

1977 *March* – The *Illuminatus!* stage play performs at the National Theatre's Cottesloe Theatre, London, to an audience including Jimmy Cauty.
May – Big in Japan form.

1978 *26 August* – Big in Japan split.
Drummond helps Julian Cope move into a flat in Toxteth, Liverpool.
Drummond forms Zoo Records with Dave Balfe.

1984 *12 May* – Bill Drummond arranges a bicycle ride which follows the shape of a pair of rabbit's ears drawn on a map of Liverpool, ahead of Echo & the Bunnymen's 'A Crystal Day' concert at St George's Hall, Liverpool.

1985 Jimmy Cauty meets Bill Drummond.
Bill Drummond meets Zodiac Mindwarp who 'teaches him about magic'.
Doctor Who is put on an eighteen-month hiatus by Michael Grade.

1986 Bill Drummond releases solo album *The Man*.
1 July – Bill Drummond issues press release to announce he has left the music industry.

1987   *1 January* – Bill Drummond and Jimmy Cauty form The Justified Ancients of Mu Mu.

9 March – 'All You Need Is Love', the first JAMs single, is released.

June – 1987: What The Fuck Is Going On?, the first JAMs LP, is released.

Summer – ABBA's lawyers not happy.

September – Remaining copies of the first JAMs album, *1987: What The Fuck Is Going On?*, burnt in a field in Sweden.

Statue of Carl Jung unveiled in Mathew Street, Liverpool.

1988   *April* – The first KLF record, 'Burn The Bastards/ Burn The Beat', released.

23 May – 'Doctorin' The TARDIS' released.

July – The original 'Pure Trance' version of 'What Time Is Love?' released.

Summer – Huge growth in the size and number of raves in locations around the M25.

Summer – Drummond and Cauty sign contract with 'Eternity'.

1989   *The Manual (How To Have A Number One The Easy Way)* by Bill Drummond and Jimmy Cauty released. Drummond and Cauty fail to complete *The White Room* movie.

1990 *February* – *Chill Out* released.
Drummond and Cauty decide to make hit records.
October – 'What Time Is Love? (Live At Trancentral)' reaches number five in the UK charts.

1991 '3am Eternal (Live At The SSL)', 'Last Train To Trancentral (Live From The Lost Continent)', and 'Justified And Ancient (Stand By The JAMs)' keep The KLF in the charts all year.
Summer solstice (23 June) – Wicker Man burnt on the Isle of Jura.
Summer – Bill Drummond flies to Tennessee to record with Tammy Wynette.

1992 *12 February* – The KLF and Extreme Noise Terror perform at the Brit Awards.
16 May – Full-page advert on the back page of the *NME* announces the end of The KLF.

1993 *3 July* – An advert in the *NME* announces the existence of The K Foundation.
18 November – Alan Moore's fortieth birthday. He informs his friends and family that he has become a magician.

1994 *January* – Alan Moore converses with a demon.
23 August – Cauty and Drummond burn a million pounds in a deserted boathouse on the Isle of Jura in the early hours of the morning.

1995 *23 August* – *Watch The K Foundation Burn A Million Quid* screened in Jura village hall.

5 November – Drummond and Cauty make a contract to end The K Foundation. The contract is signed on a Nissan Bluebird, which is then pushed over Cape Wrath.

6 November – BBC *Omnibus* documentary *A Foundation Course in Art* is broadcast.

1996 *7 March* – *Watch The K Foundation Burn A Million Quid* screened in Alan Moore's living room, Northampton.

May – Paul McGann becomes the Eighth Doctor Who.

5 June – Drummond flies to Zaire with Gimpo and Z (Mark Manning) in order to confront the Devil and reclaim his soul.

1997 *K Foundation Burn A Million Quid* by Alan Goodrick (Gimpo) and Chris Brook published.

1998 *28 November* – Kerry Thornley dies after a cardiac arrest in Atlanta, Georgia. Twenty-three people attend a memorial service in his honour.

2000 *20 July* – Greg Hill dies.

SELECTED UK DISCOGRAPHY

THE JUSTIFIED ANCIENTS OF MU MU (singles):
'All You Need Is Love' (March 1987)
'Whitney Joins The JAMs' (September 1987)
'Deep Shit' (September 1987 – unreleased)
'Downtown' (December 1987)
'It's Grim Up North (Parts 1 And 2)' (October 1991)

THE JUSTIFIED ANCIENTS OF MU MU (albums):
1987: What The Fuck Is Going On? (June 1987)
Who Killed The JAMs? (January 1988)
Shag Times (January 1989)

THE TIMELORDS (singles):
'Doctorin' The TARDIS' (June 1988)

THE KLF (singles):
'Burn The Bastards/Burn The Beat' (March 1988)

'What Time Is Love?' (June 1988)
'3am Eternal' (July 1988)
'Kylie Said To Jason' (July 1989)

'Madrugada Eternal' (February 1990)
'What Time Is Love? (Live At Trancentral)' (July 1990)
'3am Eternal (Live At The SSL)' (January 1991)
'Last Train To Trancentral (Live From The Lost Continent)'
    (April 1991)
'Justified And Ancient (Stand By The JAMs)' (November
    1991)
'America: What Time Is Love?' (February 1992)

THE KLF (albums):
Chill Out (January 1990)
The White Room (March 1991)

BILL DRUMMOND (solo album):
The Man (August 1986)

JIMMY CAUTY (solo album):
Space (June 1990)

BIBLIOGRAPHY

Beadle, Jeremy J., *Will Pop Eat Itself? Pop Music in the Soundbite Era* (Faber & Faber, 1993)

Brook, Chris, and Goodrick, Alan (Gimpo), *K Foundation Burn A Million Quid* (Ellipsis, 1997)

Cain, Susan, *Quiet: The Power of Introverts in a World that won't Stop Talking* (Viking, 2012)

Cartmel, Andrew, *Script Doctor: The Inside Story of Doctor Who 1986–89* (Reynolds & Hearn, 2005)

Cope, Julian, *Head On* (Magog Books, 1994)

Coveney, Michael, *Ken Campbell: The Great Caper* (Nick Hern Books, 2011)

Debord, Guy, *Society of the Spectacle* (Editions Buchet-Chastel, Paris, 1967)

Drummond, Bill, *From the Shores of Lake Placid and Other Stories* (Penkiln Burn, 1998)

—*45* (Little, Brown, 2000)

—*How to Be an Artist* (Penkiln Burn, 2002)

— *17* (Penkiln Burn/Beautiful Books, 2008)

— *100* (Penkiln Burn, 2012)

— and Manning, Mark, *Bad Wisdom* (Penguin, 1996)

—*The Wild Highway* (Creation Books, 2005)

Fukuyama, Francis, *The End of History and the Last Man* (Free Press, 1992)

Guiliano, Edward (ed.), *Lewis Carroll Observed: A Collection of Unpublished Photographs, Drawings, Poetry, and New Essays* (Clarkson N. Potter, 1976)

Higgs, John, *I Have America Surrounded: The Life of Timothy Leary* (The Friday Project, 2006)

Hobsbawm, Eric, *The Age of Extremes: 1914–1991* (Michael Joseph, 1994)

Jung, C. G., *Synchronicity: An Acausal Connecting Principal* (Princeton University Press, 1960)

—*Memories, Dreams, Reflections* (Fontana Press, 1995)

King, Richard, *How Soon Is Now? The Madmen and Mavericks Who Made Independent Music 1975–2005* (Faber & Faber, 2012)

Lynch, David, *Catching the Big Fish: Meditation, Consciousness and Creativity* (Penguin, 2006)

Marcus, Greil, *Lipstick Traces: A Secret History of the Twentieth Century* (Faber & Faber, 2001)

Millidge, Gary Spencer, *Alan Moore: Storyteller* (Ilex, 2012)

Moore, Alan, and Campbell, Eddie, *From Hell* (Knockabout, 2000)

— *A Disease of Language* (Knockabout Palmano Bennett, 2005)

Robinson, Pete, *Justified And Ancient History: The*

Unfolding Story of The KLF (Pete Robinson, 1992)

Sandifer, Elizabeth, *TARDIS Eruditorum – An Unauthorized Critical History of Doctor Who, Volume 2: Patrick Troughton* (Createspace, 2018)

Stone, C. J., *Fierce Dancing: Adventures in the Underground* (Faber & Faber, 1996)

Wall, Mick, *When Giants Walked the Earth: A Biography of Led Zeppelin* (Orion, 2009)

Wagner, Eric, *An Insider's Guide to Robert Anton Wilson* (New Falcon Publications, 2004)

Wilson, Robert Anton, *Prometheus Rising* (New Falcon Publications, 1983)

—*Quantum Psychology* (New Falcon Publications, 1990)

— *Cosmic Trigger*, Volume 1: *The Final Secret of the Illuminati* (New Falcon Publications, 1977)

—and Shea, Robert, *The Illuminatus! Trilogy* (Dell, 1975)

ACKNOWLEDGEMENTS

The author wishes to thank the following for their assistance, insights or blasts of enthusiasm. This book would not exist without them: Gary Acord, Jason Arnopp, Sarah Ballard, Brian Barritt, Flinton Chalk, Richard Collins, Michael Coveney, Prunella Gee, Gimpo, Jessica Gulliver, Ben Goldacre, Bea Hemming, Joanne Mallon, Tim Richards, Zoe Ross, Shardcore, Ian Simmons, C. J. Stone, Greg Taylor.

The author also wishes to thank every KLF fan who scanned an interview, digitised a track, ran an ftp server or in any other way made the entire history of The KLF available online. Much appreciated, all.

CREDITS

Weidenfeld & Nicholson would like to thank everyone at Orion who worked on the publication of *The KLF*.

Agent
Sarah Ballard
Eli Keren

Editor
Jenny Lord

Editorial Management
Jo Roberts-Miller
Jane Hughes
Charlie Panayiotou
Tamara Morriss
Claire Boyle

Audio
Paul Stark
Jake Alderson
Georgina Cutler

Design
Nick Shah
Chevonne Elbourne
Steve Marking
Joanna Ridley
Helen Ewing

Contracts
Dan Herron
Ellie Bowker
Alyx Hurst

Finance
Nick Gibson
Jasdip Nandra
Sue Baker
Tom Costello

Inventory
Jo Jacobs
Dan Stevens

Production
Hannah Cox
Katie Horrocks

Marketing
Alice Morley

Publicity
Virginia Woolstencroft
Ellen Turner

Sales
Jen Wilson
Victoria Laws
Esther Waters
Group Sales teams across
Digital, Field, International
and Non-Trade

Operations
Group Sales
Operations team

Rights
Rebecca Folland
Alice Cottrell
Ruth Blakemore
Ayesha Kinley
Marie Henckel

INDEX

John Higgs is the author of *I Have America Surrounded*, *The KLF*, *Stranger Than We Can Imagine*, *Watling Street*, *The Future Starts Here*, *William Blake Now*, *William Blake VS The World* and *Love and Let Die*. He lives in Brighton with his wife and their two children.